THE NEMECHEK PROTOCOL FOR ADD, POTS, PANS, PANDAS AND EMOTIONAL DYSREGULATION

THE HOW-TO GUIDE TO RESTORING NEUROLOGICAL FUNCTION

PATRICK M. NEMECHEK, D.O.

JEAN R. NEMECHEK, J.D.

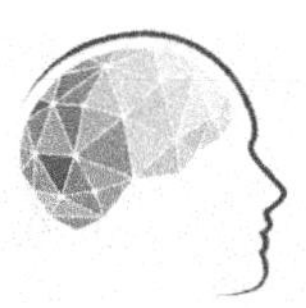

CONTENTS

PART III
VAGUS NERVE STIMULATION

PART IV

THE UPS AND DOWNS OF RECOVERY

PART V

THE SCIENCE BEHIND THE NEMECHEK PROTOCOL®

PART VI

THINKING ABOUT THE FUTURE

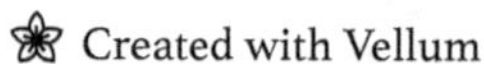 Created with Vellum

ACKNOWLEDGMENTS

My path of professional education and personal enlightenment has traveled through the seemingly diverse medical fields of HIV disease, the autonomic nervous system, and chronic inflammation, only to discover the body's enormous capacity to recover from past insults and prevent future maladies.

Through a combination of perseverance and the guidance of others who have had a substantial impact on advancing medicine (Einstein, Feingold, Tracey), I pressed forward to find new approaches that genuinely improve health rather than simply masking disease.

I can think of the many times I might have given up and become another typical clinic doctor if it were not for the support of so many patients willing to try something new. I have asked many patients to try a new approach only to have it fail, but yet, undeterred, they return asking me to try again.

Occasionally, our combined efforts would be successful, and we would work on improving their condition even further. From learning to control the ravages of wasting syndrome in HIV disease to reversing chronic brain injuries and finally helping children recover from many neurological ailments, I would not have been nearly as successful without the faith and support of my patients and their parents.

Beyond working with patients, constantly operating outside the traditional medical community is, at times, emotionally exhausting and professionally isolating. As they say, the last mile of any journey is the hardest, and it has been my wife Jean's love and faith in our shared purpose that has helped me press forward.

She is my most trusted counselor and my unwavering source of support and love. Without her, I would have never been able to finish the last mile of my journey.

Thank you, everyone, for your support.

Patrick Nemechek

MEDICAL DISCLAIMER

The information and the images contained within this publication are provided as an informational resource only and are not to be used or relied on for any diagnostic or medical or treatment purposes.

This information is not intended to be patient education and does not create any patient-physician relationship.

Please consult with a licensed healthcare practitioner to determine if any of these therapeutic approaches are appropriate for you or your child.

INTRODUCTION
A NEW ERA OF OPTIMISM FOR BRAIN RECOVERY

Fifteen years ago, when I began my research on the autonomic nervous system (ANS), my research was turning up some strange findings regarding neurological recovery after a common concussion. I saw many adults who had experienced mild to moderate concussions several years prior but who were still experiencing neurological symptoms from the accident, along with testing abnormalities of their ANS.

I found this puzzling because there are studies from the 1960s that indicated as long as someone did not bleed within their brain from their injury, they should fully recover within about three months. In other words, if your concussion was so severe you were knocked unconscious for several minutes, you were expected to recover within a few months entirely.

I was perplexed that these people were not recovering.

When I began investigating brain injuries, the prevailing scientific view was that after birth, our body can no longer produce new stem cells or new neurons. This meant there was minimal capacity for the brain to recover from injury. In other words, if a person did not spontaneously recover from a brain injury, there was little hope of any further recovery.

This confused me because thirty to forty years earlier, it was assumed the brain could recover fully. Now, the brain is viewed as the least capable organ of recovery. Nevertheless, I pushed on with my efforts to try and help these patients somehow recover from their autonomic dysfunction.

The First Breakthrough in Recovery

For the first few years, I had minimal success in helping patients improve symptomatically and objectively on their tests, looking at autonomic functioning (spectral analysis). I was trying a wide variety of neuroplasticity techniques with little results.

Then, a succession of scientific papers from 2008-2012 began to paint a picture that humans do produce stem cells not only after birth but throughout our entire lifespan. The only problem was that chronic inflammatory stress prevented these stem cells from working.

This was a critically important finding because stem cells were also viewed as vital to the body's natural repair and rejuvenation mechanisms. I decided upon a rather simplistic strategy. I thought that if I could lower inflammation enough in my patients, their naturally produced stem cells might be activated enough to allow their brain to repair their old injuries.

I set about trying a variety of supplements and lifestyle changes that I felt would lower inflammation within the brain. Within a few months, patients began to report significant improvements in their symptoms. These same patients were also finally demonstrating neurological recovery on their autonomic tests.

Over the following years, I did countless little studies comparing supplements and lifestyle changes with respect to their potency in improving symptoms and test results. The result is the present version of The Nemechek Protocol®. Yet some unbelievable recoveries I saw still seemed impossible, even with healthy functioning stem cells.

The Second Breakthrough in Recovery

Although we had clear evidence that the human body actively produced stem cells, there was little to no evidence that neurons were replaced with healthy new neurons. It was hard for me to believe that stem cells alone were responsible for the unbelievable recoveries that were occurring.

My skepticism finally resolved in 2019 with the discovery that an important region of the adult brain called the hippocampus replaced 90% of all its neurons with new healthy neurons every three weeks. The hippocampus is an important region of the brain regarding cognition, memory, and emotionality.

Additional proof of the nervous system's regenerative capacity came from studies indicating that the five hundred million neurons within the intestinal tract also replaced 90% of themselves every two weeks.

So, it seems like the 1960's viewpoint of the brain's ability to recover from most injuries was correct. The only difference between the 1960s and now is that most people nowadays are experiencing chronic inflammation, and their stem cells, repair, and rejuvenation mechanisms cannot function quickly.

Medical science is finally re-discovering that the human brain is designed by nature to fully and rapidly repair itself from all but the most severe brain injuries. With this knowledge, I started suggesting similar strategies to patients with children afflicted with a variety of childhood conditions such as autism, developmental delay, intestinal distress, failure to thrive, anxiety, sensory processing disorders, low motor tone, and even cerebral palsy.

Over the following years, several incremental changes have refined the original anti-inflammatory protocol, now known as The Nemechek Protocol®. The protocol is so ground-breaking and original that a patent (U.S. #10, 335,396) was issued in July 2019 for *Methods of Reversing Autonomic Nervous System Damage.*

My anti-inflammatory protocol was then modified for use in children after I discovered it was also effective in helping children recover from autism, developmental delay, and a wide variety of symptoms resulting from unrepaired common brain injuries.

Over time, we have discovered that The Nemechek Protocol is equally effective in helping children recover from ADD/ADHD, POTS, PANS, PANDAS, anxiety, and chronic depression. As unrelated as these conditions seem, they share a common cause, neuroinflammation primarily from dysbiosis of the small intestine, otherwise known as small intestine bacterial overgrowth (SIBO).

The unexpected success and wide application of my discovery has brought us to this point, The Nemechek Protocol® as it applies to children. This book explains the root of many medical challenges children face and offers a safe, natural, and inexpensive approach to help them recover.

PART I

HOW TO START THE NEMECHEK PROTOCOL®

1

___

NEWFOUND OPTIMISM IN THE HOPE FOR RECOVERY

More and more children are becoming affected with chronic neurological conditions carrying a variety of acronyms rarely heard of, only a few decades ago. While diagnoses such as ADD, ADHD, or OCD may be familiar to some, many children are diagnosed with new diagnoses such as ASD, ODD, POTS, PANS, and PANDAS. Seeing them struggle academically because of ADD (attention deficit disorder), increasingly missing school because of the physical challenges from POTS (postural orthostatic tachycardia syndrome), or progressively becoming increasingly anxious or depressed.

A Growing List of Pediatric Neurological and Psychiatric Conditions
Bipolar Disorder
Chronic Depression
Developmental Delay
Generalized Anxiety Disorder
ADD (attention deficit disorder)
ADHD (attention deficit hyperactivity disorder)
ASD (autism spectrum disorder)
ODD (oppositional defiance disorder)
OCD (obsessive-compulsive disorder)
POTS (postural orthostatic tachycardia syndrome)

PANS (pediatric acute-onset neuropsychiatric syndrome)
PANDAS (pediatric autoimmune neuropsychiatric disorders associated
with streptococcal infections)

Misunderstanding Leads to a Lack of Hope

Children are experiencing these medical problems because their nervous system is not functioning correctly. Consultations with physicians, psychologists, and therapists only lead to various diagnoses but no answers as to why these conditions are occurring or how to reverse them. Medications may be prescribed to control or improve symptoms, and supplements are offered with little sense of the underlying pathological mechanisms at play. The provider offers little to no hope of recovery for two primary reasons.

The first is that although they may be aware that chronic inflammation plays a role in most chronic neurological conditions, they are not given the tools to reduce the inflammation. Secondly, most physicians are still operating under the old paradigm that the symptoms of a chronic nervous system disorder cannot be reversed. This belief arose before the discovery of the brain's powerful ability to repair itself and rejuvenate or replace aging, damaged neurons.

If someone believes there is little chance to change a situation, their efforts at changing the situation often become half-hearted or non-existent. For instance, if physicians believe the brain cannot recover from symptoms after a chronic brain injury, they never wholeheartedly try to help patients fully recover. And as a result, no one recovers. The cycle of low expectations, minimal effort, and minimal success reinforces the physicians' belief that the brain is incapable of recovery. This is the classic self-fulling prophecy, a scenario with overriding implications in our efforts to help children with these chronic neurological conditions.

The modern fact is that without chronic inflammation inhibiting proper brain development and repair from injuries, most children would spontaneously recover from any neurological disorder, damage, or insult they experience. With the suppression of inflammation within the brain, the child's neuronal repair and rejuvenation mechanisms reactivate and launch them on the path of neurological recovery.

This optimism also applies to many children with a genetically based neurological condition diagnosis. I admit that reducing inflammation will not reverse the anatomical abnormalities some children display from their genetic disorder. Still, many of these children also have symptoms from unresolved neurological injury unrelated to the primary genetic condition. These secondary neurological problems are reversible. I have witnessed profound neurological improvements in these same children whose hope for improvement or recovery was deemed impossible because of the discovery of a genetic mutation.

Inflammation Reduction is the Primary Goal

Recent scientific advances teach us that the brain can fully repair severe injuries, produce stem cells, and continually replace neurons throughout life. These discoveries show that instead of being incapable of recovery, the human brain is perhaps the *most capable* organ of recovery after insults or injuries. These same studies also discovered that chronic inflammatory stress is the most common cause inhibiting recovery.

Inflammation is a normal process in which white blood cells become activated to fight infections and repair tissue. Inflammation is turned on, resolves the problem, and is naturally turned off. If it is short-lived and appropriately regulated, inflammation promotes health.

But, if inflammation is running continually in an unregulated fashion, inflammation will harm the body by activating and suppressing various genes within our DNA (e.g., diabetes mellitus, cancer, autoimmune disorders), having a direct toxic effect on the tissues (e.g., osteoarthritis, cardiovascular disease, chronic pain syndromes) as well as by inhibiting the body's natural repair mechanisms (e.g., mitral valve prolapse, post-concussion syndrome, ADD/ADHD, generalized anxiety, chronic depression, developmental delay, migraine headaches).

Sources of unnatural inflammation can be found in many aspects of our environment. Polluted air, changes in our food supply, chronic psychological stress and trauma, and chronic or recurrent infections. Most importantly, an imbalance of bacteria within the intestinal tract, SIBO, bacterial overgrowth, or dysbiosis, is the primary source of chronic systemic inflammation and neuroinflammation in children.

Knowing that inflammation is the key to many of our health problems, my priority for my patients is to first lower inflammation.

Inflammation is significantly reduced by balancing the omega-6 and omega-3 fatty acids within our tissues, reducing bacterial overgrowth in our small intestine, avoiding inflammatory oils in modern foods, and applying bioelectric stimulation of the vagus nerve. When performed correctly, inflammation is reduced enough; the stage is set for improvement and recovery for various childhood and adult neurological conditions.

2

THE NEMECHEK PROTOCOL®
OVERVIEW

The Basic Science (The Short Version)

There is growing scientific evidence that an imbalance of intestinal bacteria alongside excessive inflammation in the brain may be responsible for the features associated with autism, developmental delay, and mood disorders.

Furthermore, brain injuries from even minor head traumas in children cannot be completely repaired. These result in other common symptoms such as constipation, hyperactivity, anxiety, aggression, poor focus, fatigue, and insomnia.

The Nemechek Protocol®, as it relates to children, begins with a simple two-pronged approach that involves restoring the proper balance of intestinal bacteria and restoring a normal ratio of omega-3 and omega-6 fatty acids.

Eliminating inflammation from these sources re-activates natural brain repair and pruning mechanisms, often leading to substantial recovery from developmental delay and previously unrepaired brain injuries.

The reduction of inflammation is primarily achieved by rebalancing intestinal bacteria and balancing the intakes of omega-3 and omega-6 fatty acids.

Continue reading through this chapter to understand the critical points of the protocol. Specific dosing instructions for each component of the protocol I use with my patients will be provided.

More detailed explanations of these steps will be presented in greater detail in later chapters for those who want a deeper understanding of the science behind the protocol.

First Step – Reduce Bacterial Overgrowth within the Small Intestine

The most critical barrier to overcome when considering brain function health is the presence of excessive colonic bacteria within the small intestine.

Known as small intestine bacterial overgrowth (SIBO), bacterial overgrowth triggers the release of a large wave of inflammatory chemicals that prevent the brain from developing normally. Overcoming SIBO is the most crucial step in helping a child recover.

To emphasize the difference between the bacteria within the small intestine and the bacteria within the colon (also referred to as the lower or large intestine), there's an analogy I use: think of the bacteria from the colon as "fish" and the bacteria from the small intestine as "birds."

With SIBO, the fish live up in the small intestine with the birds. Everyone knows that fish and birds are very different animals and are not meant to live side-by-side together.

The following diagram shows the ideal balance of fish and birds, with each living within their respective environments. The small intestine has very few bacteria compared to the colon.

For every individual "bird" bacterium in the upper small intestine, one hundred million "fish" bacteria live in the lowest portion of the colon, an enormous 1:100,000,000 difference in bacterial concentrations. Because there are such small numbers of bacteria within the small intestine, it is not designed by nature to control large numbers of bacteria within the small intestine, should it occur.

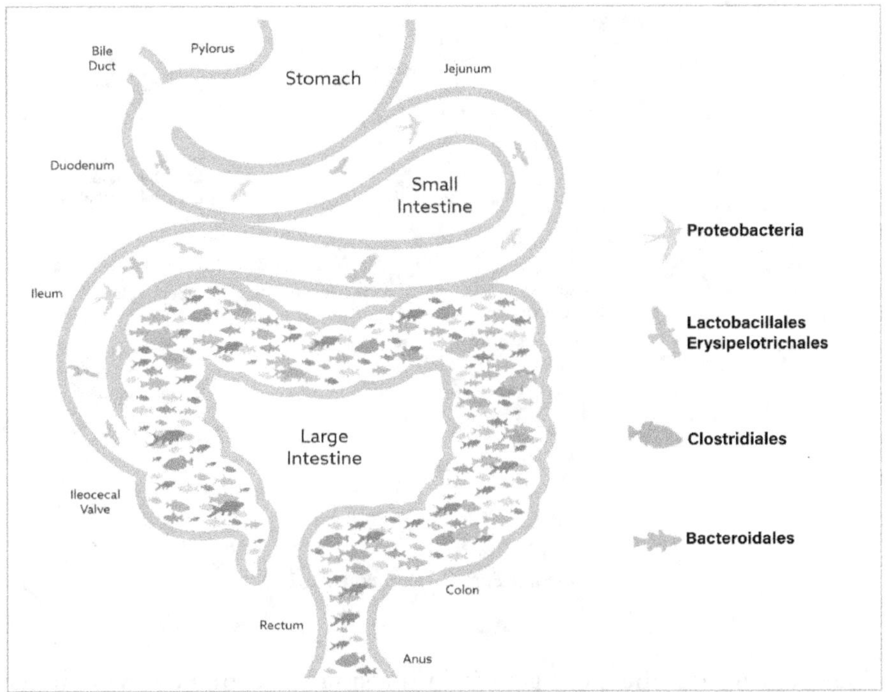

Normally Balanced Intestinal Bacteria

Bacterial overgrowth occurs when one or two species of "fish" bacteria migrate from the colon and begin replicating within the small intestine. The overgrowth from the invading bacteria results in one thousand to one hundred thousand times the normal bacteria within the small intestine.

Medical science has known bacterial overgrowth within the small intestine for approximately sixty years. This is not a recent discovery, and many decades of scientific research have been devoted to methods to help rebalance intestinal bacteria. The first clinical disorder caused by this condition is known as hepatic encephalopathy.

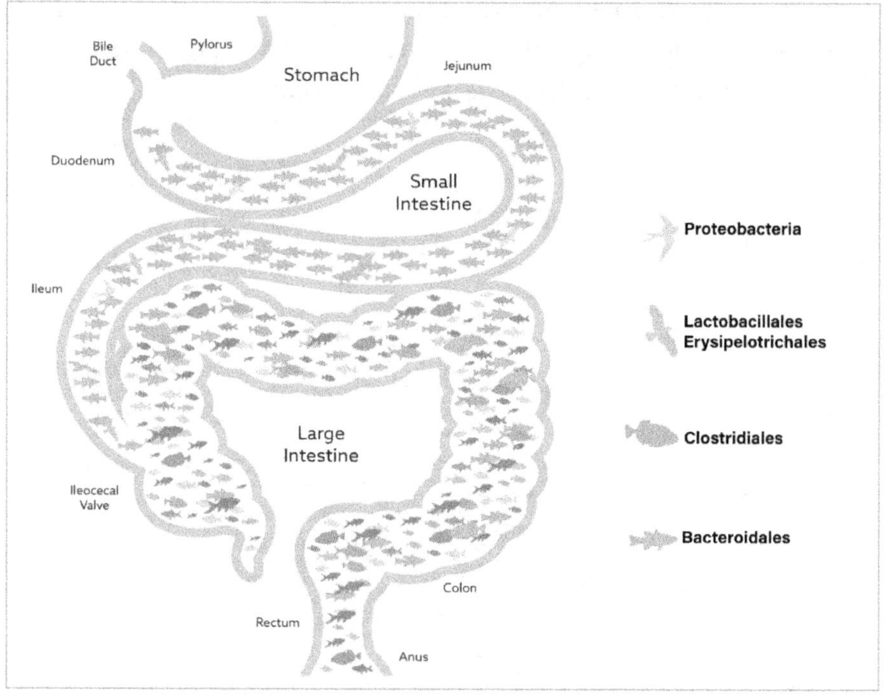

Small Intestine Bacterial Overgrowth (SIBO)

The excessive numbers of bacteria in the small intestine overwhelm its ability to contain its contents properly, and small fragments of bacteria and food molecules leak between the potential space where two cells abut (known as tight junctions) into the surrounding intestinal tissue (known as GALT or gut-associated lymphoid tissues). The failure to contain the intestinal contents is scientifically known as intestinal permeability or bacterial translocation but is more generally called "leaky gut" by laypersons.

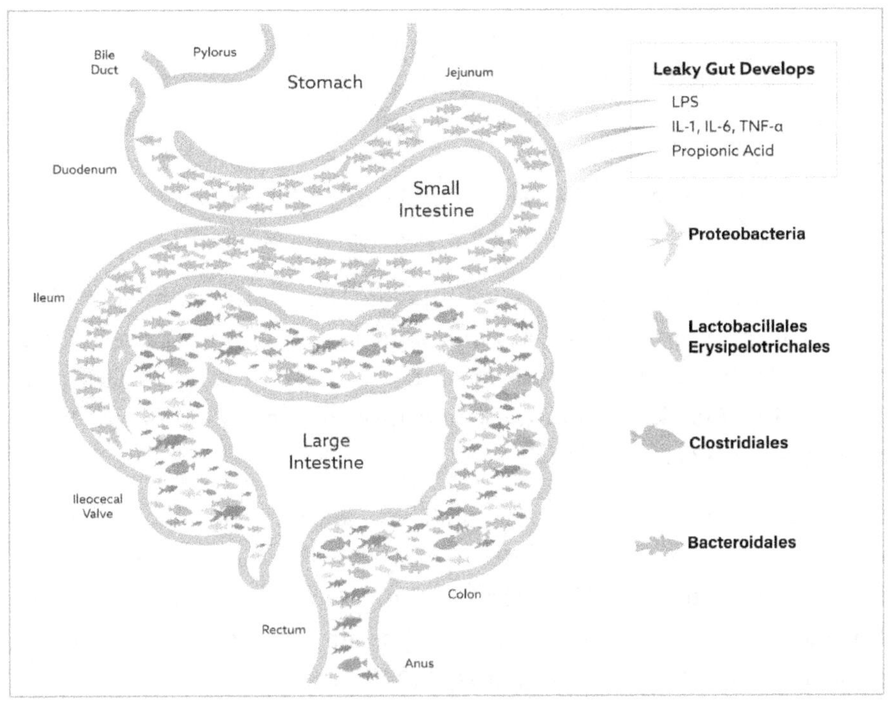

SIBO Leads to Leaky Gut (Bacterial Translocation)

The GALT tissue surrounding the small intestine is estimated to contain seventy percent of all white blood cells within the body. The leakage of bacterial cell wall fragments (LPS) and food molecules is viewed as potentially dangerous by the surrounding white blood cells and results in a substantial inflammatory reaction, releasing inflammatory chemicals into the bloodstream.

Known as cytokines, these inflammatory chemicals flow throughout the body and into the brain, preventing the brain from developing normally by interfering with natural neuronal pruning, repair, and rejuvenation mechanisms.

Of the thousand or more different species of bacteria ("fish") that typically live within the colon, overgrowth most often only occurs when one or two unique species of fish bacteria start living with the birds. The overgrowing "fish" bacteria can increase the concentration of bacteria within the small intestine by 10,000-100,000 times its typical concentration of natural "bird" bacteria.

Occasionally, the overgrowing fish bacteria within the small intestine produce large amounts of chemicals that, because of the leaky gut, can flow into the surrounding tissue and eventually into the bloodstream, causing various adverse effects. In particular, a chemical called propionic acid is suspected to leak into the bloodstream and ultimately trigger many unique behaviors often associated with autism.

Some researchers believe the production and leakage of abnormal chemicals into the bloodstream may contribute to some of the features seen in PANS (Pediatric Acute-onset Neuropsychiatric Syndrome) and PANDAS (pediatric autoimmune neuropsychiatric disorders associated with streptococcal infections).

When large quantities of propionic acid leak into the bloodstream, it can sedate children, making them behave as if they are drugged or heavily medicated. The sedating effect of propionic acid is responsible for kids losing eye contact, not responding readily, and generally behaving with very little awareness of their surroundings.

Propionic acid can also have a potentially hallucinatory effect as well. This can cause children to be almost mesmerized by rotating objects, to become obsessed with turning switches on and off, or to become completely oblivious to all other humans in the room, including their parents.

The Nemechek Protocol® uses an over-the-counter prebiotic fiber called inulin to balance the bacteria in younger children and a non-absorbable antibiotic called rifaximin to balance the bacteria in older children and adults. Reversal of bacterial overgrowth by either method leads to a rapid decline in systemic inflammation and halts the excessive production of propionic acid and its associated behaviors.

Within a few weeks of reversing bacterial overgrowth, the small intestine will naturally heal itself, leading to a rapid decline in the release of inflammatory cytokines and propionic acid. Rifaximin and inulin are not to be used in combination.

Once bacterial overgrowth is reversed and propionic acid levels decline if being produced, these children are released from the toxic, stuporous propionic acid state they have been trapped in. Within a few days, they often become more aware, have improved eye contact, and respond more readily to their name or simple commands. I refer to this early response when the propionic acid declines as "the awakening period." The awakening period is a direct effect of the drop in production of propionic acid.

Children with ADD/ADHD, POTS, depression, anxiety, older children and adults with autism, and children with developmental delay (without an autism diagnosis) tend to have little to no awakening period. This is because they have a different species of bacteria over-growing in their intestines that cannot produce propionic acid.

If a patient does not experience an awakening phenomenon within the first few weeks, it does not mean the protocol is not working. It simply means they have bacterial overgrowth with bacteria that do not produce propionic acid. The reduction of systemic and neurological inflammation that occurs with the reversal of bacterial overgrowth often does not cause immediate positive improvements. Improvement from inflammation reduction usually takes 2-3 months to happen to a significant degree.

Second Step – Rebalance the Intake of Omega-3 and Omega-6 Fatty Acids

Excessive levels of inflammatory chemicals known as cytokines prevent the brain's normal repair and pruning mechanisms from operating correctly. Balancing the intestinal bacteria substantially lowers inflammation, but improving the balance of omega-3 and omega-6 fatty acids is also required to allow the brain to recover.

Omega-6 fatty acids are natural chemicals found in plants and are required to activate healthy levels of inflammation to repair tissue or fight infection in the body. Omega-3 fatty acids are natural chemicals found in plants and animal flesh and act as a counterbalance to help turn off inflammation after it is no longer necessary.

Unfortunately, our modern food supply contains excessive inflammation-promoting omega-6 fatty acids and deficient amounts of inflammation-extinguishing omega-3 fatty acids.

An excessive amount of the omega-6 fatty acid chemical called linoleic acid is present in the food supply in the form of vegetable oils, shortening, while another omega-6 fatty acid called arachidonic acid concentrates in the meat of animals who are fed grains such as corn or soybeans. Minimizing the intake of soybean and other grain oils commonly found in processed foods goes a long way to limit the inflammatory threat they pose to your child's health.

Fortunately, another tool in the fight against inflammatory omega-6 fatty acids is oleic acid, a fatty acid found in high concentrations in extra virgin olive oil. Oleic acid can neutralize the toxicity of excessive linoleic and arachidonic acids. Consuming extra virgin olive oil (EVOO) daily will protect the body from excessive linoleic acid and reduce its negative inflammatory effect throughout the body and brain.

Increasing the intake of omega-3 fatty acids is easily achieved by daily supplementation with fish oil. Although nuts and flax also contain omega-3 fatty acids, two omega-3 fatty acids referred to as EPA and DHA are found in high concentrations of fish oil and cannot readily be supplemented in any other manner. Most importantly, DHA is the primary diet source of omega-3 fatty acids that can penetrate the nervous system.

Because of the high frequency of fraudulent fish oil and low-quality olive oil in the marketplace, careful attention must be paid to using the correct brands of fish oil and extra virgin olive oil.

3

___

STARTING THE NEMECHEK PROTOCOL

How Early Can The Nemechek Protocol® Be Started?

Before starting The Nemechek Protocol®, it is recommended that parents consult their pediatrician if their child is less than 12 months of age, if there are any other complicated medical issues for a child of any age, or if the child requires prescription medications.

Fish oil, olive oil, and inulin should be supplemented at the earliest sign of a child's developmental, behavioral, emotional, or intellectual problems. Starting the protocol in healthy-appearing children can significantly improve their chances of remaining healthy and not developing any common neurological issues occurring in children these days.

Day-to-Day on The Nemechek Protocol®

There is no particular order or timing in the day when a parent should administer the inulin, fish oil, or olive oil. They can be taken together or separately, with or without food, in the morning or the evening. In comparison, some parents prefer to start just the oils for a few weeks and then add the inulin later. If my patient is older and begins with rifaximin instead of inulin, the rifaximin must be taken in divided doses approximately ten to twelve hours apart.

The recommended brands for inulin are Nemechek Blue Organic Inulin (NemechekBlue.com) or inulin produced by NOW Foods. Gummies containing inulin are no longer recommended. For fish oil, Nemechek Silver has a high concentration of the brain-penetrating omega-3 fatty acid DHA (NemechekSilver.com). Optionally, fish oils produced by Nordic Naturals or NOW Foods are also acceptable.

Due to the unpredictable quality of extra virgin olive oil found in the market, use Nemechek Gold (NemechekGold.com) or another California Olive Oil Council (COOC) certified extra virgin olive oil (COOC.com).

These are the specific ones used with success over the years. Due to the high quantity of poor-quality or fraudulent supplements and olive oil in the marketplace, deviating from these options may cause the protocol to fail and prevent your child from recovering.

Nemechek Protocol Starter Pack (NemechekProtocol.com) is a low-stress approach to starting the protocol. It contains the proper brands of fish oil, inulin, and extra virgin olive oil, a copy of our book, and an easy-to-understand dosing guide for each ingredient. Also included is a 3-month trial subscription to Nemechek Navigator (NemechekNavigator.com), a support and education site for parents utilizing The Nemechek Protocol.

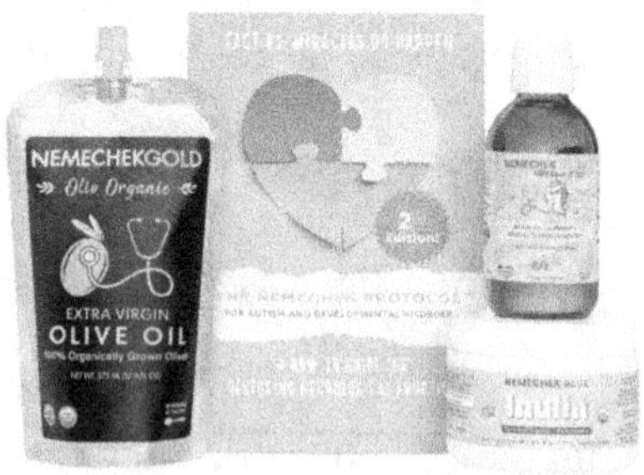

The Nemechek Protocol Starter Pack

I also recommend eliminating all additional vitamins, supplements, and remedies unless specifically prescribed by a physician for a diagnosed nutrient deficiency (e.g., iron or vitamin D deficiency).

First Step - Reduce Bacterial Overgrowth

Ingredient #1 – Inulin or Rifaximin

The prebiotic fiber inulin and the prescription medication rifaximin (Xifaxan®) are my two options to balance the intestinal bacteria. Starting the protocol with inulin is my preferred approach in younger children, while beginning with rifaximin is preferred in older children because inulin is less effective in older children.

Choosing Between Inulin and Rifaximin

- If under 8 years of age, use inulin to balance intestine bacteria.
- If between 8-14 years old, use either inulin or rifaximin to balance intestine bacteria.
- If 15 or older, use rifaximin to balance intestine bacteria.

Inulin Dosage

- Give a 1/8 teaspoon of powdered Nemechek Blue Inulin.
- It can be mixed in food or drink.
- Dosage does not change with age.

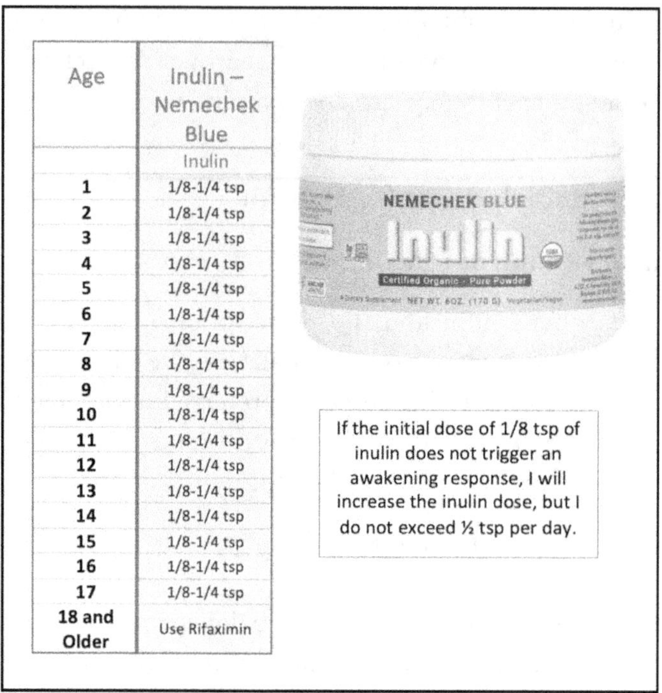

Age	Inulin – Nemechek Blue
	Inulin
1	1/8-1/4 tsp
2	1/8-1/4 tsp
3	1/8-1/4 tsp
4	1/8-1/4 tsp
5	1/8-1/4 tsp
6	1/8-1/4 tsp
7	1/8-1/4 tsp
8	1/8-1/4 tsp
9	1/8-1/4 tsp
10	1/8-1/4 tsp
11	1/8-1/4 tsp
12	1/8-1/4 tsp
13	1/8-1/4 tsp
14	1/8-1/4 tsp
15	1/8-1/4 tsp
16	1/8-1/4 tsp
17	1/8-1/4 tsp
18 and Older	Use Rifaximin

If the initial dose of 1/8 tsp of inulin does not trigger an awakening response, I will increase the inulin dose, but I do not exceed ½ tsp per day.

Rifaximin (Xifaxan®) Dosage

- 550 mg twice daily for 10 days, intermittently or monthly.
- Medication can be crushed and mixed with food or drink if necessary.
- This is a prescription medication and must be obtained through a physician.

More information on using inulin or rifaximin to reduce small intestinal bacterial overgrowth is provided later in the book.

Second Step - Rebalance Fatty Acids

Ingredient #2 – Daily Extra Virgin Olive Oil

I use California olive oil that is COOC-certified and have my patients consume the olive oil daily in its raw and uncooked form, either straight like medicine or mixed in food or drink. The minimum required amount of olive oil is listed below.

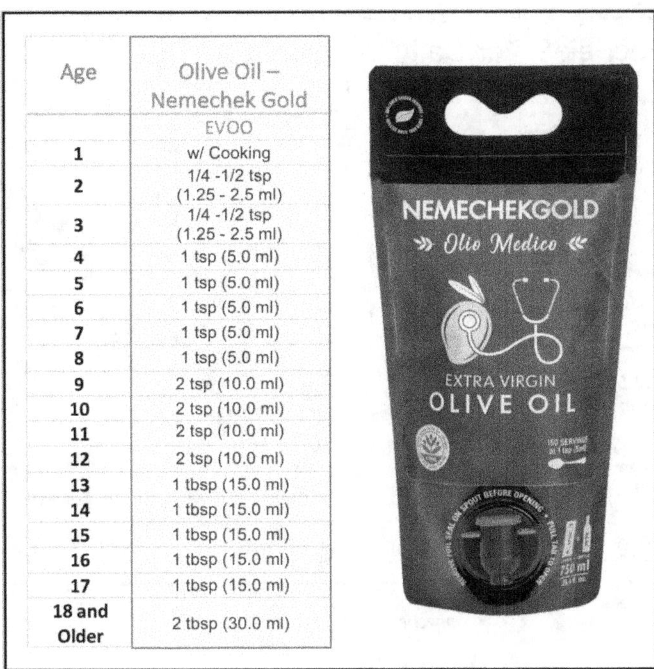

Age	Olive Oil – Nemechek Gold
	EVOO
1	w/ Cooking
2	1/4 -1/2 tsp (1.25 - 2.5 ml)
3	1/4 -1/2 tsp (1.25 - 2.5 ml)
4	1 tsp (5.0 ml)
5	1 tsp (5.0 ml)
6	1 tsp (5.0 ml)
7	1 tsp (5.0 ml)
8	1 tsp (5.0 ml)
9	2 tsp (10.0 ml)
10	2 tsp (10.0 ml)
11	2 tsp (10.0 ml)
12	2 tsp (10.0 ml)
13	1 tbsp (15.0 ml)
14	1 tbsp (15.0 ml)
15	1 tbsp (15.0 ml)
16	1 tbsp (15.0 ml)
17	1 tbsp (15.0 ml)
18 and Older	2 tbsp (30.0 ml)

Olive Oil Dosages

A listing of COOC-certified olive oils can be found in the appendix and at COOC.com. I have found that it is easier for families to buy olive oil online directly from small, regional olive farmers if COOC-certified olive oil is unavailable in the local market. Nemechek Gold (Nemechek Gold.com) is a COOC-certified extra virgin olive oil blended with your child's health in mind.

Ingredient #3 – Daily Liquid Fish Oil

When starting, use a liquid fish oil such as Nemechek Silver (NemechekSilver.com), as many children have difficulty swallowing fish oil capsules.

Nemechek Silver Daily Dose Guide

Age	Nemechek Silver, High DHA Liquid	Age	Nemechek Silver, High DHA Liquid	Age	Nemechek Silver, High DHA Liquid
1	1/4 tsp (1.25 ml)	7	1 tsp (5.0 ml)	13	2 tsp (10.0 ml)
2	1/4 tsp (1.25 ml)	8	1 tsp (5.0 ml)	14	2 tsp (10.0 ml)
3	1/2 tsp (2.5 ml)	9	1 tsp (5.0 ml)	15	3 tsp (15.0 ml)
4	1/2 tsp (2.5 ml)	10	1 tsp (5.0 ml)	16	3 tsp (15.0 ml)
5	1/2 tsp (2.5 ml)	11	2 tsp (10.0 ml)	17	3 tsp (15.0 ml)
6	1 tsp (5.0 ml)	12	2 tsp (10.0 ml)	18 and Older	2 tbsp (30.0 ml)

Nemechek Silver Fish Oil Dosages

What to Expect with The Nemechek Protocol®

Within the first few weeks of starting, many children with conditions involving propionic acid production (PANS, PANDAS, Autism) demonstrate much greater eye contact and an improved sense of awareness and connectedness. This is because the sedating effects of propionic acid have been reduced or eliminated due to a rebalancing of the intestinal bacteria. See chapter sixteen for a more in-depth explanation of bacterial overgrowth and propionic acid.

Eliminating the sedative effect will also give a child's parent a sense of how neurologically imbalanced their child is. Some behaviors may seem worse because the propionic acid was suppressing their ability to act out these behaviors as a drug might. Such behaviors might be stimming, anxiety, aggression, hyperactivity, or sleeplessness. Parents are seeing their child for the first time without being sedated.

In other words, a child's behavior may initially worsen, but that does not mean the protocol is not working. It means we have discovered a key to the potential recovery and the starting point we begin working from.

Within the following weeks to months, parents often begin noticing improvements in many aspects of any neurological impairment or delay their child has been experiencing. Although the pace may seem slower than one might have hoped, the recovery marches forward very consistently.

Patience on the parents' part is essential because there is no method to get the child to "improve faster," and efforts to do so often lead to worsening behavior or progress stopping completely.

If progress does stop or a parent feels their child is not reacting correctly to the protocol, they will need to refer to the later chapters of the book. This chapter is the short version of The Nemechek Protocol®. In contrast, later chapters are full of information to answer the inevitable questions that will arise as the child's nervous repairs and prunes itself and starts them on a path of true recovery.

4

NEMECHEK NAVIGATOR GUIDES
YOUR RECOVERY

As more and more parents opt to use The Nemechek Protocol to help their child's nervous system recover, many find they need occasional questions answered or would benefit from chatting with other parents on a similar journey. Understanding this need led Dr. Nemechek to develop the Nemechek Navigator.

The Nemechek Navigator (NemechekNavigator.com) is a web-based app that teaches and guides parents utilizing The Nemechek Protocol for their children with many neurological, behavioral, and emotional issues.

The Nemechek Navigator contains many instructional videos and a searchable database with answers to over 900 common questions parents encounter using The Nemechek Protocol for their child. Dr. Nemechek has personally provided each answer. Starting in 2024, there will also be an option to use artificial intelligence (ChatGPT) to have long-form questions answered in great detail.

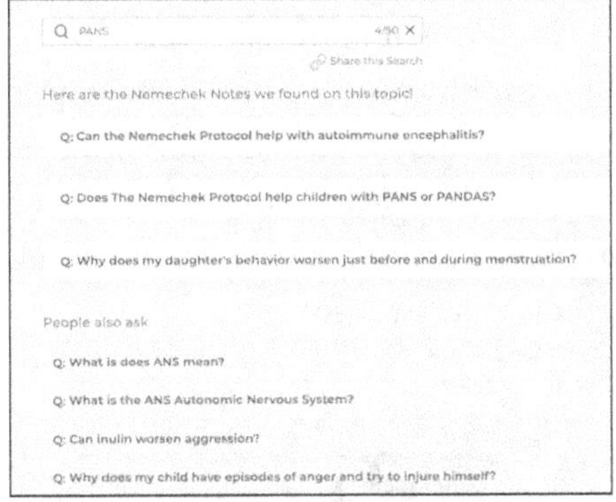

Nemechek Navigator Search Tool

The powerful Progress Tracker is a clinical tool designed to help parents assess how well the protocol is helping their child's recovery. It can also provide valuable tips on adjusting the protocol if progress is slow. Taking a Progress Tracker assessment every 90 days to measure their child's Recovery Score helps determine if their progress continues at an acceptable pace. An increasing Recovery Score indicates your child is improving at an adequate. If progress has stalled or is deteriorating, your child's Recovery Score will not increase or decrease over 90 days.

Parents are also provided dosing guides, supplement discounts, and an active parental chat community where they experience advice and support from other parents on a similar journey. Dr. Nemechek frequently posts short videos on commonly requested topics and monthly Live web video sessions, allowing members to submit questions for Dr. Nemechek to answer live.

A complimentary 3-month trial subscription to Nemechek Navigator is available with a Nemechek Protocol Starter Pack (NemechekProtocol.com).

PART II

THE FIRST THREE MONTHS

5

EVALUATING PROGRESS

Success in neurological improvement and recovery on The Nemechek Protocol® is highly dependent on maintaining a healthy balance of intestinal bacteria. Without this balance, little to no neurological recovery can occur. Lack of recovery is rarely due to inadequate fish or olive oil doses, so the adjustment of recommended olive or fish oil doses is not advised.

This section will explain how to determine if progress is occurring, how to make changes if it is not, and how to decide whether or not additional treatment with vagus nerve stimulation is warranted.

When assessing if the protocol is successful, the first question is whether the use of inulin has effectively rebalanced intestinal bacteria. If not, inulin needs to be switched to rifaximin. If the child has already been using rifaximin, the regimen will be increased from occasional or monthly cycles of rifaximin to a continuous, non-stop rifaximin dosing regimen.

The second question is whether neurological recovery occurs across all areas that seem injured, dysfunctional, or delayed. Suppose the child is experiencing only partial improvement (significant improvements in many areas but little to no improvement in a few others). In that case, five minutes of daily vagus nerve stimulation is added to broaden the neurological recovery further. A thorough discussion of the science and use of vagus nerve stimulation can be found in chapters 11 and 12.

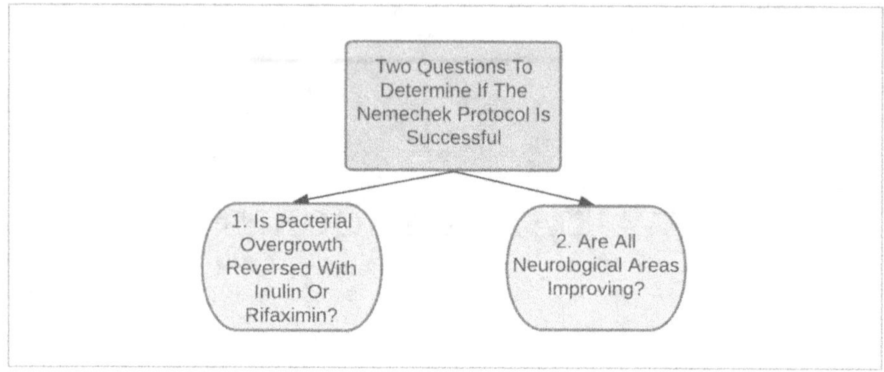

Determining if The Nemechek Protocol is Successful

As simple as this sounds, answering these two questions can sometimes be complicated because many events can occur after starting the protocol that can impede progress and mask recovery but do not indicate improper dosing. Examples might be beginning the protocol, but six weeks later, the child develops an infection that takes two rounds of antibiotics, and then another four weeks to recover from the effects of the illness and antibiotic treatment for it.

Another example might be that during the first few months of the protocol, the family moves, and the child experiences many stressors, including changing to different schools with different routines and new teachers and therapists. Both examples are unavoidable situations that can impact recovery, especially early on.

If there are intervening events, the parents account for these and factor them into our decision-making process before deciding if a particular step in the protocol is working or not working.

The Initial Response Patterns to The Nemechek Protocol®

The Nemechek Protocol® may initially bring about two patterns of treatment response within the first three months:

1. Significant improvement in the pace of recovery.
2. Little to no improvement in the pace of recovery.

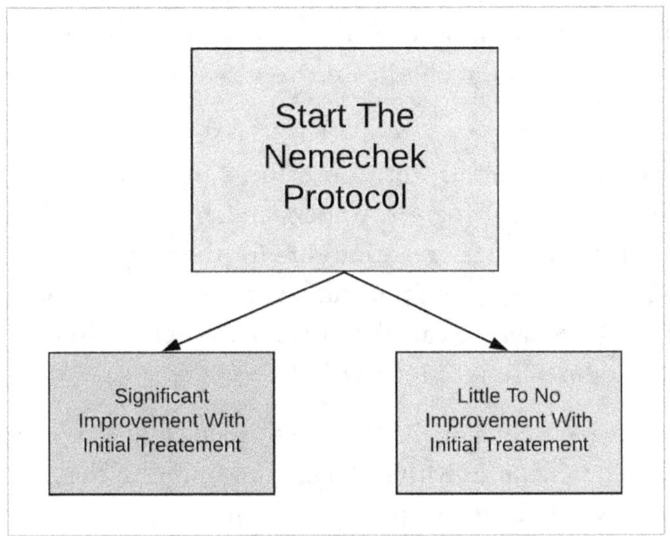

Initial Response Patterns

Making an objective determination about the child's progress is essential in getting the most out of The Nemechek Protocol®.

Several aspects of the child's development need to be considered. Assess their receptive and expressive language skills, awareness, emotional lability, intestinal function, hyperactivity, social interaction, and motor skills. Sometimes, it is helpful for a parent to consult with their child's teachers and therapists about their observations now compared to when they first started to help determine which response category the child falls into.

Teachers and therapists can greatly assist because their curriculum or programs are often modular with chapters and skill levels. As professionals who interact with the child frequently, they are in a unique position to observe if the child's pace of learning or developmental improvement has increased or plateaued.

Many parents will use the Progress Tracker within Nemechek Navigator to help determine if their child's progress is on track or if changes to the protocol are required. Taking a Progress Tracker assessment every 90 days to measure their child's Recovery Score helps determine if their progress continues at an acceptable pace. An increasing Recovery Score indicates your child is improving at an adequate. If progress has stalled or is deteriorating, your child's Recovery Score will not increase or decrease over 90 days.

It is important for parents not to overfocus on their child's speaking ability when assessing progress. Understandably, conversing with their child is often the parent's greatest desire for their child's recovery. Still, receptive and expressive communication are possibly the most complex neurological processes we can observe and, as such, often take the most extended amount of time to recover fully.

Once parents have categorized how well their child has responded to either inulin or rifaximin within the first few months, the remainder of this chapter will help them understand what to do next to maximize their recovery.

The following sections in this chapter are organized based on a child's response to treatment. They will either consistently improve or show minimal to no response to inulin or rifaximin.

Significant Improvement Scenarios

If inulin or rifaximin is effective in balancing intestinal bacteria and the fish oil and olive oil are correctly dosed, parents should observe improvements in multiple areas of development over the first three to six months. The forms of progress seen include cognition, communication, meaningful play, emotional control, socialization, motor function, receptive and expressive language, and intestinal function, which are common in most children.

If a significant pace of recovery has begun and the inulin seems well-tolerated, there is no need to adjust the dose of inulin, fish oil, or olive oil. The fish and olive oil doses will only need to be adjusted about every one-to-two years as the child ages. The exception is inulin; its dose does not increase over time, even with substantial changes in the size or age of the child.

However, in some cases, neurological improvements are not uniform across all areas, with one or two areas of concern that do not show signs of improvement. Sometimes, they may show an initial response that is not maintained, with the results proving to be only temporary. Each of these outcomes is shown below.

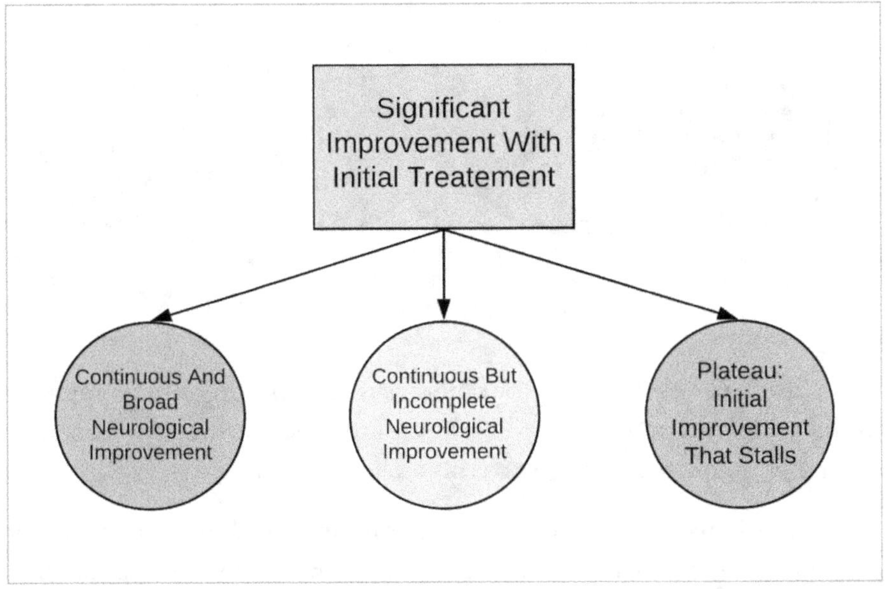

Patterns of Initial Improvement

Little to No Improvement Scenarios

Occasionally, it is difficult to see the initial gains in children being treated with inulin because of overlapping anxiety, hyperactivity, and aggression revealed during the awakening. These issues can arise when inulin has effectively stripped away the excessive propionic acid, which shows the true extent of the child's underlying neurological imbalance. In some children, the increase in anxiety, aggression, and hyperactivity is so extreme that their inulin must be discontinued.

This situation is referred to as "inulin intolerance." If the increase in these behaviors is tolerable, the inulin can be continued, and the negative behaviors will begin resolving within 1-2 months as the nervous system continues to recover.

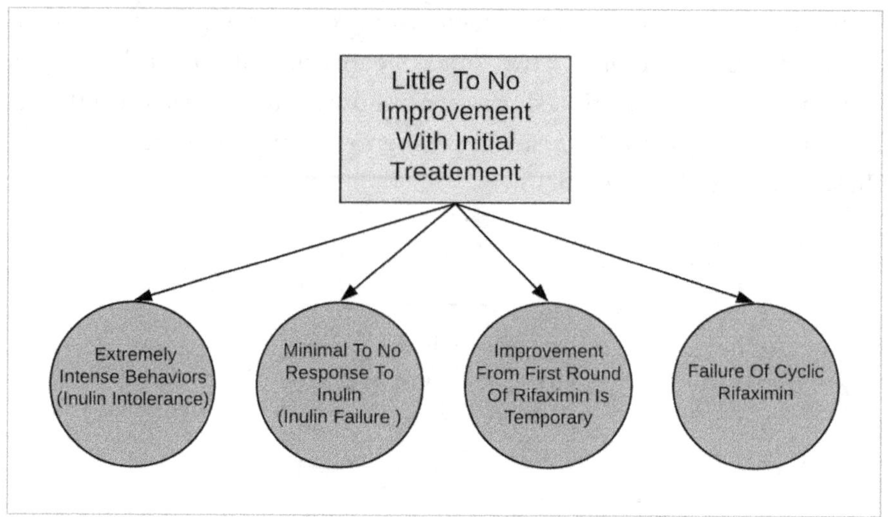

Patterns of Little to No Improvement

If the inulin is well tolerated, but there is no significant improvement in the neurological recovery rate after 3-4 months, you need to consider the inulin ineffective and refer to this as "inulin failure."

Sometimes, the child's lack of progress on inulin is due to poor quality or possibly fraudulent inulin. It is not uncommon to witness patients who showed no response to the protocol after many months of using inulin but suddenly experienced an awakening within a few to several days of switching to an approved brand of inulin. The authenticity of the product is a variable I must always consider.

Finally, suppose there is no progress within several months after taking rifaximin intermittently or on 10-day monthly cycles. In that case, the child is most likely experiencing rapid relapsing of bacterial overgrowth within the small intestine and will require continuous, twice-daily rifaximin to maintain a consistent pace of recovery.

The primary cause of rapid relapsing of bacterial overgrowth within the small intestine is often due to slow forward propulsion of the small intestine. Fortunately, intestinal motility improves, and continuous rifaximin can be transitioned to monthly or intermittent 10-day courses of twice-daily rifaximin.

6

MANAGING SUCCESSFUL RECOVERY

The most common response to The Nemechek Protocol® is a continuous, broad-level state of recovery that can continue for years. Inulin easily maintains intestinal bacterial balance and protects against relapse despite exposure to antibiotics, intestinal illnesses, anesthesia, slow intestinal motility, and other causes of intestinal bacterial overgrowth.

For these reasons, inulin is my preferred initial method of balancing the intestinal bacteria. The fact that inulin is inexpensive and readily available worldwide is also a prominent factor. Unfortunately, some children may experience inulin failure, a plateauing of their progress when the inulin seemingly fails to work.

Once a child develops inulin failure, they will require further treatment with rifaximin to balance their intestinal bacteria. By age fifteen, it is preferred to start children on rifaximin because the chances of lasting response to inulin are small.

If rifaximin is not readily available, starting a child of any age on inulin along with fish oil and olive oil is recommended because the combination might still be enough to result in a positive shift in recovery, even in older children. Once rifaximin becomes available, the inulin can be stopped if deemed ineffective.

When initially treating with rifaximin, parents need to be patient because they may not notice any improvements for four to eight weeks. Because rifaximin is classified as an antibiotic, many parents expect a more rapid recovery. Still, after either inulin or rifaximin, recovery in these children occurs slowly but steadily. Unlike other antibiotics the parents are familiar with, rifaximin rebalances the intestinal bacteria, which allows the nervous system to begin recovering, a process that will continue after the course of rifaximin is completed. It is essential to know that rifaximin has an excellent safety profile because it does not enter the bloodstream.

Children initially treated with rifaximin tend to be older, often will have less of a recognizable "awakening," may have relatively more significant degrees of developmental or maturity delay depending on how long their condition has been ongoing, and significantly worse focus or emotional dysregulation because of a more substantial number of cumulative brain injuries occurring over a more extended period. For all these reasons, older children sometimes appear to recover "more slowly" than younger children. The actual truth is the pace of recovery is the same, but some older children have a more significant neurological deficit to recover from.

Suppose the child has responded to a single course of rifaximin. In that case, there is a chance that additional treatment with other antibiotics, intestinal illnesses, general anesthesia, or slow intestinal motility from underlying autonomic dysfunction may trigger a relapse in intestinal bacterial overgrowth, which will halt recovery.

With the relapse in intestinal bacteria, parents may see a return of some of the symptoms that had been improving after rifaximin or simply an overall plateauing in the pace of their neurological recovery. Suppose there are no apparent circumstances (severe illness, emotional stress, head injury, sinus infections, dental problems) to account for the behavior change. In that case, the child must be re-treated with a course(s) of monthly or continuous rifaximin.

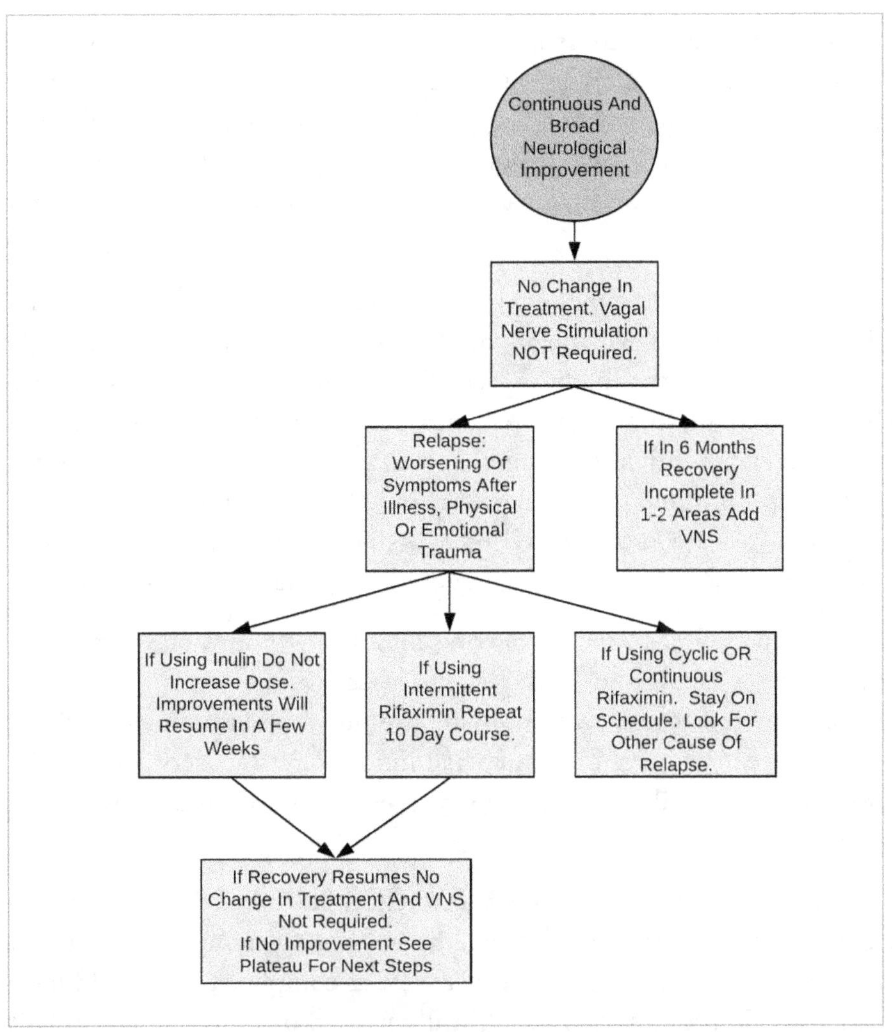

Managing Continuous and Broad Recovery

Waiting approximately 3-4 weeks before repeating rifaximin is necessary because the worsening of symptoms might instead be from a mild intestinal disturbance (virus, medicine, tainted food) or an emotional, physical or inflammatory brain trauma, and these would predictably show signs of recovery before the waiting period is complete.

Chronic, low-grade sinus or dental infections are very common events that can cause a temporary and prolonged worsening of symptoms that might be misconstrued as a relapse but are not. A mild runny nose, cough, or flair of allergies can cause enough neurological stress to worsen anxiety, hyperactivity, aggression, and stimming. A simple ten-day course of nasal corticosteroid spray (e.g., OTC fluticasone) can improve the symptoms and lead to a positive trajectory of improvement once again.

Once excessive inflammation is substantially reduced, immune function improves and will begin more effectively in clearing low-grade infections from the body, especially around the teeth and gums. Increasing dental pain from the improved immune function is also a frequent cause of deteriorating behavior, especially if it occurs a month or two after improving the balance of intestinal bacteria with rifaximin. Dental X-rays are strongly advised as visual examination by the dentist often fails to see the underlying issues causing the behavioral changes.

Emotional traumas such as moving into a new home, starting a new school or a change in therapist, increased home stress (pandemic, divorce, or separation), and bullying are just a few examples of situations that can cause a temporary halt in recovery. Recovery may not be noticed again until the stress-causing scenario has been dealt with or a new routine is established.

Parents must monitor all aspects of their child's neurological development to ensure they recover. Sometimes, after six months, parents will realize that their child's recovery was not as complete as it should have been or that progress has significantly slowed or even seemed to halt altogether. As stated previously, assessing the Recovery Score with the Progress Tracker or getting feedback from teachers and therapists is of great assistance in determining if the child's progress has hit a plateau or is deteriorating.

As shown in the graph below, if a slow, continuous, and broad level of neurological recovery is present, no change in treatment is required.

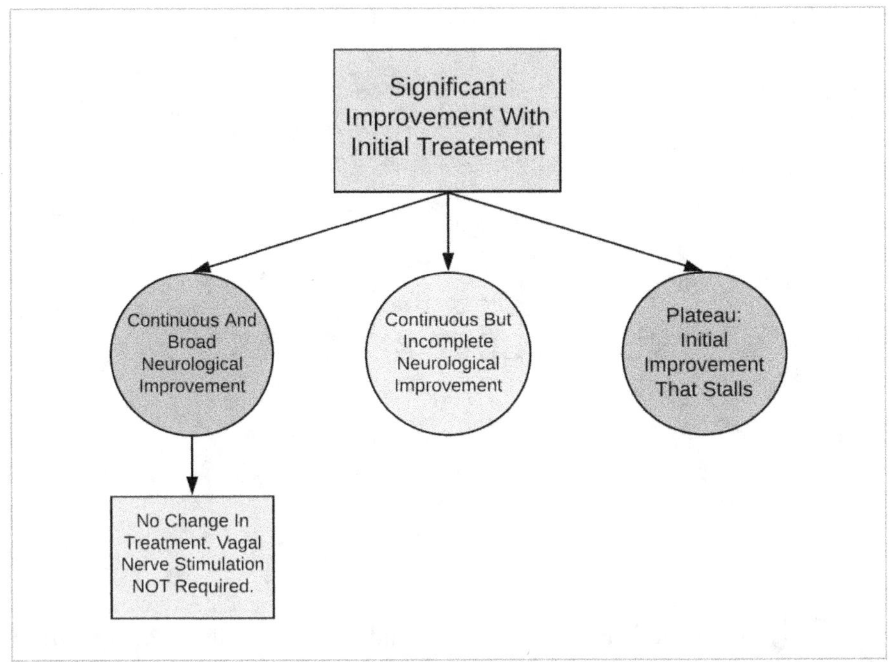

Patterns of Improvement

Sometimes, the child will continue to recover, but after several months, it becomes apparent that their recovery is incomplete. If incomplete recovery occurs, additional changes to the protocol are then required.

7

INCOMPLETE RECOVERY

Occasionally, recovery is partial or incomplete. An example might be when, despite improvements in comprehension, expressive communication, and socialization, the child has little to no gains in another neurological aspect, such as gross motor skills. Or, it could be a child with improved speech, socialization, and constipation, but their intense hyperactivity and tantrums have shown no improvement.

If recovery continues in some areas but not others, adding five minutes of transcutaneous auricular vagus nerve stimulation (taVNS) per day is recommended. This will reduce inflammation within the brain, further allowing the remaining areas to begin recovering.

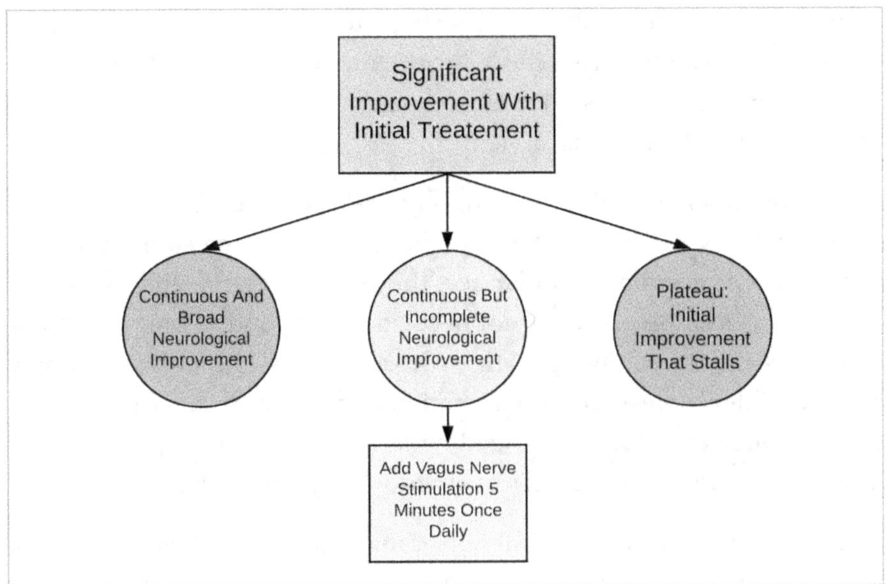

Managing Incomplete Recovery

Vagus nerve stimulation does not increase the speed of recovery, but it lowers inflammation further to help more areas of the nervous system begin recovering. Often, within 6-8 weeks of starting vagus nerve stimulation, the lagging neurological aspects also begin to improve in most children.

Many parents may keep extensive notes, charts, and diaries, logging their child's daily functioning and dosages. While keeping track of dosage changes is essential, it is recommended to chart neurological progress no more than *once a month* or only when there is a sudden change in behavior or function. Since neurological recovery is slow, all children will experience "good days and bad days." Charting too frequently might lead to the misinterpretation of the routine ups and downs in a child's behavior as a relapse and an unnecessary change in the regimen, not to mention unnecessarily adding to the parents' anxiety.

Overfocusing on behavioral changes that occur in the short term is a common mistake and often leads to unnecessary changes in therapy. Remember, even the behavior of neurotypical children can fluctuate daily. Having a bad day or week is usually of no consequence, and efforts to determine the causes of each good or bad event will often lead to false conclusions, errors in treatment, and emotional exhaustion for the parent. The key is focusing on net improvements over a few months, not days or weeks.

Also, remember that although two children with similar neurological issues, such as ADD or PANS, may have begun at the same time and started the protocol at a similar age, they can have very different paths of recovery because one does not necessarily respond to the protocol as readily as the other. Overgrowth with varying species of bacteria may result in differing levels of inflammation and other presence or absence of propionic acid production, leading to better or worse eye contact or awareness and varying degrees of emotional dysregulation.

Differing frequency and severity of brain trauma (physical, emotional, and inflammatory) will result in different levels of cumulative brain injury each child is experiencing and often present as poor focus, hyperactivity, anxiety, aggression, emotional lability, gastroesophageal reflux, constipation and even premenstrual syndrome (PMS). Likewise, genetic differences between the two children can result in different brain sensitivities to chronic inflammation, leading to varying degrees of disability due to or recovery from a similar injury.

The Addition of Vagus Nerve Stimulation

The science of vagus nerve stimulation (VNS) will be described in greater detail in later chapters, but to understand how it is used with The Nemechek Protocol®, essential aspects of its use will be discussed here.

Vagus nerve stimulation (VNS) improves recovery by reducing inflammation within the child's brain, allowing the brain's natural repair, pruning, and rejuvenation mechanisms to work more effectively throughout the entire brain.

Stimulation of the vagus nerve can be done by surgically implanting a device in the chest or placing an electrode clip to the front and back of an area of the ear called the concha. Stimulation through the skin of the ear is referred to as transcutaneous auricular VNS (taVNS) and uses such low currents that the child cannot feel any electrical sensation.

Transcutaneous auricular VNS only needs to be done five minutes per day on either ear and can be done while the child is awake or asleep. Transcutaneous auricular VNS has a proven safety record over decades of use for treating epilepsy and depression. Although five minutes of taVNS per day seems insignificant, it can potentially lower systemic inflammation for 24-36 hours.

Remember, the primary goal of The Nemechek Protocol® is to lower inflammation enough to allow the nervous system to repair itself.

In summary, taVNS is not required for all children because many can fully recover without it. If a child seems to be recovering fully, vagus nerve stimulation is unnecessary, and its use will not speed up recovery. However, if certain aspects of their neurological impairment are lagging behind other areas' recovery, taVNS is strongly recommended. Overall, the older the child, the more likely taVNS will be beneficial in a more complete neurological recovery.

8

RECOVERY PLATEAU

Another response pattern parents might observe is that the child is experiencing significant improvement, but after several months, the pace of recovery dramatically slows and may even stop altogether. Hitting this plateau is generally easier to notice than one might think. Parents, therapists, and teachers will often all share the same observation that the child's progress rate has reached a near standstill.

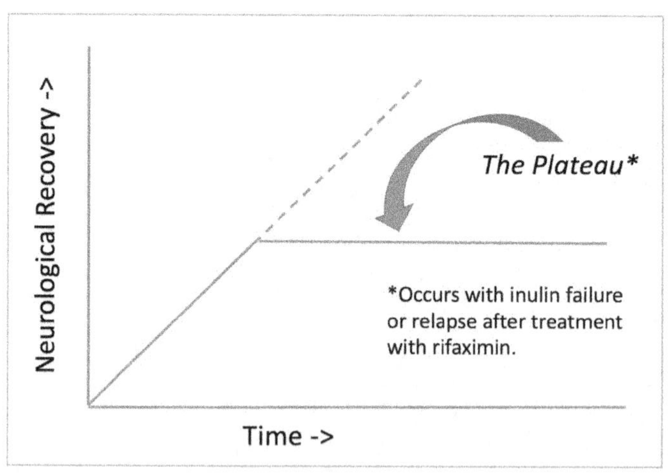

The Recovery Plateau

If a plateau is being considered, look for new factors that might disrupt intestinal balance or cause recent brain trauma. This could be a new supplement or probiotic that has been introduced, a significant new trauma (physical, emotional, or inflammatory), or a new chronic infection such as low-grade sinusitis or a dental infection.

Factors That Interrupt Recovery When Using Inulin

- Physical Brain Injury (concussion, subconcussive event)
- Emotional Trauma (bullying, abrupt routine change, loss of a loved one)
- Inflammatory Trauma (acute infection, surgery, vaccination)
- Recent Infections or Antibiotic Use
- Addition of New Supplement, Remedy
- Addition of Probiotic
- Dental Infection or Pain

Emotional traumas are more common than most parents might believe. Frequently, a child's progress is temporarily interrupted because of an emotional event that an adult thinks is minor but can be significant to a child. The distress associated with a change in a familiar therapist or teacher, their school, bullying or ongoing conflict with peers, a family member moving out of the home, jet lag after a long flight, or a parent intermittently leaving home for work-related travel to be enough trauma to plateau a child's progress for some time. After the event triggering an emotional trauma resolves or becomes part of the new everyday life pattern, the child will often regain their prior level of progress within 2-6 weeks.

If there is no further improvement and the plateau continues for a few months, discontinue using other supplements, herbal remedies, chelation agents, homeopathic products, or probiotics if used. Treat potential infections and examine the child's teeth with X-rays if this has not been done recently. Recovery should begin again within a couple of weeks after eliminating the offending event or after the physical or emotional trauma.

A common source of interference with recovery is a chronic sinus infection that can present subtly with nothing more than a chronic runny nose or a slight cough. Once or twice daily treatment with the OTC nasal corticosteroid fluticasone for 1-2 weeks is a safe and simple remedy for chronic sinus infections. It will not disrupt intestinal bacterial balance like common antibiotics might.

As long as the patient is using approved brands of inulin, fish oil, and olive oil, switching brands or making subtle changes in dosage will likely not restart progress after a plateau has been reached and may trigger more symptoms, leading to confusion about the true source of the relapse.

Too often, parents will increase and decrease dosages after minor changes in their child's behavior. Quickly changing dosing like this only serves to make the protocol more complicated. It also creates false conclusions about common fluctuations in behavior that would eventually correct themselves if nothing were done.

"The single most important factor resulting in no improvement or a plateau in the rate of improvement is a loss of balance of the intestinal bacteria, not the dose of fish or olive oil."

If all efforts to find any ongoing source of interference have failed, the bacteria overgrowth of the small intestine has likely returned despite continued use of inulin. Once it is determined the patient has "inulin failure," stop the inulin and switch the patient to rifaximin as the new method to balance the intestinal bacteria.

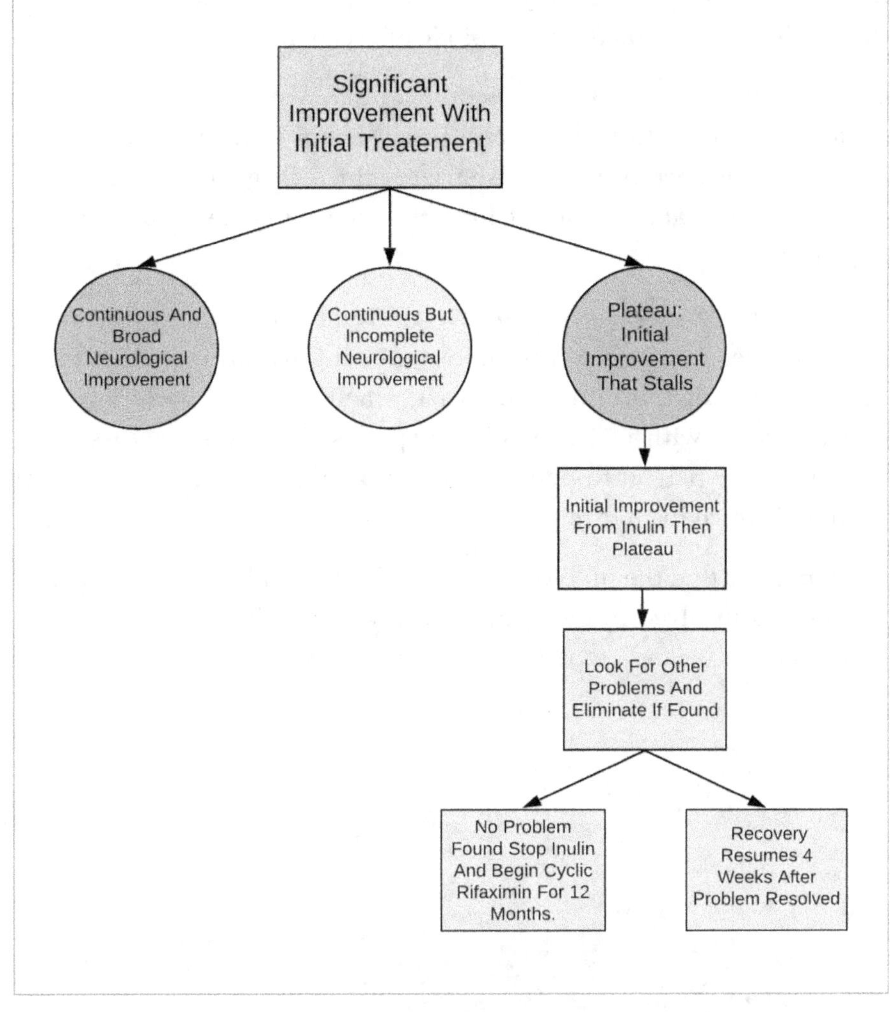

Managing the Plateau on Inulin

As mentioned, the precise reason why inulin failure occurs is unknown, possibly because a different species of bacteria unresponsive to the prebiotic effects of inulin is now inhabiting the small intestine.

Remember, the intestinal microbiota (the collection of all intestinal bacteria) comprises a thousand or more species, each with potentially different responses to the prebiotic effects of inulin.

A child's blend of intestinal bacteria naturally changes as children age ten and older. Young children with bacterial overgrowth of the small intestine may tend to initially be overgrown with a species of bacteria that positively respond to the prebiotic effects of inulin.

Given enough time or some other unknown factor, a different bacterium not controlled by inulin may begin growing in the small intestine. This bacterium can also trigger the leakage of pro-inflammatory cytokines that flow into the brain, which causes the child's recovery to plateau.

In adults, 50-75% of cases of bacterial overgrowth occur with only a single species of colonic bacteria overgrowing within the small intestine. In most of the remaining cases, small intestine bacterial overgrowth occurs with just two colonic species. The overgrowth species can vary from person to person. Similar detailed studies have not yet been performed in children.

Now, imagine that the prebiotic effects of inulin inhibit the single bacterial species involved in overgrowth in a young child. We will refer to this species as bacteria type A.

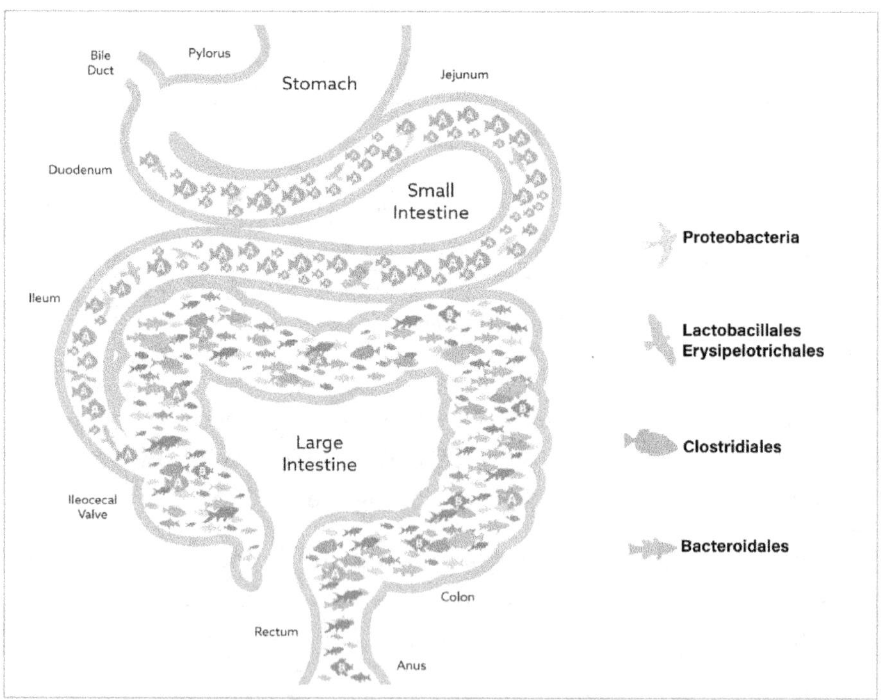

Because adding inulin inhibits bacteria A, it adequately controls the overgrowth, allowing neurological recovery. However, a thousand other species remain within the colon, many of which are not controlled by inulin.

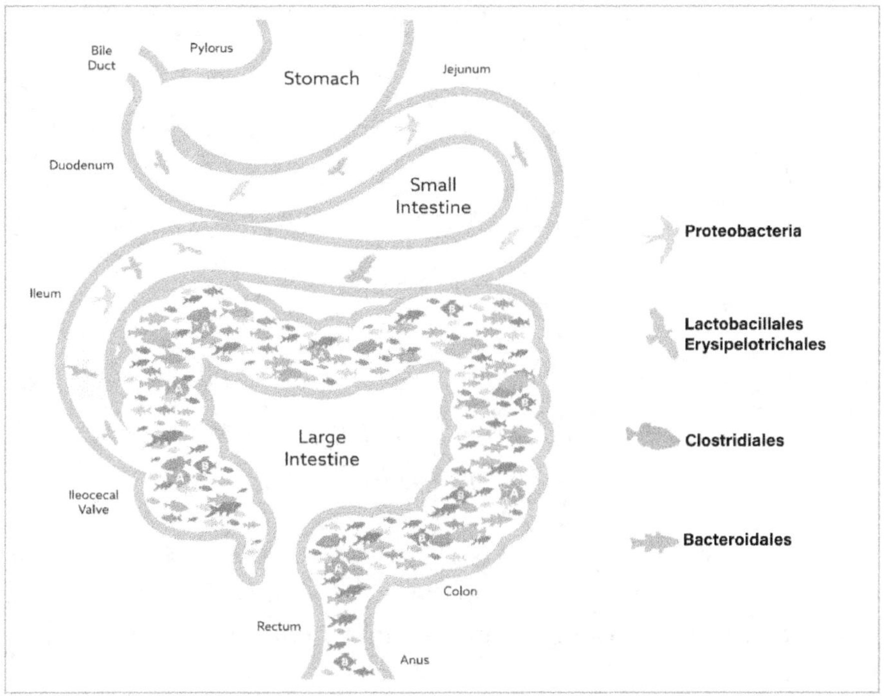

Intestinal Bacteria Rebalanced Because of Inulin

Over time, as the child's intestine bacteria naturally evolves, an inulin-resistant species (species B) may eventually migrate into the small intestine, grow uncontrolled, and become the predominant species of overgrowth bacteria resistant to inulin.

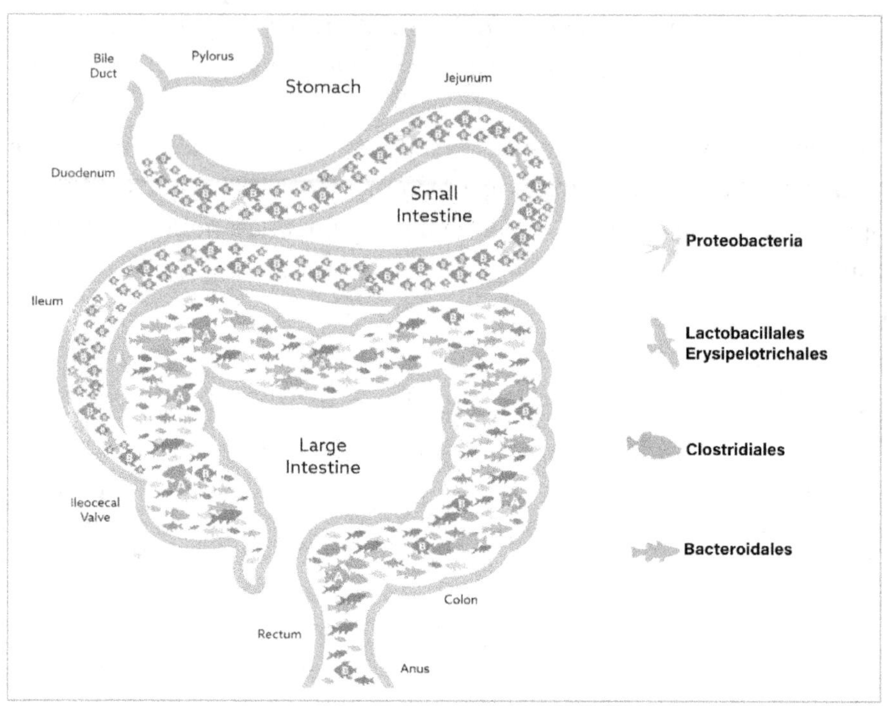

*Overgrowth with Bacteria Type B that are Resistant
to the Effects of Inulin*

The inulin-resistant overgrowth will once again trigger the same events that lead to excessive inflammation and halting prior recovery, inhibiting the recovery process and resulting in the recovery plateau.

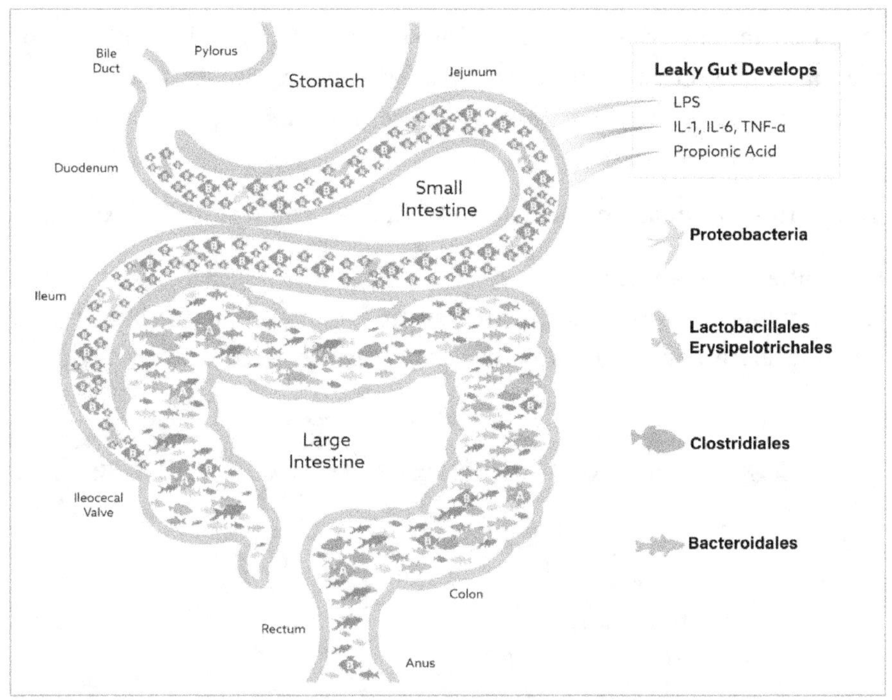

*Leakage of Inflammatory Cytokines can
Flow into the Nervous System and Inhibit Recovery*

Suppose a patient is suspected of experiencing inulin failure and has hit the plateau. In that case, the best treatment course is discontinuing inulin and initiating monthly cycles or continuous twice-daily rifaximin.

Unlike other common antibiotics, rifaximin does not damage intestinal bacterial biodiversity, and the development of long-term bacterial resistance to rifaximin is rare even with continuous, daily dosing over a year or more.

Rifaximin is a unique antibiotic, and some researchers have suggested that it be put into a new medication category called "eubiotic." This term is used because rifaximin has a neutral effect on the gut microbiome, unlike most other antibiotics.

Because rifaximin is not absorbed into the bloodstream, it is difficult for rifaximin to interact with other medications abnormally, irritate other organs such as the liver, or cause systemic side effects.

Managing a Plateau in a Child Previously Treated with Rifaximin

In a patient previously treated with a single round of rifaximin whose recovery has been halted, the same approach of looking for factors that might interrupt or trigger a relapse of bacterial overgrowth is required.

<u>**Factors That Interrupt Recovery After Rifaximin Use**</u>

- Physical or Emotional Trauma
- General Anesthesia
- Treatment with Antibiotic
- New Supplement Added
- New Probiotic Added
- Chronic Infection
- Abdominal Surgery
- Colonoscopy

Suppose the recovery of a child previously treated with a single round of rifaximin seems to slow or even stop. In that case, this plateau in their recovery is due to a relapse of bacterial overgrowth within the small intestine. They must be re-treated with rifaximin or shifted to more regular dosing twice daily for repeated monthly ten-day cycles or non-stop continuous rifaximin. This plateau is similar to what can occur with inulin failure.

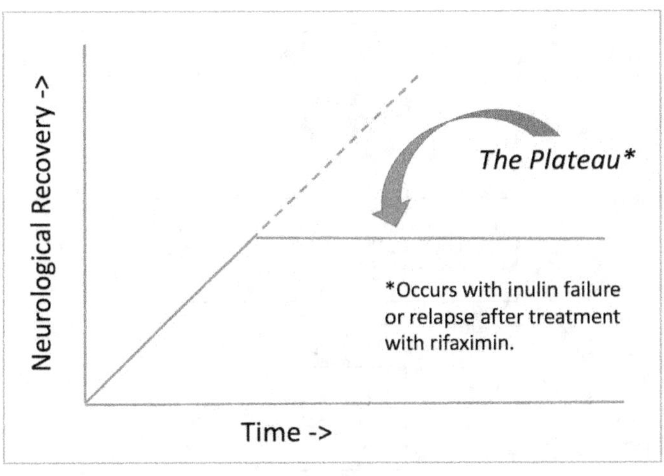

The Plateau

The rifaximin plateau is similar to what can occur with inulin failure. After increasing the frequency of rifaximin dosing, the child should begin experiencing renewed neurological recovery within six to eight weeks.

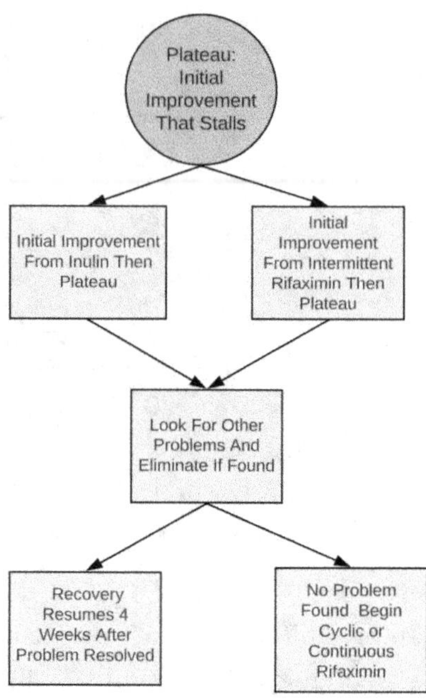

Comparison of Managing the Plateau while on Either Inulin or Rifaximin

Because of the high safety profile of rifaximin, Dr. Nemechek's preference when managing a plateau is to shift the child to continuous rifaximin until they have fully recovered. Rifaximin is proving to be an extremely safe and effective approach to maintaining a consistent path of recovery.

Relapse of Bacterial Overgrowth within the Small Intestine

The four major factors contributing to small intestine bacterial overgrowth are loss of biodiversity of the gut microbiome, decreasing acidity within the small intestine, slow intestinal motility, and external factors.

The loss of bacterial species of the gut microbiome has been occurring slowly over many generations as additional damage to gut bacteria from antibiotics, preservatives, pesticides, etc., is passed on from mother to child and subsequently from female children to their children.

The proper acidity (i.e., pH level) of the small intestine is a byproduct of the stomach delivering hydrochloric acid when the stomach empties, as well as the natural production of short-chain fatty acids produced by bacteria that usually inhabit the small intestine (The "birds" as discussed in previous chapters). Potent antacids belonging to the proton pump inhibitor class (PPIs; e.g., omeprazole) so dramatically reduce the production of hydrochloric acid within the stomach that they are now associated with higher risks of developing bacterial overgrowth within the small intestine.

Slow intestinal motility is also a well-known predisposing risk factor for bacterial overgrowth. It can occur secondarily from autonomic nervous system (ANS) dysfunction from acute events (acute brain injury or concussion, cumulative brain injury) and medical conditions (chronic inflammatory stress, scleroderma, chronic renal failure).

External factors can also trigger bacterial overgrowth, including certain medications, some digestive supplements, general anesthesia, medical procedures (gall bladder surgery, appendectomy, hysterectomy, stomach or bowel resection), and acute intestinal infections.

Causes of Recurrent Bacterial Overgrowth

Low Biodiversity
Slow Intestinal Motility
Proton Pump Inhibitors
Use of Antibiotics
Abdominal Surgery
General Anesthesia
Acute Intestinal Infections

The most common cause of repeated relapse is from slow motility of the intestinal tract due to underlying autonomic dysfunction, often from previous brain injuries. The ANS influences the forward propulsion of the intestinal tract. The intestinal tract's forward propulsion slows down if the ANS becomes damaged. Brain injuries can be relatively minor, but because of the cumulative brain injury phenomenon, they will build upon each other, resulting in substantial intestinal slowing due to their cumulative effect. See other chapters for more information on cumulative brain injury.

Rapid relapsing is common in adult patients, and they often need to be treated with repeated courses of rifaximin. After three to six cycles of rifaximin, their autonomic nervous system function and intestinal motility improve enough that their need for repeated rifaximin slows or stops.

The chronic use of antacids known as proton pump inhibitors (PPIs) is also a frequent cause of relapse of bacterial overgrowth. The flow of stomach acid into the small intestine is an essential barrier to the overgrowth of bacteria within the small intestine. PPI antacids result in a profound reduction of stomach acid production and can result in the overgrowth of bacteria within the small intestine.

PPIs may be prescribed to children because of severe gastroesophageal reflux. They cannot simply be stopped because of the potential damage to the child's esophagus and the pain the child might experience. Since esophageal reflux can cause permanent scarring and narrowing of the esophagus, I recommend not stopping PPI therapy without consulting the prescribing physician.

Another contributing factor to recurrent bacterial overgrowth is the low biodiversity of intestinal bacteria (low number of intestinal bacterial species). In studies of adults with recurrent *Clostridium difficle* enterocolitis (a form of bacterial overgrowth with a single, toxic bacterial species), the subjects with the lowest biodiversity are most apt to relapse or not respond to antibiotic therapy.

Although the list of precipitating factors for recurrent bacterial overgrowth is small, expect the list to grow as more and more relapse-triggering environmental factors are identified.

9

LITTLE TO NO IMPROVEMENT

Strategies for Managing Inulin Intolerance, No Response to Inulin or Rifaximin, and Failure of Rifaximin Cycling

The following graphic illustrates that the initial response to The Nemechek Protocol® may be intolerable, nonexistent, or temporary. Determining which applies to the patient's scenario helps me guide parents when presenting the information outlined in this section.

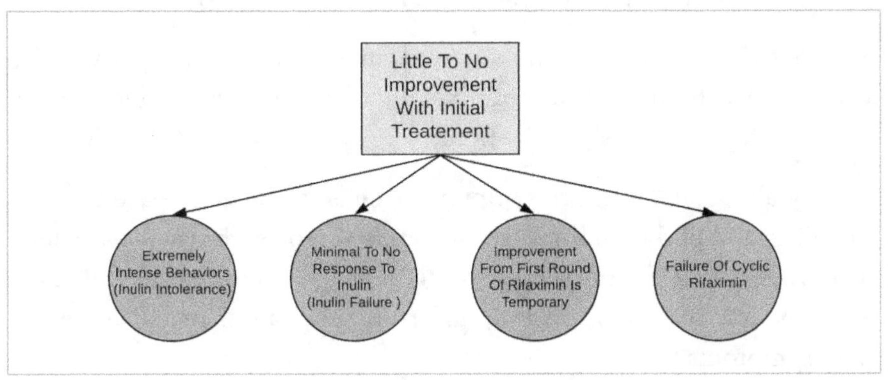

Patterns of Initial Treatment Failure

Managing Inulin Intolerance

Occasionally, some children will react intensely to inulin, even at extremely low doses. The most common intense side effects of inulin are increased hyperactivity, anxiety, insomnia, and maybe even aggression, which can sometimes be managed by lowering the dosage of inulin and still maintaining the pace of recovery. Some children will have these reactions even at doses as low as 1/32 tsp or 1/64 tsp of inulin daily. The difference between the awakening and inulin intolerance is that any immediate increase in negative behaviors will begin to decrease after four weeks if this is the awakening. If this is intolerance, the negative behaviors will continue for several months until the inulin dose is reduced or discontinued altogether.

In other cases, parents have mistakenly been increasing the inulin to doses of one-to-two teaspoons per day to increase the recovery rate or force certain aspects of recovery, such as speech, to occur. These extremely high doses of inulin can also trigger the same anxiety, aggression, and hyperactivity in their children.

The anxiety, aggression, and hyperactivity noted by parents are then mistakenly called a "second awakening" when, in fact, it is simply what I refer to as inulin intolerance. The reason for such an extreme reaction to inulin is unclear, but it is clinically consistent with suboptimal brain blood pressure with resulting suboptimal oxygen delivery.

Hyperactivity, increased hunger, and increased thirst are reflexive responses by the brain that often result in improved brain blood pressure and oxygen delivery to the brain.

Anxiety and aggression are symptoms triggered by the release of noradrenaline, the body's natural fight (aggression) or flight (panic, anxiety) hormone. Noradrenaline increases blood pressure in the brain and alleviates the low oxygen stress but, unfortunately, causes negative fight or flight symptoms.

At this point, the best option is to discontinue inulin entirely and treat the patient with monthly or continuous rifaximin. Rebalancing the intestinal bacteria with rifaximin does not result in the same adverse response and is equally effective at reducing bacterial overgrowth.

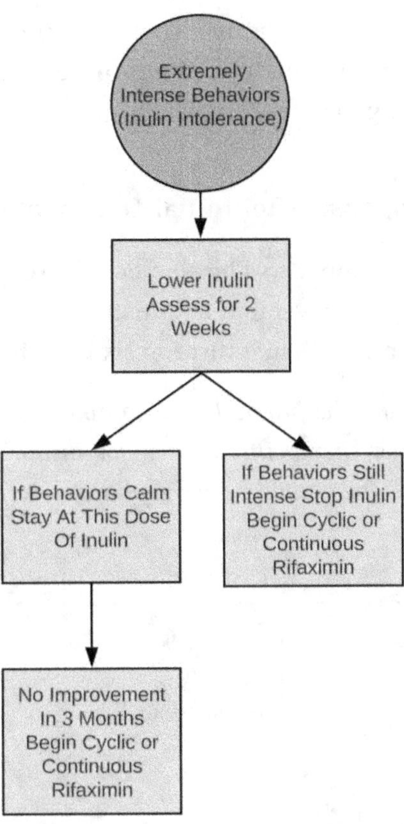

Managing Inulin Intolerance

The reason why repeated monthly or continuous twice-daily rifaximin is recommended is that pediatric patients often have a relapse of bacterial overgrowth within four to eight weeks of the first round of rifaximin. This seems to happen so commonly that when starting rifaximin after inulin failure, repeated ten-day courses of cyclic rifaximin each month or continuous rifaximin are recommended.

For example, if the child receives the first round of rifaximin from April 4th through the 13th, they will receive another round from May 4th through the 13th, June 4th through the 13th, and so on.

Cyclic rifaximin dosing has been a breakthrough in establishing a consistent path of recovery for my patients with autism and developmental delay.

The improvements seen by the twelve-month time point are often so impressive that many parents opt to continue cycling rifaximin until their child is behaving in a neurotypical fashion.

Minimal to No Response After Initial Treatment with Inulin

The least common response to The Nemechek Protocol® in my patients is that no significant improvement in autistic or developmental issues is observed after the protocol's first three to six months.

Children initially failing the protocol may continue to have minor improvements because of other therapeutic efforts (for instance, speech or occupational therapy). Still, there will be no significant increase in the pace of recovery.

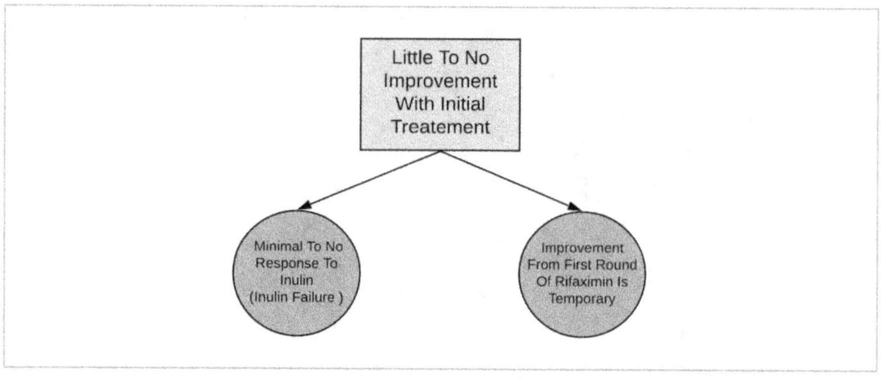

Patterns of Little to No Response to Initial Therapy

A word of caution before deciding that that initial use of inulin did not work. Many parents tend to over-focus on wanting to see improvements in speech or socialization initially. They will overlook improvements in receptive communication, fine or gross motor skills, anger control, or sensory-seeking behaviors.

The ability to speak is highly complex and does not start to recover until complex levels of receptive communication skills have developed. Likewise, learning to socialize with unfamiliar children often only occurs after learning to socialize with the child's parents, siblings, and unfamiliar adults.

The intense desire to see their child communicate normally and play with other children is natural for the parents. Still, unfortunately, these are some of the most complicated behaviors to master and often occur later or last, not sooner, in the recovery process.

If there has been no substantial increase in recovery despite taking inulin and no interference from probiotics, antibiotics, supplements, or a chronic illness, then the child has experienced inulin failure. Treatment with rifaximin is then recommended. Inulin as monotherapy is not restarted after initiating treatment with rifaximin.

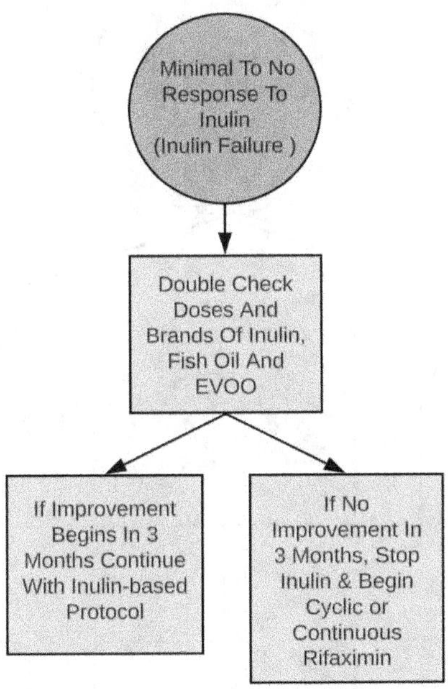

Managing Little to No Response to Inulin

Minimal to No Response after Initial Treatment with Rifaximin

Sometimes, after a patient is treated with rifaximin, there is no improvement, or the child seems to relapse within a few days or weeks. These children are experiencing a rapid relapse of bacterial overgrowth within the small intestine. These rapid relapses are likely due to slow intestinal motility from underlying autonomic dysfunction (see chapters ten and fourteen).

My most effective approach in this scenario is to begin cycling rifaximin with monthly ten-day courses of rifaximin for a minimum of twelve months. The point of cycling is to keep the bacterial overgrowth suppressed enough to allow the child's nervous system to continue recovering.

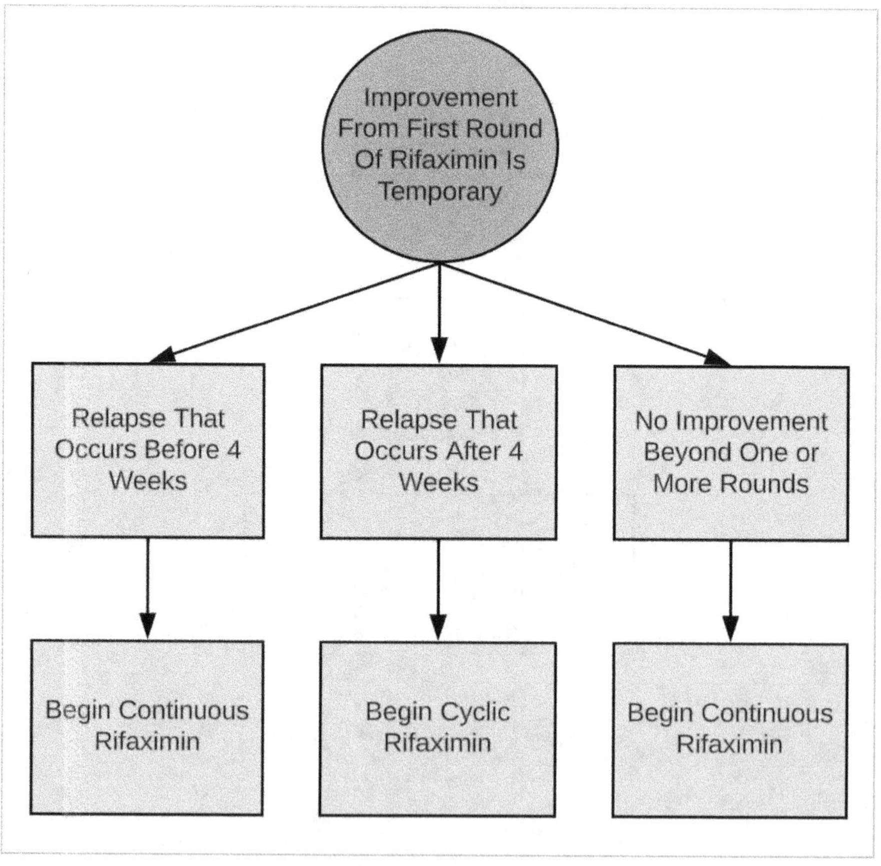

Managing Poor Response after Starting Rifaximin

Managing Failure of Rifaximin Cycling

Even with monthly rifaximin, some patients still will not show evidence of recovery, and this is because they are relapsing even before the next course of rifaximin has begun.

If a patient is not showing any improvement after three months of rifaximin, I start these patients on non-stop, twice daily, continuous rifaximin along with five minutes of daily vagus nerve stimulation.

The children are relapsing rapidly because of slow intestinal motility, often from autonomic nervous system damage. Adding vagus nerve stimulation will help ensure their intestinal motility can improve so that continuous rifaximin can ultimately be discontinued.

The first cases requiring continuous rifaximin involved extremely violent, older children (sixteen-to-twenty years of age) with autism. These patients would significantly decrease their violent tendencies while on rifaximin but then relapse within a few days of finishing the course of ten days. Increasing the course of rifaximin to fourteen or twenty-one days was not more effective in preventing the relapses.

After starting on the continuous, twice-daily rifaximin, their violent behavior declined and did not increase again. Over time, their behavior improved so much that the dosages and number of psychiatric medications they had been described were reduced and often discontinued. In several such cases, the parents have opted to stay on continuous rifaximin, fearing that the violent relapses might occur again.

After twelve months of continuous therapy, consider reducing rifaximin therapy to the monthly cycle of ten-day courses. If recovery stops because of relapsing bacteria, restart continuous treatment for the patient for another six months and then try reducing to monthly cycles again. With more time, the monthly cycles of rifaximin might also be discontinued, with rifaximin only needing to be used occasionally.

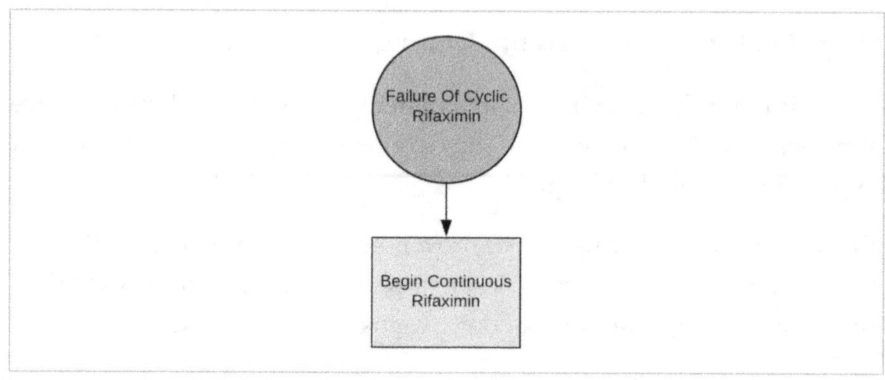

Managing Failure of Cyclic Rifaximin

Daily, continuous rifaximin has been safely used for almost thirty years in patients with advanced liver cirrhosis who develop hepatic encephalopathy. Patients with hepatic encephalopathy are continuously placed on twice-daily rifaximin to prevent dangerous ammonia production. Studies indicate the continuous use of rifaximin does not lower the bacterial biodiversity within the gut microbiome.

Although bacterial resistance to rifaximin rarely occurs, the opposition quickly disappears after discontinuing rifaximin for only a few weeks. The rifaximin can then be restarted with the same positive effect.

In review, after initiating the protocol with the appropriate fish oil and olive oil and starting to balance the intestinal tract with either inulin or rifaximin, observe and make note of the degree of recovery that occurs in the following three months.

If there is a significant suppression of bacterial overgrowth, the child will experience notable improvements. If most, but not all, aspects of their neurological problems are improving, adding five minutes of daily vagus nerve stimulation is necessary to encourage all developmental issues to begin recovering.

If there is only a temporary improvement, minimal improvement, or treatment with inulin causes too many side effects, the flow charts presented earlier in this chapter will help you understand how to determine the dosing of rifaximin in single, cyclic or continuous dosing strategies to move my patients forward in the recovery process.

Managing Continous Rifaximin Failure

Unfortunately, approximately 10-20% of children treated with rifaximin will have a very slow rate of recovery or no recovery at all. The reasons for the lack of response to rifaximin can be broken down into a few categories: bacterial overgrowth with bacteria not sensitive to rifaximin's antibacterial effects, poor small intestine motility, and non-bacterial forms of leaky gut (i.e., increased intestinal permeability), other non-intestinal sources of inflammation and other triggers for negative behaviors obscuring rifaximin-related improvements.

Reasons for Lack of Rifaximin Response
Poor Intestinal Motility
Bacteria Insensitive to Rifaximin
Non-Bacterial Forms of Leaky Gut
Non-Intestinal Sources of Inflammation
Other Issues Obscuring Improvement

Which issue is affecting an individual patient is difficult to determine because of the lack of specific and sensitive testing methodologies in the community setting. The lack of testing leaves us presently with the option of trying a variety of safe options that have been shown to significantly improve the pace of recovery in several children under Dr. Nemechek's care.

But clues are available to guide one to try one option over another. For example, suppose a child does not improve after a switch to rifaximin but was previously recovering on an inulin-based protocol. In that case, adding inulin back combined with rifaximin can be helpful, although inulin and rifaximin were ineffective. Alternatively, using a different prebiotic fiber instead of inulin, such as partially hydrogenated guar gum (PHGG) combined with rifaximin, might be more successful at suppressing bacterial overgrowth, leading to further recovery.

Poor intestinal motility of the small intestine is a common risk factor for bacterial overgrowth. A mobility agent such as pyridostigmine can improve intestinal motility and partially reverse SIBO. Unlike other motility agents, pyridostigmine can also boost blood pressure and lower inflammation via different mechanisms that might incrementally help with recovery.

Individuals with particularly severe constipation whose rifaximin is not very effective may also be experiencing slow motility of the small intestine and would benefit from adding pyridostigmine.

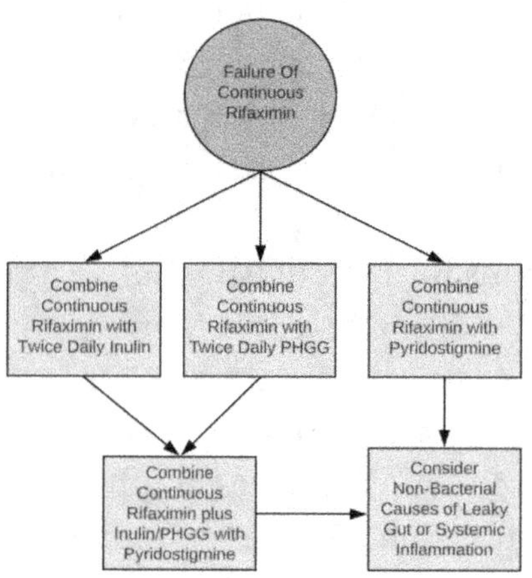

Managing Failure of Continuous Rifaximin

As our understanding of how inflammation plays a significant role in most chronic neurological conditions, the focus on the intestinal tract as a source of this inflammation has identified some non-bacterial causes of increased intestinal permeability of the small intestine (i.e., leaky gut).

Sugar alcohols such as erythritol and artificial sweeteners such as saccharin and aspartame damage the lining of the small intestine, increasing intestinal permeability and systemic inflammation. Erythritol is a common additive to sweeten Stevia as well as monkfruit products.

Although the inulin or rifaximin may effectively reverse bacterial overgrowth within the small intestine, intestinal permeability may persist because of these sugar alcohols and other artificial sweeteners in an individual's diet.

A persistent elevation of pro-inflammatory cytokines within the body may result in a relative deficiency of l-glutamine, an essential amino acid required by the small intestine as a primary fuel source. If glutamine deficiency persists, the small intestine may experience the death of mucosal barrier cells, leading to intestinal permeability and often a perpetuation of systemic inflammation.

Intestinal permeability from glutamine deficiency can be triggered by uncommon conditions such as severe burns, chemotherapy, radiation therapy, uncontrolled HIV replication, and massive physical trauma. A more frequent cause of non-bacterial leaky gut has been detected in patients hospitalized with SARS-CoV-2 infection (i.e., COVID-19).

Non-Bacterial Causes of Leaky Gut
Severe Burns
NSAID Enteropathy
Cancer Chemotherapy
Cancer Radiation Therapy
Chronic HIV Replication
Massive Physical Trauma
Hospitalization with COVID-19
Sugar Alcohols (Erythritol)
Pregnancy With or Without Obesity
Artificial Sweeteners (saccharin, Sucralose aspartame)

Most of these conditions are self-evident and are either being treated or are required to treat cancer. The consumption of sugar alcohols and artificial sweeteners is not apparent but can easily eliminated from the diet. Whether or not the systemic inflammation common in COVID-19 patients with chronic symptoms (i.e., Long COVID) results from glutamine has yet to be determined. However, if confirmed, supplementation with oral glutamine would be a preferred choice to heal the intestinal tract barrier.

Finally, there is the possibility that neurological recovery is limited because of excessive systemic inflammation from non-intestinal sources. Examples might be excessive exposure to 2.5-micron particles (secondhand smoke, cleaning products, hydrocarbon leakage from a stove) within the home, inflammation triggered internally by an autoimmune disorder, gum disease, or severe vitamin D deficiency.

10

WHEN AND IF TO STOP THE NEMECHEKPROTOCOL

After a few years on The Nemechek Protocol®, many children will recover enough to reach a neurotypical state. The next obvious question is which protocol components can be stopped and which must be continued.

In my adult patients recovering on the protocol, most will experience a partial relapse of their prior cumulative brain injuries if they stop or decrease any of the components (fish oil, olive oil, vagus stimulation, and maintaining a balanced intestinal tract).

I think recurrence in cumulative brain injury will similarly apply to the children treated with the protocol, with a significant exception that involves a particular white blood cell in the brain called a primed microglia. I will discuss primed microglia further in this chapter.

The brain learns to speak, socialize, and process sensory inputs by pruning away neurons. Improvement in developmental function occurs as excessive neurons within the brain are pruned away. Therefore, a relapse would require an increase in the overall number of neurons. There is no medical evidence that once pruned away, more neurons would accumulate with increased inflammatory stress.

But why do the cumulative brain injuries recur after stopping the protocol? Understandably, many people mistakenly assume that recovery from a brain injury is like healing a broken bone. Once the injury is healed, you no longer need the treatment or the arm cast in the case of a fracture.

A significant difference between a chronic brain injury and a forearm fracture is that a brain injury has become established because of the formation of a permanent population of harmful cells called primed microglia.

Microglia are a population of special white blood cells that only live in the brain. They are involved in the normal pruning of neurons during the developmental process and in repairing neurons after injury. Unfortunately, bacterial overgrowth can alter microglia's behavior, leading to a recurrence of cumulative brain injury if the protocol is stopped.

Primed Microglia Contribute to Relapsing from Chronic Brain Injury

Primed microglia are formed after lipopolysaccharide (LPS) from bacterial overgrowth (SIBO, small intestine bacterial overgrowth) leaks into the bloodstream and eventually migrates to the brain and encounters healthy microglia.

LPS transforms healthy microglia into harmful inflammatory microglia, referred to as primed microglia. They are also referred to as primed M1-microglia.

Unlike healthy microglia that are replaced with new normal functioning microglia every few months, primed microglia never die and constantly leak inflammatory cytokines into their surrounding area.

The inflammatory stress these inflammatory cytokines create prevents the neurons in the same area from being repaired and will magnify the damage in future injuries.

The protocol's combination of vagus nerve stimulation, olive oil, and high omega-3 fatty acid DHA concentrations helps control the damaging inflammatory behavior of primed microglia through a process called phenotypic shifting.

As long as these ingredients are given consistently in the correct dosages, the primed microglia change their behavior and start helping with the repair process. Maintaining the primed microglia in a helpful, repairing mode (i.e., M2-microglia) also reduces their production of damaging inflammatory cytokines and improves the ability of nearby neurons to recover.

At present, there is no known treatment to eradicate primed microglia. Therefore, they need to be controlled over the long term to maintain one's recovery from a previously unresolved brain injury. There is growing evidence in animal studies that eliminating primed microglia may be possible someday. Most of this work is looking at chemical compounds known as CSFR1 inhibitors.

Vagus nerve stimulation, fish oil, and olive oil will all need to be continued for the long term until other methods of eliminating primed microglia are found.

There is another reason why some of The Nemechek Protocol® ingredients should not be stopped. Since there is no effort by the food industry to remove the excessive amounts of inflammatory linoleic acid from the food supply, the need for olive oil in our diet to protect us from these omega-6 fatty acids will remain.

Similarly, the lack of anti-inflammatory omega-3 fatty acids in the food supply necessitates long-term supplementation with omega-3 fatty acids sourced from fish and other marine sources to assist our cells in regulating inflammation.

As fish stocks in the oceans become increasingly depleted, other forms of omega-3 fatty acids may need to be produced from algae or other recombinant technologies.

On the distant horizon is the hope of pharmaceutical therapies that can rid the nervous system of these permanently damaging primed microglia. A class of agents known as Csf1R inhibitors show promising results, permanently halting the chronic inflammatory damage from primed microglia in animal trials.

Potential Relapses in Children Differ from Adults

Children's situation is not straightforward because they have recovered from cumulative brain injuries and developmental delays. Although both require a normal microglial function to recover, a unique difference in children's recovery prevents developmental delay relapses.

Children who have recovered from cumulative brain injuries often relapse similarly to adults. The most common symptoms associated with cumulative brain injuries that might return in children include hyperactivity, toe-walking, anxiety, OCD, fearfulness, aggressiveness, rage events, flight events, increased hunger and thirst, poor focus, and concentration, including ADD and ADHD, constipation, abdominal cramping and heartburn or reflux, and insomnia.

Relapsing from developmental delay is a different matter. To realize their developmental milestones, a child needs to prune away fifty percent of the neurons within their brain. Synaptic pruning is the brain's way of removing unnecessary connections that are not needed, which strengthens the ones that are required to mature and lock in a new developmental skill.

Once pruned away, these neurons are gone forever, never to return. Developmental delays occur when there is incomplete or slowed pruning of the brain's neurons.

The Nemechek Protocol® resolves developmental delays by allowing the microglia to begin finally pruning away the excessive neurons, leading to developmental gains. There are fewer neurons when your child has recovered developmentally than when they were delayed.

For this reason, I do not believe true relapses after recovery from a developmental delay are possible. These children do not "unlearn" the developmental milestones they have reached. Since recovery from developmental delay involves permanently removing neurons, relapse from developmental delay cannot occur because the neurons would need to be added back, which is not believed to be possible.

I have often heard that a child has "lost" this or that developmental function, and I understand the comment from the parent's perspective. In truth, the prior gains are still present but not visible to the parent and not accessible to the child often because of the child's increased anxiety, worsened focus, and toxic effects of propionic acid.

This phenomenon is no different from an adult who cannot think or speak clearly in front of an audience (i.e., stage fright). With more practice at public speaking, the adult can finally speak well, even when anxious or under stress. Similarly, a child with continued recovery will ultimately be able to use more complex speech even when feeling anxious.

Long Term Challenges of Maintaining a Healthy Balance of Intestinal Bacteria

Reversal and prevention of bacterial overgrowth in the small intestine (SIBO) is required for recovery from developmental delay and brain injuries in children. If SIBO returns, the inflammatory stress from this is so great that all recovery stops. After recovery, maintaining a healthy balance of intestinal bacteria in children (and adults) can be challenging.

The three known factors involved in relapses of bacterial overgrowth of the small intestine are the slowing of intestinal motility, intermittent disruption of the intestinal bacteria by infections or medications, and low intestinal biodiversity.

Slowed Intestinal Motility

Spontaneous relapses from slowed intestinal motility are due to underlying autonomic dysfunction from cumulative brain injury. With time on the protocol, the autonomic dysfunction leading to relapses in this manner will substantially improve during the child's recovery. Slow intestinal motility is the most frequent cause of relapsing bacterial overgrowth in children and adults.

Disruption of Intestinal Balance

Intermittent disruption of bacterial balance often cannot be avoided because it can be triggered by common infections (viral and bacterial gastroenteritis) or necessary medications (antibiotics, chemotherapy, proton pump inhibitors). Regrettably, this source of relapse will continue until medical science discovers how to treat infections without gut-damaging antibiotics or manage severe acid reflux without proton pump inhibitors.

Low Intestinal Biodiversity

Low biodiversity is known to predispose people to spontaneous bacterial overgrowth only when the level of biodiversity is severely depleted. In studies of *Clostridium difficle* enterocolitis, frequent relapses of bacterial overgrowth occur when the individual's intestinal gut microbiome has been depleted to about 70% of typical bacterial species.

Treatment requires a fecal microbiota transplant (FMT), essentially a human stool transplant. Most studies of FMT in patients with higher levels of biodiversity (>80%) seem to have little to no benefit. Most biodiversity studies in children with autism or developmental problems do not indicate severe depletion of biodiversity. Because of this, I do not recommend FMT. In addition, I have been involved in caring for many children who have received FMT but still had frequent relapses of bacterial overgrowth, so FMT was of no benefit to them in their neurological recovery.

Long Term Inulin to Prevent Bacterial Relapses

As a child ages, there is an increasing tendency for inulin to be unable to control bacterial overgrowth. By twenty years of age, inulin is ineffective in controlling bacterial overgrowth enough to obtain a substantial degree of brain recovery.

The reason for this is not precisely understood but most likely has to do with the tendency of overgrowth in adults from a bacterial species whose growth is not suppressed by inulin.

The long-term use of daily inulin in children is very safe and inexpensive and controls SIBO as long as it remains effective. Eventually, the inulin will likely fail as the child ages, and bacterial overgrowth will return.

At this point, the child will need to be transitioned to intermittent courses of rifaximin to control any symptoms of bacterial overgrowth.

Managing Bacterial Overgrowth with Rifaximin

Many children under my care today receive monthly courses of rifaximin (during cyclic rifaximin) to prevent the relapsing of bacterial overgrowth. A smaller proportion of children receive rifaximin non-stop without any intermittent breaks in treatment ("continuous rifaximin"), and an even smaller proportion receive intermittent rifaximin only as needed for recognizable relapses.

Over time, from treating neurotypical adult patients, I have learned that their intestinal motility will improve, and bacterial overgrowth relapses will become less frequent so that we can taper off rifaximin. This seems to hold true for children as well.

My overall approach is to reduce the frequency of rifaximin in children as they recover. If a child was only able to experience recovery with continuous, non-stop rifaximin therapy because they were relapsing very quickly, I found it will take a minimum of twelve months of rifaximin before intestinal motility recovers enough that the rifaximin can be changed from continuous to the less intense schedule of monthly cycles of rifaximin.

After another six to twelve months on cyclic rifaximin, there is a good chance the child can be tapered off rifaximin to just intermittent rifaximin.

Likewise, if a child's recovery improved with cyclic rifaximin, I recommend a minimum of twelve monthly cycles before shifting to intermittent rifaximin.

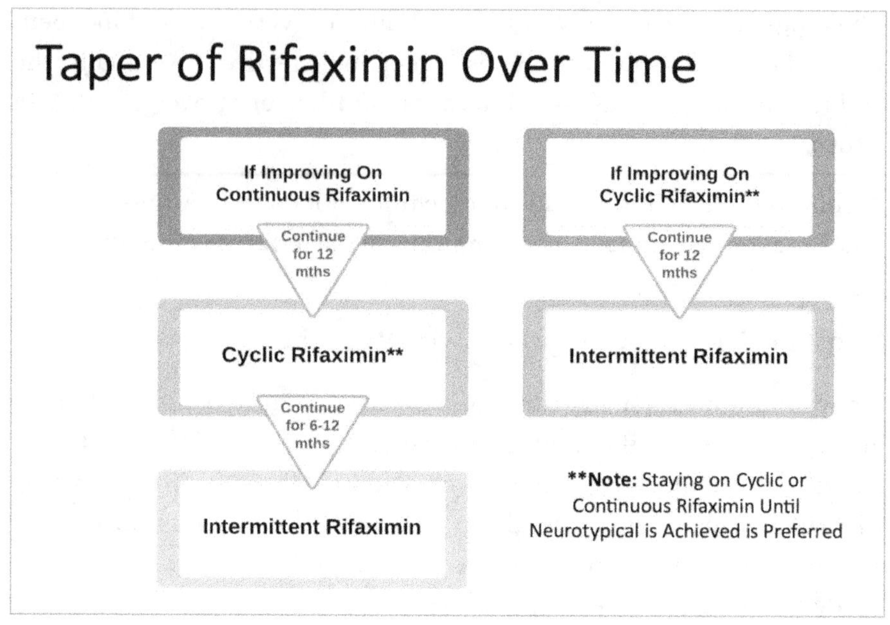

Considerations on the Reduction of Rifaximin Dosing

Many parents are opting to use rifaximin for even longer than twelve months to prevent any delays in recovery from the inevitable relapses. As of this writing, some older children with autism have been treated with cyclic and continuous rifaximin for up to five years without complication.

PART III

VAGUS NERVE STIMULATION

11

THE USE OF VAGUS NERVE STIMULATION IN CHILDHOOD DISORDERS

This chapter will explain in greater detail vagus nerve stimulation (VNS) and the role it plays in The Nemechek Protocol®.

The vagus nerve is one of the most important nerves in the body. Commonly referred to as the tenth cranial nerve, it runs down either side of the neck, fusing below the breastbone to form a single trunk and branching out to the body's organs and blood vessels.

Generally, nerves are often visualized as a strand of insulated biological wire that carries electrical impulses from the brain to different body areas. However, the vagus nerve is much, much more complex.

The vagus nerve comprises approximately 60,000 separate nerve fibers bundled like a fiber-optic cable. These nerves transmit information and instructions as electrical impulses, and these signals travel from the body up to the brain and from the brain down to the body.

About 80% of the information and instructions carried by the vagus nerve travels from the body upwards into the brain in what is referred to as afferent fibers. The remaining 20% of information on the vagus nerve travels downward from the brain to the body to help regulate inflammation and other organ functions. These downward brain to the body fibers are called efferent fibers.

The autonomic nervous system (ANS) has two branches or controlling arms: the parasympathetic and sympathetic. These branches allow the brain to regulate every aspect of bodily function.

The vagus nerve is the main conduit of signals from the parasympathetic branch. The sympathetic branch runs through the spinal cord and sends out smaller branches between each pair of vertebrae. Signals carried by the sympathetic branch travel both upwards and downwards.

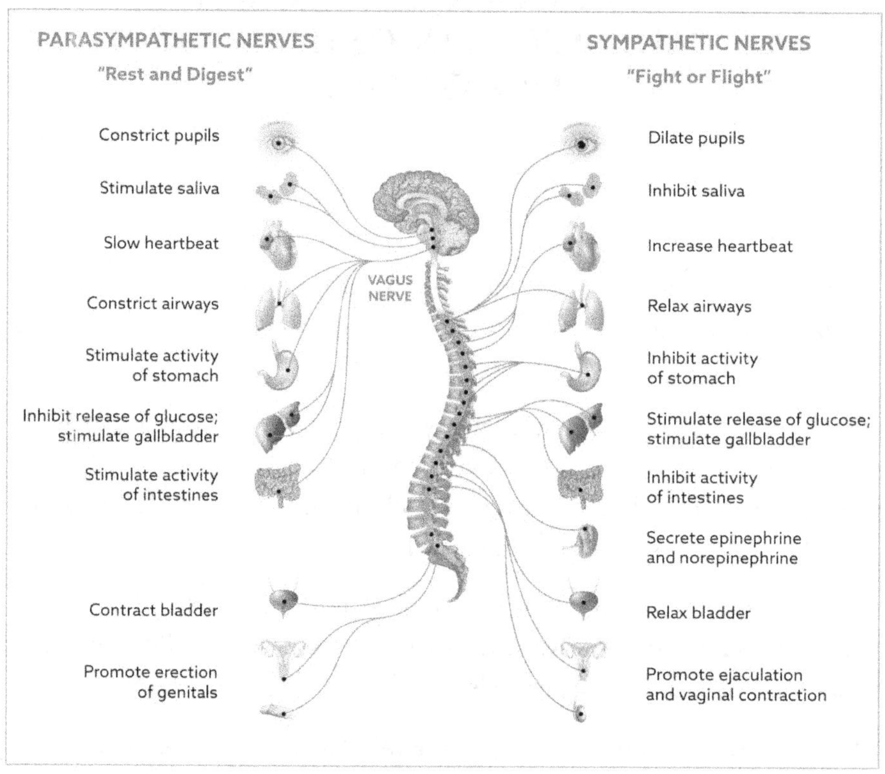

The Parasympathetic and Sympathetic Branches of the ANS

Through parasympathetic pathways of the vagus nerve, the brain "listens" to how the organs are functioning and monitors the body's stress level (infection, injury, or toxins) as various signals are sent upwards.

Various regions of the brain interpret signals from the vagus nerve. The brain interprets the signals and responds by sending signals downward through the efferent fibers of the vagus nerve, the sympathetic fibers in the spinal cord, and by releasing hormones from the pituitary glands.

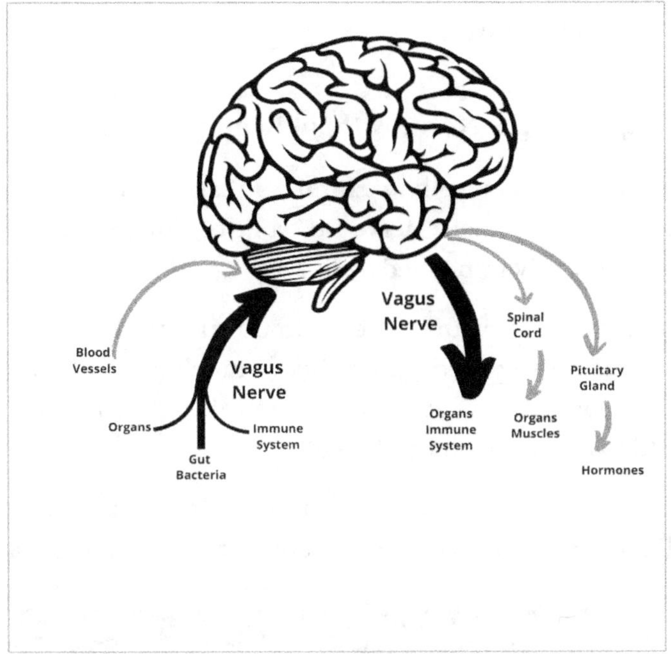

Flow of Signals To and From the Brain

This circular pattern of "listening" through the vagus nerve and then "responding" through the vagus nerve, spinal cord, and hormones is how the brain regulates the body's organs when things are functioning normally and when there is a dangerous threat in the area, or if the body is suffering from an infection or an injury.

The Beginnings of Vagus Nerve Stimulation

In the 1990s, research suggested that vagus nerve stimulation might be a helpful approach to controlling seizures. Researchers developed an implantable vagus nerve stimulating device similar to a pacemaker used to increase the heart rate of an ailing heart.

When used for vagus nerve stimulation, the wires are wrapped around the vagus nerve, and the electrical impulses stimulate the vagus nerve instead of the heart. These devices send pulsations of electricity and stimulate the vagus nerve 24 hours daily. Vagus nerve stimulators have astonishing remission rates of 50-75% per year for treatment-resistant epilepsy and depression.

Stimulating the Vagus Nerve without Requiring Surgery

A breakthrough in controlling chronic inflammation with electrical stimulation of the vagus nerve to control inflammation without requiring a surgically implanted device.

As the vagus nerve runs from the brain down into the neck, a branch from the vagus nerve called the *auricular* branch (auricular is the Latin word for the ear) extends out to the center of the ear in regions of the ear referred to as the concha and tragus.

The vagus nerve can be externally stimulated by directly placing a very mild and imperceptible electrical current on the skin in these areas.

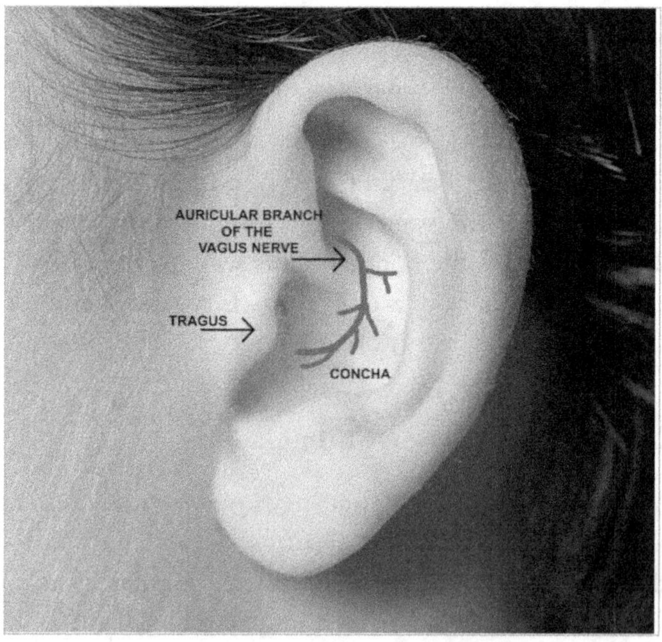

Auricular Branch of the Vagus Nerve

This method is called transcutaneous auricular (meaning across the skin of the ear) vagus nerve stimulation or taVNS. Five minutes of tVNS is highly effective in lowering systemic inflammation throughout the body for over twenty-four hours.

Avoiding the surgery of implanting a VNS in the chest eliminates the risk of surgery-related infections and complications from anesthesia and dramatically reduces the cost of VNS. taVNS brings the positive health benefits of the treatment into the reach of individuals affected by chronic inflammatory disorders.

Modern Vagus Nerve Stimulation

In the last twenty years, over 120,000 vagus nerve stimulators have been successfully implanted in the United States for epilepsy and depression. In addition to the remarkable improvement in controlling these disorders, vagus nerve stimulation is a powerful method to suppress unhealthy levels of chronic inflammation.

Chronic inflammation is now understood to be the primary cause of various common medical conditions. Inflammation causes illness by turning on or off genes associated with diabetes mellitus, cancer, and autoimmune disorders.

Inflammation causes direct tissue damage and is essential in developing strokes, heart attacks, nerve damage (neuropathy), and chronic pain from fibromyalgia, arthritis, fasciitis, tendonitis, and bursitis.

Lastly, chronic inflammation within the central nervous system impairs the nervous system's natural repair mechanisms. It is primarily responsible for developing Alzheimer's dementia, Parkinson's ataxia, chronic depression, schizophrenia, PTSD, and bipolar disorder.

<u>General Effects of Chronic Inflammation</u>

- Trigger Genetically Associated Disease State
- Direct Damage to Tissue within the Body
- Impairment of Tissue Repair Mechanisms
- Suppression of Stem Cell Function
- Impairment of Immune Function

In children, chronic inflammation impairs the brain's ability to correctly prune neurons, which is required for normal development and leads to developmental issues such as sensory impairment, apraxia, and communication problems.

Inflammation also prevents a child's brain from naturally repairing itself after an injury, in a process referred to as cumulative brain injury (CBI) or repetitive minor traumatic brain injury (rmTBI)

As investigations into the chronic inflammatory model of the disease continue to develop, our understanding of how chronic inflammation can negatively affect a child's health continues to grow.

<u>Specific Effects of Chronic Inflammation on Children</u>

- Developmental Impairment
- Autism Spectrum Disorders
- Intellectual, Communication Disorders
- Visual Impairment
- Sensory Perception Disorder
- Low Muscle Tone
- Focus and Concentration Issues
- Hyperactivity
- Headaches, Functional Abdominal Pain
- Aggression and Self Injurious Behavior
- Constipation, Bloating and Heartburn
- Chronic Depression, Bipolar Disorder, Anxiety
- Schizophrenia
- Epilepsy
- Growth Impairment
- Chronic or Recurrent Joint or Muscle Pain

Given the wide variety of harmful effects of chronic inflammation on the human body, vagus nerve stimulation's ability to suppress inflammation is being tested in various conditions other than epilepsy and chronic depression with generally positive results.

In my experience with children, tVNS dramatically improves the ability of all areas of the central nervous system to develop correctly and improves the brain's ability to recover from cumulative brain injury.

12

____

WHEN TO ADD THE VAGUS NERVE STIMULATION

After balancing the intestinal bacteria with either inulin or rifaximin and initiating the proper fish and olive oil doses as described in The Nemechek Protocol®, the next step is to monitor the child's recovery over the following three to six months. It is essential to monitor the patient to determine if all aspects of the child's neurological impairments progress toward recovery.

Over a three to six-month period, many children will begin to experience improved recovery rates from developmental delay and cumulative brain injury effects.

Several aspects of neurological recovery should be monitored to assess the effect of the protocol and if vagus nerve stimulation is indicated. Items to track include speech, sensory, attention/focus, meaningful play, socialization, aggression, self-injurious behaviors (SIBs), motor skills/tone, intestinal function, and low brain blood pressure symptoms.

<u>Items to Monitor to Determine Recovery</u>

Speech
Sensory
Socialization
Attention/Focus
Meaningful Play
Aggression/SIBs
Motor Skills/Tone
Intestinal Function
Receptive Communication
Expressive Communication
Symptoms of Low Brain Blood Pressure

Usually, all aspects of development, function, and behavior will steadily improve, but occasionally, a child might have one or two areas that do not seem to improve.

For instance, a child might experience remarkable improvements in emotional control, motor function, and improvement in sleep and intestinal function. Still, expressive language and socialization do not seem to improve after several months.

If, after being on the proper doses of fish oil, olive oil, and either inulin or rifaximin, the child has one or two areas that are not improving, then the child may benefit from adding VNS.

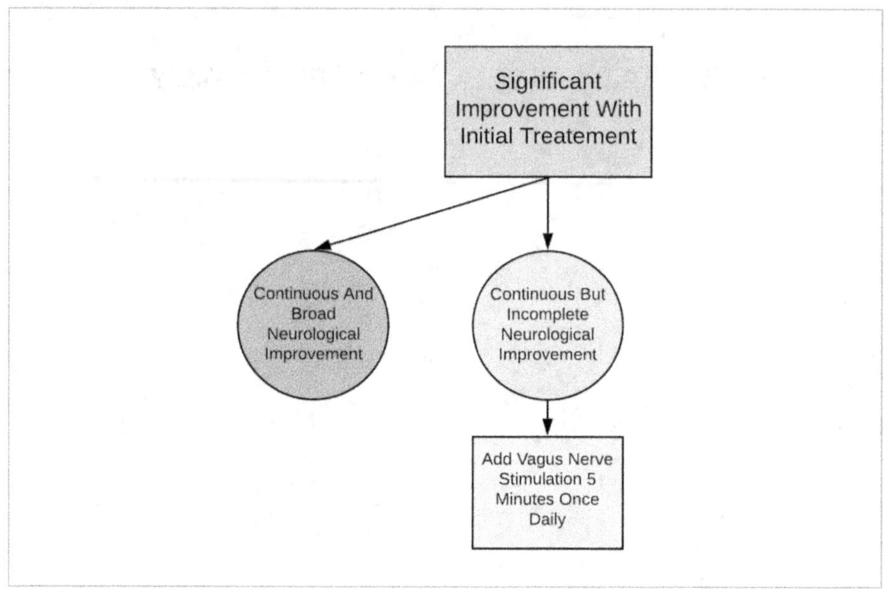

The Addition of Vagus Nerve Stimulation

Transcutaneous VNS assists all developmental areas to recover through its combined effect on suppressing the adverse effects of inflammation on neuronal pruning and repair and its ability to expand neural networks.

The use of taVNS is generally recommended in young patients four years and older demonstrating incomplete neurological recovery. Children under four seem to have a much greater chance of recovery without taVNS, but they may also be candidates for taVNS if they show signs of incomplete recovery.

Benefits of Vagus Nerve Stimulation in Non-Developmental Conditions

There are several other areas in which taVNS may help patients that are not directly related to traditional developmental delay. For instance, vagus nerve stimulation can improve some genetically triggered illnesses, such as tinnitus, post-concussion syndrome, spinal cord injury, schizophrenia, and cerebral palsy.

<u>Other Potential Benefits of Vagus Nerve Stimulation</u>

Schizophrenia
Cerebral Palsy
Post-Concussion Syndrome
Reduction or Elimination of Tinnitus
Stroke and Spinal Cord Injury

A growing number of adult studies are even evaluating VNS as a method to improve recovery after ischemic and thrombotic strokes and traumatic spinal cord injuries. Since cerebral palsy is related to brain cell damage from the lack of oxygen, the same benefits are seen in stroke and spinal cord injury recovery and cerebral palsy.

Finally, the most intriguing but least studied effect of VNS is on genetic remission in chronic inflammatory disorders. Some genes are activated or de-activated by increasing levels of inflammatory stress, leading to altered cellular function and triggering what is outwardly diagnosed as a particular disease.

Examples such as diabetes mellitus type 2, rheumatoid arthritis, and many common cancers (breast, colon, prostate, brain) are believed to be activated by chronic inflammation.

In about 10% of children who appear on the autism spectrum, an abnormal gene is detected. The parent is told their child is "at risk" for developing a particular disease, including autism, associated with the gene. It is important to emphasize that the child will only develop the illness if the identified gene is turned on or activated, which is often caused by inflammation.

Furthermore, animal studies suggest that if inflammation is lowered enough, many previously active disease-causing genes can be shut off, resulting in a genetic remission.

We have witnessed this several times in adults with Hashimoto's thyroiditis and Crohn's disease, and genetic remission might be responsible for the recoveries seen in some children with various congenital abnormalities known to be associated with autism.

Use of Vagus Nerve Stimulation for Other Inflammatory Conditions

As previously discussed, the health of children and adults is negatively affected by the chronic presence of inflammatory chemicals called pro-inflammatory cytokines. These chemicals are rising worldwide as people age in a process often referred to as inflamm-aging.

Released by white blood cells, inflammatory cytokines circulate in the bloodstream and encounter every body cell. The cytokines trigger the activation of molecules such as HMGB-1 and NF-kB, ultimately responsible for turning on the genes responsible for common diseases like insulin resistance (diabetes), most cancers, and autoimmune disorders such as rheumatoid arthritis and Crohn's disease.

Chronically elevated pro-inflammatory cytokines also cause direct damage to the tissue, resulting in chronic pain syndromes, nerve damage (neuropathy), strokes, and heart attacks. The chronic production of these cytokines impairs stem cell function and other natural repair mechanisms.

In children, chronic inflammation is responsible for inflammatory bowel disease (Crohn's and ulcerative colitis), triggering the genes responsible for other autoimmune disorders such as juvenile arthritis or type 1 diabetes mellitus. Inflammation also causes chronic joint and muscle pain (arthritis), worsens inflammatory skin conditions such as eczema and psoriasis, increases the frequency of epileptic seizures, and can damage peripheral nerves, leading to neuropathy.

Transcutaneous auricular vagus nerve stimulation (taVNS) can significantly reduce inflammation and thus improve these genetically driven disorders. Considering how safe and well-tolerated taVNS is in children, this component of The Nemechek Protocol® provides an opportunity to enhance and potentially reverse genetically linked childhood illnesses.

Because of its ability to lower inflammation even further, I routinely recommend the addition of taVNS in any child with autism or developmental delay who is experiencing an incomplete recovery using my protocol, is requiring continuous rifaximin to control bacterial overgrowth, or is requiring the use of prescription medications to control behavior or enhance focus and attention.

Other indications of taVNS in children might include an uncontrolled inflammatory or autoimmune disorder and poorly controlled epilepsy.

Expansion of Neural Networks

Another benefit of taVNS results from its ability to help the brain reestablish and expand neural pathways known as neural networks.

The brain functions by sending signals from one area of the brain to another. The concept of a single thought or function between two brain areas does not occur through a single linear pathway. Communication pathways in the brain occur simultaneously through a collection of neurons known as a neural network.

Furthermore, the more neurons engaged in achieving the desired function within a particular neural network, the brain's ability to carry out the desired command or instruction becomes more effective.

When a person practices playing a particular musical score over and over on the piano, the neural networks required to read the music and move their fingers appropriately on the keyboard expand. The expansion of the neural network occurs as more and more neurons are crowdsourced to perform a collection of tasks that allow the individual's piano-playing skill to improve.

Likewise, suppose they cease practicing that particular piece of music. In that case, their neural network for that piece of music and for playing the piano will shrink, and their performance will worsen in direct proportion to the reduction of that neural network.

Transcutaneous auricular VNS can increase the brain's ability to build and expand these neural networks in a process called cortical plasticity.

Electrical Dosing and Failures After Vagus Nerve Stimulation

The initiation of taVNS to The Nemechek Protocol® jump starts a new pattern of neurological recovery in children. It is also a significant component of autonomic recovery as applied to adults. The purpose of vagus nerve stimulation is to begin substantial recovery in those few areas not yet improving with only fish oil, olive oil, and a balanced intestinal bacteria (inulin or rifaximin).

As a general observation, taVNS is often required in patients older than fourteen to realize a broader, more complete neurological recovery.

The dosage of electrical stimulation can vary greatly depending on the individual's age and the medical condition we are trying to improve. The electrical stimulation parameters vary by intensity, frequency, and timing of electricity cycling on and off and total time on the device per each twenty-four-hour period. The variables for taVNS treatments include amperage, bandwidth, frequency (Hz), the cycling pattern (off/on), and the clip's position on the ear.

The vast majority of children and young adults less than thirty years of age will only require five minutes of continuous transcutaneous vagus nerve stimulation per day. At the proper settings, five minutes of taVNS is enough to significantly reduce inflammation throughout the body for at least twenty-four hours.

Five minutes of taVNS has also been shown to cause the unhealthy primed M1-phenotype microglia to change their behavior and begin acting like the healthy M2-microglia that can once again prune and repair neurons. In children with ADD or ADHD, POTS, PANS, PANDAS, depression, anxiety, or aggression disorders, the M1-to-M2 phenotypic shift is essential to recover fully. More information on shifting between the M1 and M2 phenotypes is found in later chapters.

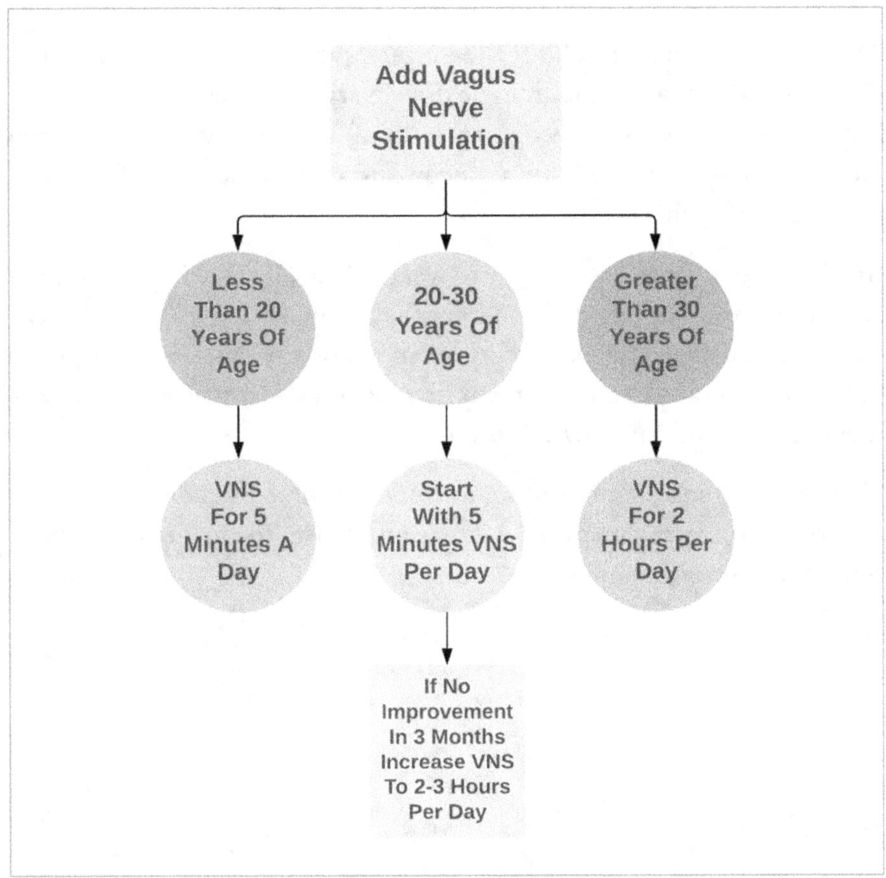

Different Vagus Nerve Stimulation Time Requirements

The general recommendation is to start with five minutes of taVNS per day between the ages of twenty and thirty. When combined with the core aspects of The Nemechek Protocol®, most adults in this age range will begin to experience significant neurological recovery within three months. Still, occasionally, there may be some young adults who are an exception.

Often, the neurological deficits begin to improve within six weeks. Although the impact of taVNS on inflammation and microglia behavior occurs immediately, it usually takes a few weeks for the improvements to accumulate enough that they become recognizable by the parent or caretaker.

The older the patient is (child -> teenager -> young adult -> older adult), the slower their rate of neurological recovery may seem. But as a rule, improvement should be recognizable in all patients after one to three months as long as there have not been any substantial interruptions or traumas during this time.

In adults between twenty and thirty years of age, if there is no recognizable improvement after three months of daily five-minute taVNS sessions, consider the possibility of a relapse of bacterial intestinal imbalance and retreat with rifaximin. Also, look for interfering supplements and discontinue them if present.

If neither of these is present and a repeat course of rifaximin fails to restart neurological recovery, increasing taVNS to one hour daily is sometimes recommended.

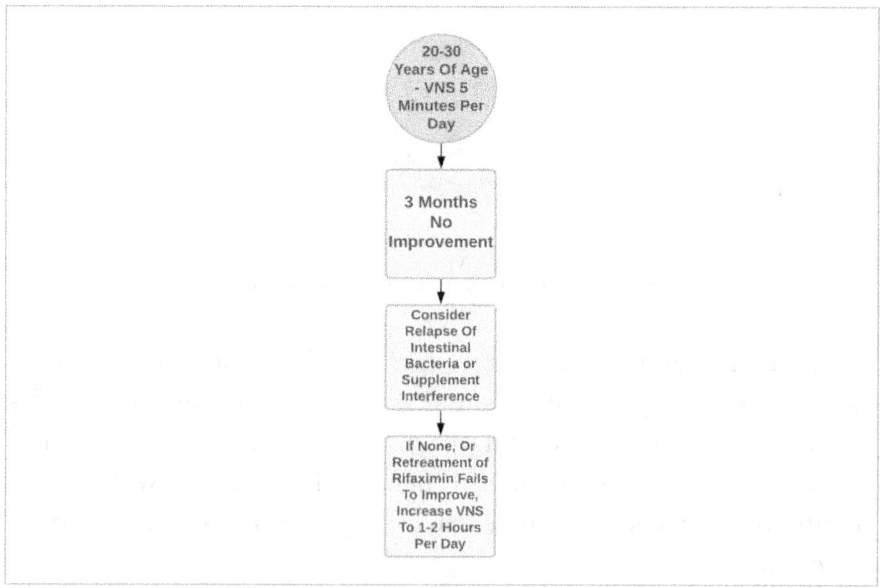

Adjustment of Therapy Patients 20-30 Years of Age

The need to increase taVNS to more than five minutes per day rarely occurs in children under twenty. Within this age group, if there is no significant improvement, the cause of no neurological improvement is likely due to a relapse of intestinal bacteria overgrowth rather than the taVNS not being effective.

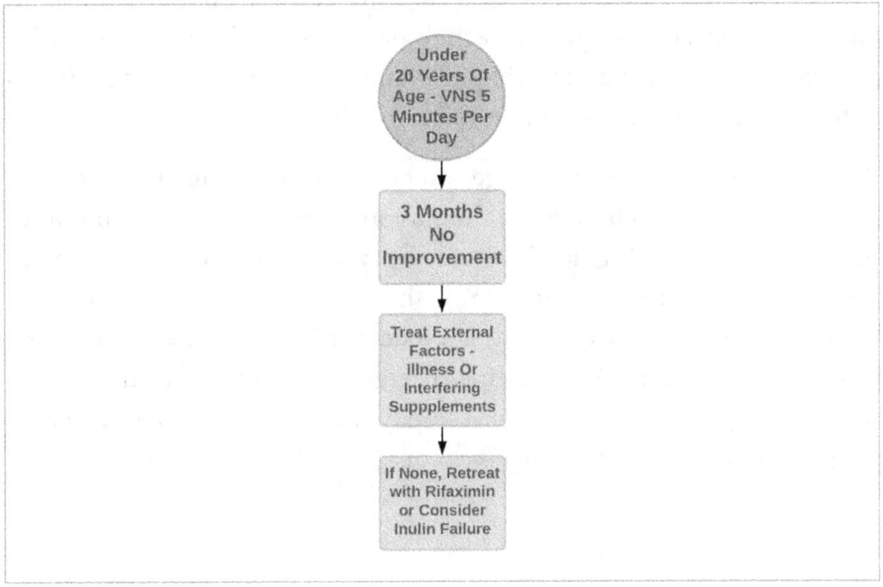

No Adjustment of VNS in Younger Patients is Recommended

This scenario would need to be addressed with another round of rifaximin, initiating cyclic or continuous rifaximin, or if the patient is on inulin, replacing inulin with rifaximin. Again, always look for external factors such as an intensely stressful situation, supplements, homeopathic remedies, or a probiotic that might prevent or mask recovery.

There is an exception to the five minutes of taVNS per day rule in children under twenty-five. On occasion, parents will notice that after just five minutes of taVNS, their child may experience a prolonged calming effect that can last for a few hours.

In these cases, taVNS should be used at least once daily to control inflammation and an additional two to three five-minute increments to manage anxiety.

When the taVNS is increased beyond five minutes per day in adults, the electrical current needs to cycle on and off in a particular manner to avoid a problem called habituation. Habituation means that the nervous system begins ignoring the electrical stimulating signal as we commonly do with "white noise" or background noises in a room.

After a few years of closely following the recovery patterns of adult patients using taVNS, Dr. Nemechek has developed a highly effective proprietary cycling pattern that prevents habituation but retains its potent ability to reverse cumulative brain injury.

Patients over thirty years of age almost universally need one to two hours of cycling vagus nerve stimulation to recover from cumulative brain injury or to further their recovery from autism and developmental delay. Just as in children, if there is little to no improvement within a few months of starting cyclic taVNS, the most interfering factor as a relapse of the intestinal bacterial or some other interfering supplement, or a homeopathic remedy, probiotics, recurrent herpes simplex, chronic dental infection or high dosages of vitamins or minerals.

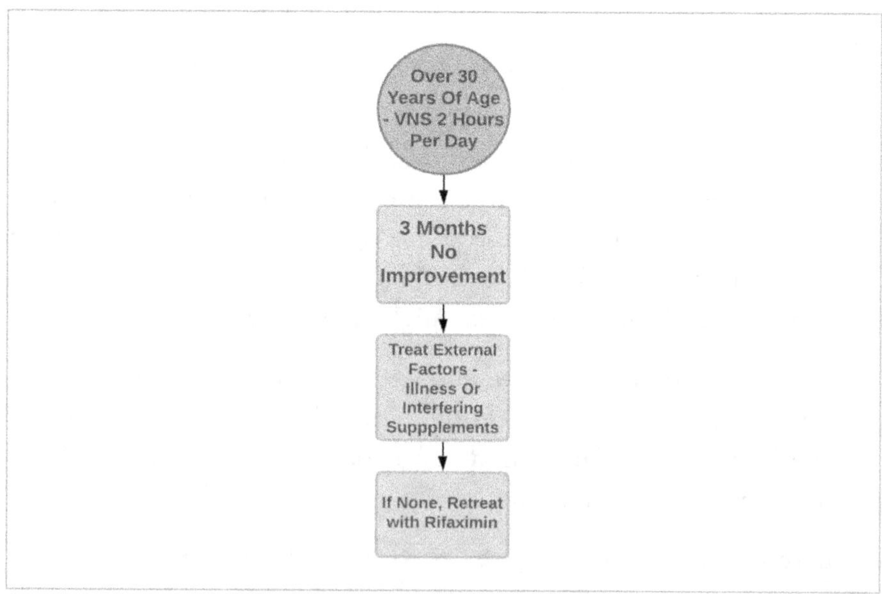

Adjustment of Therapy Patients Over 30 Years of Age

Increasing the taVNS above two hours per day will not solve these problems and should not be attempted. taVNS should never be programmed or conducted by yourself without the specific guidance of your physician. The vagus nerve is capable of being permanently damaged if stimulated improperly.

Time Course for VNS Therapy

At the time of publication of this book, the specific number of years of taVNS therapy required for children with autism or any form of developmental issue is unknown. At the same time, data is collected on the children under my care who have been on taVNS long enough to determine if or what kind of relapse might occur if taVNS is discontinued after recovery.

The two primary effects of taVNS are to restore neurological pruning, which helps the child develop and mature, and secondly, to help repair damage to the autonomic nervous system and neural networks that occur from cumulative brain injury.

It is believed that the developmental pruning process during childhood is unidirectional, meaning that once the child has pruned off a branch of a neuron, just like a branch of a tree, they will not replace it with a new one and increase the number of unorganized neurons again.

Children would not regress from a developmental milestone standpoint if taVNS were discontinued (i.e., a child who has regained speech or socialization skills would not lose these skills once the brain is pruned correctly).

My research using taVNS as part of The Nemechek Protocol® in adults for recovery autonomic dysfunction from cumulative brain injury demonstrates that after discontinuing taVNS, many adults will have a return of some of their autonomic symptoms (constipation, fidgetiness, headaches, poor focus) they experienced previously. Yet many also become less consistent with the other components of the protocol at the same time, so it is unknown if the symptoms return because of the absence of any single element or the lack of several.

The return of symptoms occurs slowly and is often apparent within four to eight weeks. In addition to a return of their symptoms, evidence of their prior autonomic damage as measured by autonomic spectral analysis will also return on repeat testing.

Therefore, once a child patient has reached developmental maturity and behaves neurotypically, consider discontinuing taVNS while continuing fish and olive oil and maintaining intestinal bacteria balance with either inulin or rifaximin.

Either the recovery from cumulative brain injury (resolution of ADD, hyperactivity, anxiety, aggression, constipation, heartburn) will persist, or they might notice a return of some of these symptoms within the eight weeks after discontinuation.

If the symptoms do not return, the taVNS is no longer required. If a child seems to be relapsing, re-initiation of taVNS is warranted.

Suppose the child also has another non-developmental health condition (inflammatory bowel disease, epilepsy, or cerebral palsy) that has improved because of the addition of taVNS. In that case, it is not advised to stop taVNS because these other conditions are often more than likely to return with discontinuation of taVNS.

PART IV

THE UPS AND DOWNS OF RECOVERY

13

THE PROCESS OF RECOVERY

Generally, the gains from your child's neurological disorder steadily accumulate with only occasional setbacks from colds, additional brain traumas, or other illnesses.

As mentioned in Chapter 1, the first change often seen during the first few weeks with my young patients is described as "the awakening" period, an increased level of awareness and functioning due to the initial decline of the toxic effects of propionic acid. The awakening can improve some behaviors while temporarily worsening others.

Only children who experience bacterial overgrowth from propionic-producing bacteria (Autism, PANS, PANDAS) might experience the awakening. Children with ADD, ADHD, depression, or anxiety often will not.

But from this point forward, normal neuronal repair begins the recovery process, and the child will start improving month by month, year by year.

It helps to view a child whose bacteria is producing propionic acid as a child under the effects of a sedative such as Valium (diazepam). All their behaviors are blunted or subdued; they may seem calmer and sleep through the night, but they do not respond readily when spoken to, may seldom speak unless encouraged, and may not be aware of their surroundings.

In the case of autism, the sedative affecting the children is the elevated tissue levels of propionic acid made by the overgrowth of bacteria within the child's small intestine, which then leaks into the bloodstream. Reversing the bacterial overgrowth reduces the sedating propionic acid from the body, and the child becomes more cognitively alert. Children diagnosed with PANS or PANDAS demonstrate a similar clinical response to balancing of the intestinal bacteria.

Children in the awakening period become more aware of their surroundings. They are often more tolerant of being touched or held and communicate more but may also seem more anxious or sleep less. The older the child, the less noticeable the awakening period.

The True Extent of Brain Dysfunction

If the child also has underlying brain injuries from physical, emotional, or inflammatory traumas, parents may see more angry outbursts, hyperactivity, anxiety, and stimulation behavior after the awakening period.

This is because the sedating effect of propionic acid has suppressed these behaviors, and as the propionic acid levels decline with the reversal of bacterial overgrowth, the sedating effect wanes, and the behaviors become more apparent. The children are not worse; they are finally awake.

After reversing bacterial overgrowth, neuronal repair depends on the additional reduction of inflammation with fish oil, COOC-certified California olive oil, decreasing the omega-6 vegetable oils from the diet, and incorporating vagus nerve stimulation when necessary.

The Pace of Recovery

The vital point to remember is that a child's brain can repair past injuries and continue the path of development once the inflammation is consistently controlled.

Nothing can be done to speed up the brain's natural ability to recover. Hoping to speed up the brain's repair process is similar to someone wanting to speed up the recovery of their broken arm. A broken arm will not heal faster by doing anything "extra." It is the same with brain recovery.

Like brain tissue, bone tissue has its own naturally determined rate of recovery, and there is no known way to improve upon the natural rate. It is important not to compare a child's behavior today with yesterday but instead compare them today to how they were one or two months ago or when they first started the protocol.

Keeping a longer timeframe when assessing the pace of recovery is essential because it prevents a parent from getting distracted by some of the everyday ups and downs in the recovery process.

Over Focusing and Misinterpreting

Some of the first changes to occur after starting the protocol might be in a child's skin condition or the speed of their digestive tract. Usually, if a child has eczema or psoriasis, the skin will noticeably improve. The Nemechek Protocol® reverses bacterial overgrowth, which often stops chronic diarrhea or sometimes a perceived worsening of constipation.

Constipation, Poor Focus and Autonomic Dysfunction

The autonomic nervous system (ANS) is a large portion of the nervous system that controls and coordinates all organ functions, emotional regulation, metabolism, hormonal production, and most of the immune system.

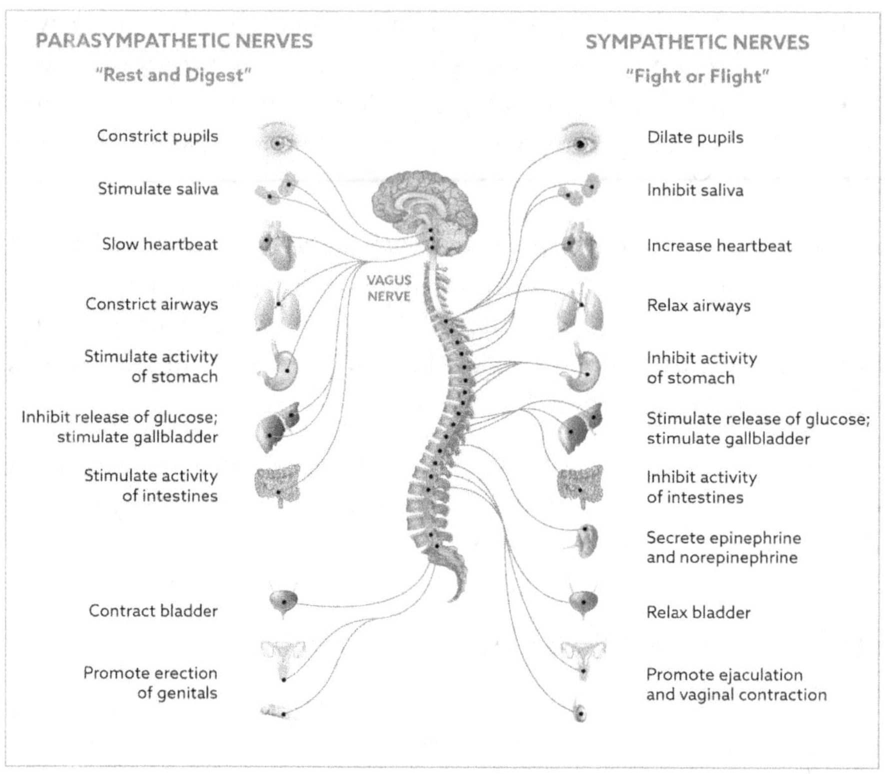

The Autonomic Nervous System

In a child, chronic inflammation prevents the brain from fully repairing damage to the autonomic nervous system from head banging, accidental falls, intense emotional traumas, inflammatory trauma from surgery, allergy testing, adverse vaccine reactions, and potentially a chemical injury from propionic acid if it is leaking into the bloodstream.

The residual damage from new injuries accumulates on top of damage from prior injuries in a process known as cumulative brain injury (CBI). Cumulative brain injuries eventually cause enough damage to the autonomic nervous system that the child will start to experience symptoms.

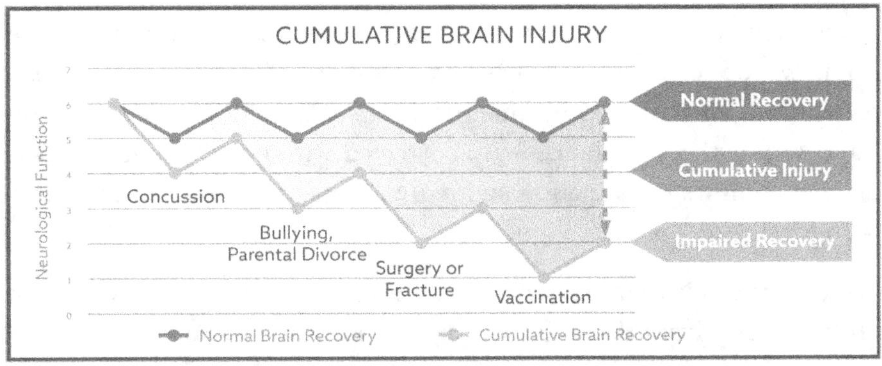

Cumulative Brain Injury from Brain Injuries

A common problem after the reversal of bacterial overgrowth is the appearance of constipation in children. From an autonomic viewpoint, constipation is the nervous system's inability to push the stool's contents forward on that conveyor belt. It is a common symptom that develops after a physical brain injury. Understand that inulin or rifaximin did not "cause" constipation; they stop diarrhea or loose stool that masks the underlying neurological constipation.

Studies in adults find that 50-70% of adults will develop constipation within the first week after a mild-to-moderate concussion (i.e., head injury). The source of constipation is often greatly influenced by the autonomic nervous system, not solely caused by the colon.

Understanding the mechanics that drive digestive tract propulsion can help parents understand the changes they see in their children during the treatment of bacterial overgrowth. Bacterial overgrowth may lead to either constipation, diarrhea (an increased rate of stool production), stool urgency, heartburn after particular foods, frequent bowel movements, or all the above.

Suppose a child has an increased rate of stool production from bacterial overgrowth (i.e., diarrhea) while at the same time having inadequate forward stool propulsion from autonomic nervous system damage (i.e., constipation). In that case, they may seem to have a regular stool pattern. The liquid stool of diarrhea essentially treats the slow movement of stool in constipation.

Not understanding that this somewhat normal stool pattern may be from two opposing imbalances that present a "false" normal bowel pattern and can lead to improper decisions. Therefore, once the bacterial overgrowth is rebalanced and corrected with either inulin or rifaximin, the child's constipation suddenly seems to "be caused by" these therapies.

What happens is that the diarrhea (an underlying bacterial overgrowth problem) resolves, thereby making the underlying constipation (an autonomic nervous system problem) more prominent. Eventually, the underlying constipation will improve as the patient's autonomic nervous system recovers.

The Nemechek Protocol® shifts the patient's microglia into repair mode, reduces brain inflammation, and stimulates brain stem cell production and neuron regeneration. When the microglia begin to function and the inflammation declines, the repair of the autonomic nervous system begins in earnest. The improvement of autonomic nervous system function allows the digestive conveyor belt to move more naturally again.

Supplements and Prescription Medicine

Children are being over-treated with many supplements for oxidative stress, mitochondrial defects, digestion, biofilm, folate problems, yeast overgrowth, parasites, and other metabolic disturbances.

Although many of those types of supplements may have improved something initially, they do not significantly impact the overall pattern of bacterial overgrowth, brain trauma symptoms, and autonomic nervous system dysfunction. As a cautionary note, many supplements can impede or even reverse recovery.

The Nemechek Protocol® does not use any of these products because none of them impact the reversal of bacterial overgrowth, microglial activation, or excessive levels of brain inflammation.

Many supplements are ineffective in allowing complete recovery because many of these products often only address the downstream effects of the much more significant and overwhelming issue of metabolic inflammation.

Metabolic inflammation is the term used to describe the broad adverse effects that the chronic elevation of pro-inflammatory cytokines within the bloodstream has on cellular function. Metabolic inflammation must persistently suppressed throughout the body for cells to begin functioning more normally.

I often speak of metabolic inflammation as if water is flooding a valley because the dam upstream is broken and no longer holds back the water. When the dam breaks, the homes and fields downstream of the dam become flooded from the excessive water flow.

The water in my example is meant to represent the massive release of pro-inflammatory cytokines associated with bacterial overgrowth, the deficiency of the dietary omega-3 fatty acids, the excessive nutritional intake of omega-6-rich oils and foods, and often damage to the inflammation-controlling vagus nerve.

Certain efforts, such as placing sandbags around a home or pumping water out of a basement, may benefit the flooded area, but they do not address the primary problem, which is the broken dam. Sandbags and basement pumps are like many supplements used to address mitochondrial dysfunction or the depletion of antioxidants. The real problem remains. The dam needs to be repaired, and once that occurs, the sandbags and basement pumps are no longer required.

Once metabolic inflammation is reduced with The Nemechek Protocol®, the need for supplements addressing mitochondrial dysfunction and antioxidant depletion disappears.

Regarding all prescription medications or prescription supplements (e.g., iron, Vitamin D3, injectable Vitamin B12, or leucovorin), parents should never under any circumstance reduce or stop those without first consulting their child's managing physician. - Dr. N

Understanding Bacterial Terminology

Our understanding of the diversity of microbes living within the human intestinal tract is rapidly expanding, and a few phrases (dysbiosis, low biodiversity, SIBO, and bacterial overgrowth) may seem similar but are all slightly different.

Dysbiosis is a general term referring to any change in the blend of living microbes within the intestinal tract. It does not explicitly apply to only bacteria, and it may refer to viruses, protozoan, or archaebacteria, nor does it apply to any specific region of the intestinal tract (i.e., colon vs. small intestine).

In addition to an imbalance of one type or species of a microorganism to another, dysbiosis may also refer to the absence of certain species thought to inhabit the human intestinal tract normally. The extinction or loss of species is referred to as low biodiversity.

SIBO (small intestinal bacterial overgrowth) implies the patient has an overgrowth of bacteria within the small intestine. These bacteria usually live in the colon (the lower intestinal tract); they have migrated upward and live in the wrong place.

The "gold standard" test for determining bacterial overgrowth is a procedure that requires a long endoscope to be passed into the small intestine to sample bacteria within the jejunum portion of the small intestine. Then, the sample needs to undergo quantitative culturing, DNA identification, and metabolic activation testing of the species in the sample.

This testing is not recommended because it is expensive, impractical, generally unavailable outside of a research study, and unnecessary to achieve improvement using The Nemechek Protocol®. Furthermore, the testing will commonly need to be repeated may need to be repeated several times should any recovery issues arise.

Some people undergo a "SIBO breath test" looking for a SIBO diagnosis, but the breath test is prone to many sources of error. Within my practice, I stopped using SIBO breath testing on my patients to determine overgrowth because unacceptably high false positive and false negative results made it clinically useless.

The Misconception of Feeding "Bad" Bacteria and Yeast with Inulin

It is difficult to imagine the hundreds of thousands of bacteria within our digestive tract that are causing our brains and bodies so much trouble. Common questions from parents of my patients are whether inulin feeds "bad bacteria" and yeast.

Inulin is a safe prebiotic fiber that produces enough bacterial rebalancing, propionic acid reduction, and inflammation reduction to allow a child to become more alert and restart the process of neuronal pruning and development.

Inulin is present in large amounts in garlic and onions, and these foods have been historically safe to feed children over millennia. Combining inulin with fish and olive oil is nothing more than the same ingredients a child might have when consuming fish soup in ancient Rome.

Starting with an inulin-based protocol in children is generally recommended because it is often effective, safe, inexpensive, and does not require a prescription. Inulin is widely available from several manufacturers. Inulin is also appealing as a natural fiber since many parents understandably fear using more antibiotics.

Intestinal Symptoms and Stool Testing

When children are experiencing occasional intestinal issues, I always consider whether some other common mechanism is causing their intestinal symptoms.

Things to consider include viral infections, injury to the autonomic nervous system, reaction to other medications or supplements, or tainted food. Adverse reactions to these events should resolve within one to two weeks without necessitating changes in dosage or the discontinuation of inulin.

Occasionally, patients have chronic diarrhea, loose stools, or an oily film in the stool. These things generally occur for two reasons. The first is that bacterial overgrowth injures or stresses the intestinal tract. Their intestinal tract will begin to repair itself within two to three weeks after starting inulin or treatment with a course of rifaximin. Because of the rapid healing, patients do not need special "gut-healing" supplements or special diets.

The second reason is that their intestines may not be accustomed to absorbing the volume of oil used in The Nemechek Protocol®. The intestinal tract alters its ability to absorb oils depending on the amount of oil or fat in the person's diet.

To improve oil absorption in my patients, first decrease their amounts of fish oil and EVOO to a lower dose that allows their stools to normalize somewhat. Then, slowly increase their dose of fish oil, followed by olive oil, a little every week until they reach the full dose in about three to four weeks.

Although testing the stool for bacteria and yeast is commonly performed by other practitioners, the interpretation of the results should be viewed with a great deal of caution. The first issue is that approximately 90% of the bacterial species that live within the intestine cannot be grown by standard laboratory techniques.

Culture results from a stool specimen will only potentially grow 10% of all the species present. Concluding the balanced health of the intestinal bacterial blend from only 10% of the population is bound to be inaccurate. Accurate identification of bacteria species can only be done by quantitative DNA sequencing techniques.

The second issue is that a stool sample from the colon's last part (i.e., rectum) contains a vastly different blend of bacteria and cannot be compared to a sample aspirated from the small intestine. The adverse health effects of bacterial overgrowth are due to excessive bacteria growing in the small intestine, not due to changes in the balance of bacteria within the rectum.

Analysis for bacterial overgrowth of the small intestine (SIBO) requires a sample of fluid from within the small intestine, and this sample can only be obtained by endoscopy (EGD; esophagogastroduodenoscopy) and is generally only performed for research purposes. Because of the complexity, cost, and risk, obtaining samples by endoscopy is not recommended.

On rare occasions, a simple stool test might detect parasitic organisms called protozoans (like Giardia) or helminths (worms). Detection of one of these organisms might require treatment depending on the organism found, the nature of the patient's symptoms, and the potential adverse effects of the treatment. Infection with these types of organisms tends to occur when consuming contaminated water or foods or walking barefoot in contaminated areas.

The Risk of Running Unnecessary Tests

By the time most people come to my office for a consultation, many have been misled, over-charged, and even harmed physically and emotionally by excessive and unnecessary laboratory tests (enzymes, food intolerance, infectious disease antibody levels, metabolic panels, genetic panels) or physical testing (CT/MRI scans, EEG, etc.).

The modern era of medicine has seen an excessive dependence on various tests to help determine the cause of the patient's symptoms. The interactions with providers can quickly become nothing more than a timely and expensive guessing game. The traditional and most effective method of diagnostics in medicine is a thorough history and examination to determine the most probable cause of a person's symptoms.

Physicians should not order testing until they have determined the one or two conditions most likely responsible for the patient's symptoms. Any ordered tests should be specific to either rule in or rule out these conditions. A common example is when a clinician orders several different antibody panels looking for various organisms, all of which would cause vastly different symptoms. When done this way, this indicates the doctor is lost diagnostically.

Tests ordered should be based on the patient's particular symptoms. If the patient is not exhibiting symptoms suggestive of EBV or Babesiosis, these antibody levels should never be ordered. An unnecessary test can return a false positive result, and now the entire clinical treatment strategy is moving down the wrong path.

Broad panels of tests for random things that do not change the patient's course of care should always be avoided. The question that needs to be asked when ordering tests is whether the test result will change the treatment strategy.

Procedures such as colonoscopies, MRI scans, or EEG should only be ordered if the results will alter the course of treatment. These tests should never be performed to "take a look" because they all can potentially harm the child physically or emotionally.

Restricting Foods in the Diet

The restriction of foods in the diet is unnecessary when treating children with The Nemechek Protocol® other than foods known to cause severe allergic reactions (peanuts, shellfish, etc.) or obvious intolerance (milk causing diarrhea, etc.) in the patient.

If a child has been on a restrictive diet before starting The Nemechek Protocol®, the reintroduction of previously intolerant foods can often occur a few weeks after starting the inulin or after completing the course of rifaximin.

An obvious exception to this is foods such as peanuts that may have previously caused a severe allergic reaction in the child. These should never be re-introduced. Parents should discuss reintroduction with their primary care physician if there are any questions about the severity of past food reactions.

Unfortunately, many children have developed a limited pattern of food preferences (the so-called picky eaters). While this can be frustrating and worrisome for parents, it resolves over time.

Adding vitamins to "ensure they get everything they need" is not advised. The importance of a wide variety of foods is less critical than most people think, and the high rate of fraud in the supplement industry increases the potential for harm.

Some studies suggest the symptoms of gluten intolerance seem to occur because of an abnormal inflammatory reaction against gluten. This inflammatory reaction may result from parasympathetic weakness of the autonomic nervous system and is not directly related to bacterial translocation (leaky gut).

As the child starts recovering neurologically, the autonomic nervous system begins to recover, and gluten intolerance often slowly resolves without needing to remain on a gluten-free diet.

Physical, Occupational and Speech Therapies

Continuing therapy while a patient is on The Nemechek Protocol® is recommended. Still, as the child improves, many of these therapies become unnecessary and can trigger negative behaviors in the children.

My experience has taught me that once the child is showing overall signs of neurological recovery on The Nemechek Protocol® and they have overcome their primary obstacle with therapy, the therapy should be curtailed or stopped. The child should be allowed to recover independently. Everyday social interactions with parents, siblings, and others are ample stimulation and role-modeling to allow for continued normal development.

During the pandemic, when schools were closed and children were no longer receiving ABA, OT/PT, or speech therapies, many children experienced continued gains, and many times, much to their parents' surprise, gains much greater than when actively receiving therapy.

Monitoring Propionic Acid Levels

Although there are tests available that can measure propionic acid levels in the bloodstream and urine, there are no set standards we can use to determine if a level is too high or low, like our interpretation of blood sugar (glucose) levels. Furthermore, propionic acid is rapidly absorbed by cells, where its toxic effect occurs internally. Therefore, testing for propionic acid is not recommended.

In ten years or more, it is anticipated that chemicals other than propionic acid will be discovered to be released into the bloodstream. Remember, a major aspect of The Nemechek Protocol® is to reverse the bacterial overgrowth in the small intestine, and this would predictably eliminate the production of any chemicals produced from the overgrowing bacteria.

Successful rebalancing of the intestinal bacteria will reduce both inflammatory stress and the decline in the abnormal production of chemicals, whether it is propionic acid or something else.

Suppose a child under my care has any features resembling autism, PANS, PANDAS, POTS, ADD/ ADHD, a mood disorder, or any other developmental issue. In that case, they will be started on The Nemechek Protocol® because, with any of these diagnoses, the patient has a good chance of improvement or recovery regardless of a propionic-related test result.

The protocol focuses on restoring neurological function by reducing inflammation within the nervous system and eliminating any bacterial toxins if they are being produced. These conditions will similarly improve because they all occur due to abnormal neuronal pruning, repair, and rejuvenation mechanisms.

The Genetic Wildcard in Recovery

First, the specter of a "genetic disorder" implies it is irreversible and leaves many parents feeling that recovery is impossible. Many parents are being counseled that there is little hope for their child to improve because of these genetic test results. This is false.

Secondly, demonstrating a genetic abnormality is not proof that the abnormality is *the cause* of any particular problem with the child.

Another fact is that finding a gene for any particular medical condition does not mean the gene is necessarily active. A typical example is that many people with brown eyes may carry a gene for blue eyes. They have the gene for blue eyes, but it has not been activated. A wide variety of children have recovered with The Nemechek Protocol® despite tests demonstrating the presence of abnormal genes or genetic deletions or repetitions.

While the anatomic issues (small cranium, musculoskeletal issues with arms or legs, etc.) associated with some genetic abnormalities do not improve, most children will experience significant *neurological* gains with The Nemechek Protocol®.

14

MANAGING ANXIETY TANTRUMS, OCD AND AGGRESSION

In my pursuit to help reverse patients' health problems, it is crucial to identify the underlying mechanisms driving these problems rather than prescribing medications that often mask the problems. Masking or controlling symptoms with drugs is not necessarily improper, nor should it be considered "bad" medicine; often, it is the best we can do with the scientific knowledge at hand.

However, many chronic conditions result from excessive inflammation, and unbalanced intestinal bacteria are often a contributing source of the inflammation. Typical medications used to treat these conditions only treat the downstream effects of inflammatory damage but not the underlying source of inflammation.

A significant difference between treating children (especially kids with a communication disability) and adults is that children often do not talk about symptoms they are experiencing or might be unable to communicate their symptoms in the same manner that most adults can.

For example, a child might have a simple runny nose and an occasional cough for a few weeks. However, because there is no high fever, their symptoms are often interpreted as allergies or a mild virus, and no further evaluation is entertained.

An adult may have the same symptoms but can also volunteer they have headaches, muscle aches, occasional chills, and a sore throat. The adult is then diagnosed with a sinus infection and might be offered antibiotics or a nasal steroid spray. The child might have had the same additional symptoms but could not provide these added clinical information that changed the treatment approach.

The same problem occurs when treating, diagnosing, and managing conditions like anxiety, tantrums (emotional fits), OCD-like behaviors, and overly aggressive reactions. Because we cannot question the child about what they are experiencing, it is often impossible to be sure what they are feeling (e.g., anxiety versus fear, frustration versus anger).

Because the clinical history is sometimes limited when treating children, I approach these problems from a mechanical injury perspective. In other words, what neurological pathways may be broken to result in these behaviors?

Anxiety and aggression can be very appropriate or inappropriate depending on whether truly threatening circumstances are present (e.g., being face-to-face with a growling dog) or not (e.g., sitting still for an extended period during school or a car ride). Appropriate reactions are often readily apparent and generally not of concern. Inappropriate reactions are unpredictable and frustrating to the child and their parents.

Various situations and physical conditions can trigger the release of the "fight or flight" hormone noradrenaline (norepinephrine). Its release causes adults and children to feel anxious, aggressive, or fearful and causes them to want to flee from the triggering situation.

Rebalancing intestinal bacteria with inulin or rifaximin can sometimes result in a significant decline in anxiety and aggression. If the symptoms persist after rebalancing intestinal bacteria, the excessive emotional responses are most commonly due to unrepaired damage to the autonomic nervous system (cumulative brain injury).

Excessive emotional reactions can occur after rather severe injury to the limbic system of the central nervous system. In blast-induced neurotrauma experienced by soldiers, limbic system injuries are thought to be due to the combination of the concussion of the blast and the twisting of the head from the explosion. Luckily, damage to the limbic system is otherwise very uncommon in routine concussions.

Some medications can trigger the release of fight-or-flight hormones if the medications lower blood pressure and oxygen delivery to the brain. Medications most capable of this include blood pressure-lowering medications used to try to control anxiety (clonidine, guanfacine, propranolol) as well as some psychotropic medications (risperidone).

The focus of this chapter is on the behaviors in children labeled as anxiety, panic attacks, OCD, or aggression that result from autonomic dysfunction.

A Mechanical View of Anxiety

As discussed elsewhere in the book, bacterial overgrowth in the small intestine results in three discreet pathological processes: the release of abnormal amounts of propionic acid, the release of pro-inflammatory cytokines, and the activation of an abnormal population of cells in the brain known as primed microglia.

While the release of propionic acid is responsible for a portion of features that are unique to autism (loss of eye contact and awareness), the pro-inflammatory cytokines and primed microglia both directly impair the brain's natural ability to prune and repair the brain.

Remember, cumulative brain injury (CBI) is the inability to fully repair the brain after mild to severe brain injuries, leading to residual damage from a recent injury to be added to residual damage from past injuries. Although any portion of the brain can become damaged after a head trauma, damage to the autonomic nervous system often results in noticeable symptoms.

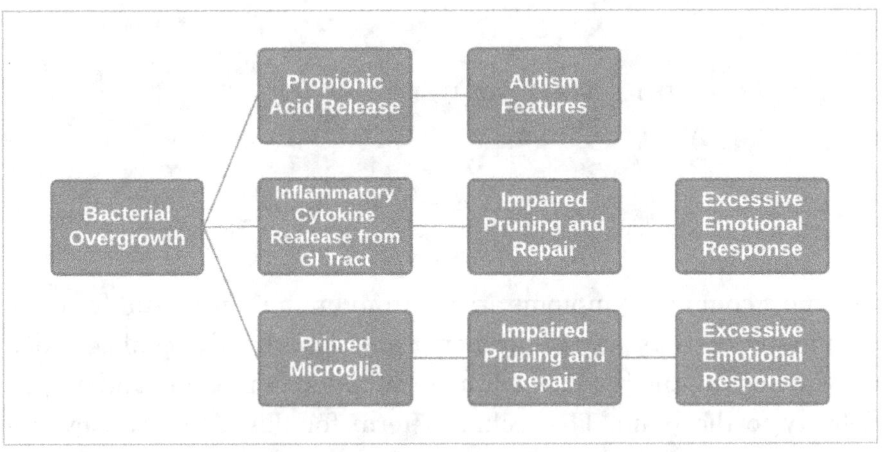

Bacterial Overgrowth Triggers Three Pathways that Contribute to Emotional Problems

The autonomic nervous system (ANS) controls all aspects of the body's involuntary physiological functioning. It controls the immune system, regulates hormone production and metabolism, intestinal tract motility, blood pressure, heart rate, and the proper intensity of emotional responses.

Furthermore, the autonomic nervous system can be injured through various traumas besides physical injuries. There is growing evidence that the brain can also sustain cellular damage after significant emotional traumas or after the release of inflammatory cytokines from surgeries, fractures, vaccines, and even after a stroke within the brain. Any of these traumas can potentially increase damage to the autonomic nervous system.

Mechanisms of Injury to the Nervous System

- **Physical Injury:** concussion or sub-concussive events

- **Inflammatory Injury:** surgery, vaccinations, fractures

- **Emotional Trauma:** moving to a new home, change in trusted therapist, bullying

The most common symptoms arising from brain injury result from the autonomic nervous system not being able to correctly regulate blood pressure within the brain, resulting in suboptimal pressure and oxygen delivery to the brain. The technical term for this is cerebral hypoperfusion.

The low brain pressure and inadequate release of oxygen commonly result in symptoms like headaches (migraine, cluster, or tension), chronic and unexplained fatigue, difficulty with concentration and focus (often diagnosed as ADD or ADHD), hyperactivity, insomnia, and increased thirst and hunger with particular cravings for salty or sweet foods.

Most importantly, low brain blood pressure can result in the periodic release of the fight-or-flight hormone noradrenaline. Noradrenaline is released from nerves of the sympathetic branch of the autonomic nervous system, not from the adrenal gland, as its name might suggest.

As the phrase "fight or flight" suggests, noradrenaline can cause aggressive, anxious, and frightened behaviors that sometimes manifest as the need to escape or flee. This need to escape is often referred to as elopement in children. Growing scientific evidence shows that children with autism, developmental disorders, and attention-learning deficits suffer from autonomic dysfunction and low brain blood pressure.

Anxious, Hungry, Hyperactive, and Aggressive Responses

The ANS has evolved in all animals, including humans, to help keep them alive in the wild. Primitive apes and stone-age humans had no modern concept of how much they needed to eat or drink, but they survived because the ANS would make them feel hungry or thirsty.

The ANS tells us to sleep and when to wake. The ANS scans the environment for signs of danger and constantly gives feedback about safety or danger. These signals are often called our "sixth sense" or "inner voice" when a situation strikes us in an uncomfortable manner.

If the ANS is injured, the loss of proper blood pressure and oxygen delivery to the brain is an urgent issue because the brain only has one second of reserve oxygen and is worried about passing out and dying from a lack of oxygen. The urgency and physical reaction to the suboptimal oxygen supply can sometimes be as intense as one might feel if they were drowning. The brain will seek ways to improve blood pressure and oxygen delivery to survive.

The brain learns that liquids or foods containing salt or sugar will boost blood pressure to the head and help improve oxygen delivery to the neurons. This drives the constant need in some children to eat or drink, and if they do not get enough, they begin to act irritable and angry. Some parents jokingly refer to this combination of hungry and angry as "hangry."

Likewise, movement of the leg muscles will increase blood pressure and oxygen delivery to the brain. We have all witnessed an individual in a cafe or at a desk at work whose feet or legs are tapping or bouncing incessantly. In children with autism, the low blood pressure problem is responsible for their hyperactivity and toe-walking behaviors, which, through the contraction of muscles, pushes blood upward into the brain.

The contraction of the leg muscles while moving or standing up on their tippy toes also helps squeeze blood flow upward towards the brain, improves oxygen delivery to neurons, and helps to dampen their uncontrollable fight-or-flight impulses.

The brain subconsciously drives the movement of the muscles to prevent itself from passing out and possibly dying. Some children will improve blood flow to their brains by lying flat or even hanging their heads upside down off the edge of a sofa or a bed.

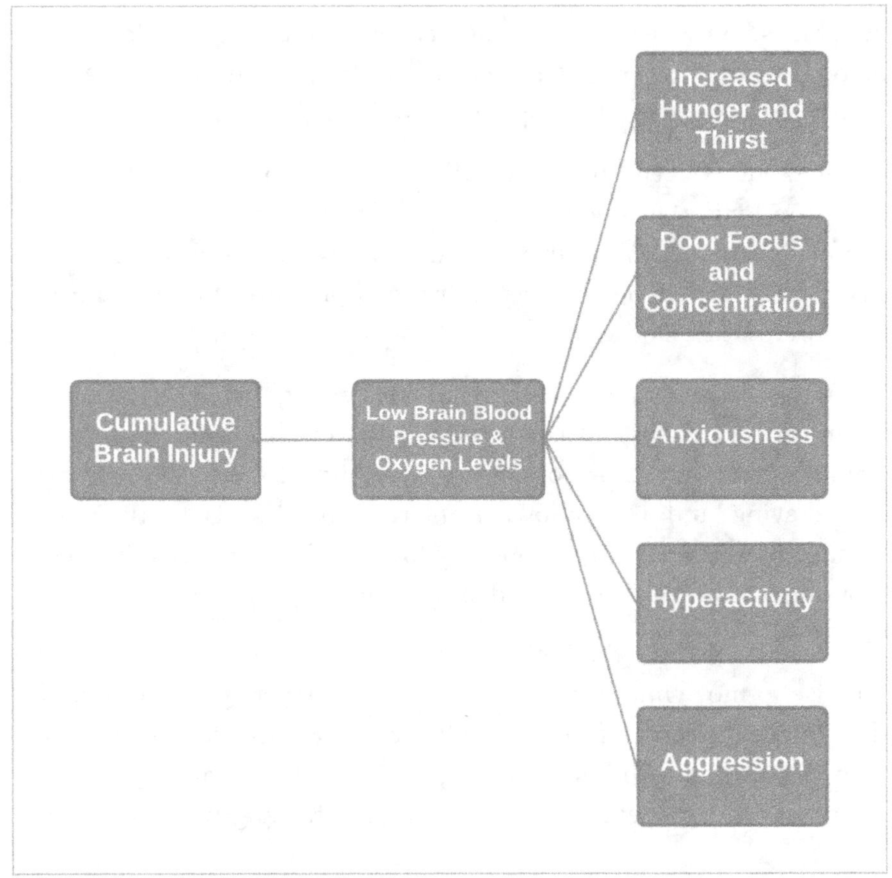

Low Brain Pressure Causes Multiple Symptoms

If a neurotypical seventh-grade boy sustains injuries resulting in low brain blood pressure, he may act a little restless or fidgety in class and sometimes be seen tapping his feet. If the brain pressure is low enough, it might affect his focus and concentration, and he will be diagnosed with attention deficit disorder (ADD).

He may snack on some salty or sweet foods in his backpack. Although he feels restless, he doesn't leave his chair. At his age and maturity level, he has enough impulse control to remain seated because he knows he will be in trouble with his teacher if he gets up and wanders about.

If that boy were in first grade instead of seventh grade, he would not be as able to control his impulses because of his immaturity. He would hop out of his chair whenever his brain needed to move his muscles to drive blood pressure and oxygen delivery. He is also labeled as having ADHD if he is also having trouble staying focused and paying attention.

An elementary-aged child once told me that when they sat in their chair too long, their vision began to fade and would temporarily go completely black. What they are describing is the slow decline in oxygen delivery to the brain as their blood pressure slowly declines in their brain while sitting still.

The child understandably became anxious or frightened and would get up from their chair and move around the classroom to prevent this from recurring. To those observing the child, it seems as if they are misbehaving and not following instructions. But from the child's perspective, they are simply obeying the brain's command to use body movement to improve blood and oxygen delivery to the brain.

The release of the fight-or-flight hormone norepinephrine drives the impulse to move muscles. As the name implies, the primitive impulse the child experiences from the fight or flight hormones is extremely powerful and, in addition to making the child restless and hyperactive, can cause them to feel unusually anxious, fearful, angry, and aggressive.

Recognizing Low Blood Pressure Issues in Children

The hyperactivity and anxiousness, anger, or aggression described are the same reasons young children with autism, developmental disorders, ADD, ADHD, anxiety, depression, PANS, or PANDAS may have difficulty sitting still or focusing. It is often why some with aggressive tendencies suddenly pull hair, scratch, or bite when frustrated.

The exact process that triggers autism and developmental issues is also responsible for the inadequate repair of brain trauma, cumulative brain injury, and the resulting low brain blood pressure. These children are often unable to sit still because their brain is fearful that they may die of lack of oxygen if they do.

They walk, toe walk, run, climb, and bounce to generate blood pressure in their brains. Some arm flapping might also generate blood pressure to the head via the large upper arm blood vessels. Some children are constantly hungry or thirsty, which will defy willpower or even the instruction of the parents to stop eating or drinking.

The low blood pressure phenomenon is widespread. The child's anxious, disruptive, and aggressive behavior often escalates the longer they are required to sit still. If fed something salty or sweet, encouraged to drink about 2-4 oz. of water within five minutes. These steps increase blood pressure and oxygen delivery to the brain and relieve the fear of drowning that the brain was beginning to experience.

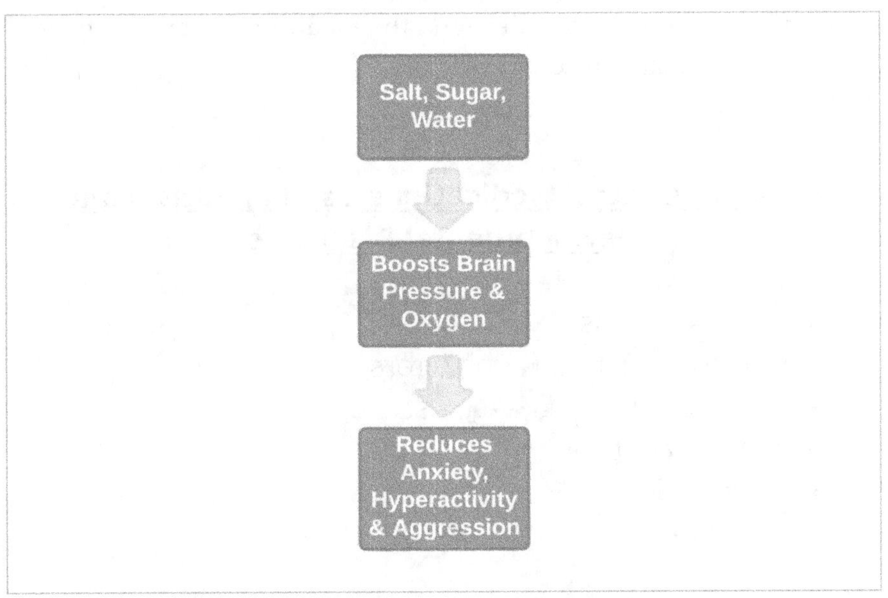

Salt, Sugar and Water Can Reduce Anxiety

Other extenuating circumstances can temporarily worsen a child's underlying brain blood pressure problems: lack of sleep, mild sinus or gastrointestinal infections, fever, emotionally stressful situations, and pain (dental or abdominal) are all able to temporarily worsen a child's blood pressure issues and trigger the symptoms I have described.

Sometimes Exercise, Salt, Sugar, and Water are Not Enough

Through practical experience, most parents learn that exercise, food, or liquids will help make their children better able to focus and less irritable or anxious. But sometimes, the low brain blood pressure issues are to such an extent that these simple steps have little to no effect on helping calm their child. In certain circumstances, prescription medications can control anxiety, hyperactivity, or aggressive behaviors.

What and when to be used is best decided by the patient's managing physician. My discussion of these medications is intended to guide physicians and parents to understand the medications commonly used and not as a particular recommendation.

<u>Behavior Control Medications Used in Autism and Developmental Disorders</u>

- Benzodiazepine
- Antihistamines
- Serotonin Reuptake Inhibitors
- Alpha-2-Adrenergic-Agonist
- Anti-Psychotic Agents
- Blood Pressure Boosting Drugs

Typically, these medicines are chosen to suppress the anxious behavior irrespective of the cause of the anxiety. Anxiety can be suppressed using a class of medications known as serotonin reuptake inhibitors, such as fluoxetine (Prozac®) or sertraline (Zoloft®). Hydroxyzine (Antivert®) is an antihistamine prescribed to help with mild anxiety.

Also, more potent benzodiazepine medications, such as alprazolam (Xanax®), might be used for emergencies involving severe anxiety and aggression. These medicines can be highly effective but should be used cautiously because of the potential for addiction.

Some children are placed on alpha-2-adrenergic-agonist medications traditionally used to lower anxiety for common daytime problems such as generalized anxiety and stage fright. Common examples include propranolol (Inderal®), guanfacine (Tenex®, Intuniv®), and clonidine (Catapres®).

<u>Drugs that Reduce both Anxiety and Lower Blood Pressure</u>

- Propranolol (Inderal®)
- Guanfacine (Tenex®, Intuniv®)
- Clonidine (Catapres®)

Ironically, these medicines were initially developed to lower blood pressure by blocking the effects of noradrenalin (norepinephrine). These medications are used to lower anxiety in children by blocking the effects of noradrenaline. Still, in doing so, these medications can sometimes worsen anxiety and aggression by lowering the blood pressure in the brain even further. This may have the unintended effect of trapping the child in an emotional rollercoaster of fluctuating anxiety and aggression.

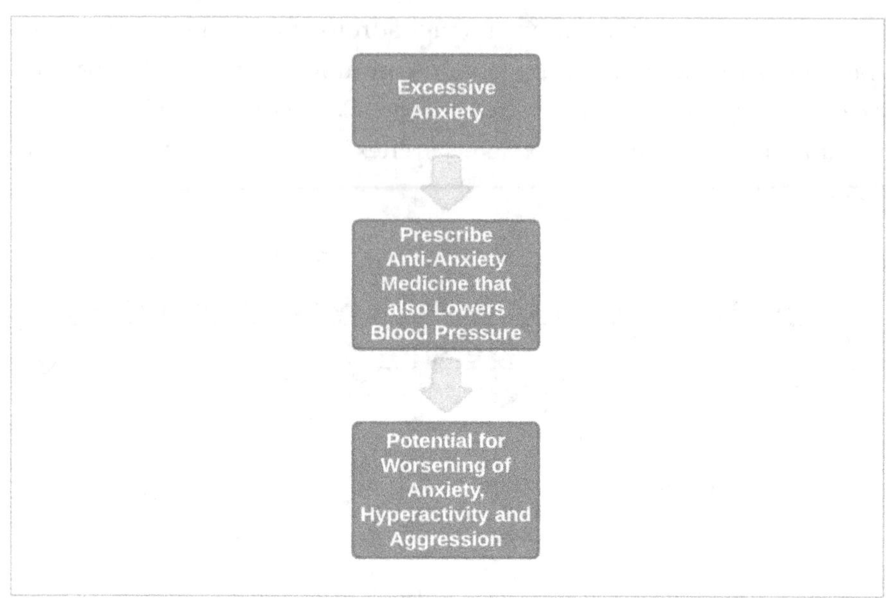

Potential Worsening of Anxiety with Medications

When more intense anxiety involves aggressive behavior, potent anti-psychotic medications are sometimes used. These medications work through uncertain mechanisms and are employed to control behaviors. These drugs can also cause severe side effects such as tardive dyskinesia, psychosis, and suicide. They should be prescribed only by physicians as a last resort. Some common examples are aripiprazole (Abilify®), quetiapine fumarate (Seroquel®), haloperidol (Haldol®), and risperidone (Risperidol®).

Children who respond to The Nemechek Protocol® should be closely monitored by their physicians so these medications may be properly adjusted and tapered off as their autonomic nervous system recovers.

Boosting Blood Pressure to Reduce Anxiety and Aggression

Contrary to traditional anti-anxiety medications, I have found the use of medication to increase brain blood pressure to be very effective in reducing anxiety and aggression in many children.

Drugs that boost blood pressure have been known to help calm anxious, hyperactive children. The medicines used to raise blood pressure work by stimulating the sympathetic branch of the autonomic nervous system (sympathomimetics) or increasing saltwater retention in the body (fludrocortisone).

Several medicines (Ritalin®, Adderall®, and Concerta®) commonly used for attention deficit disorder (ADD) or attention deficit hyperactivity disorder (ADHD) improve the child's behavior by boosting blood pressure into the brain as well as directly stimulating the brain (similar to caffeine).

Drugs that Boost Blood Pressure and Stimulate the Brain
- Amphetamine/dextroamphetamine (Adderall®)
- Lisdexamfetamine dimesylate (Vyvanse®)
- Atomoxetine hydrochloride (Strattera®)
- Methylphenidate (Quillivant XR®)
- Methylphenidate (Focalin XR®)
- Methylphenidate (Concerta®)
- Methylphenidate (Ritalin®)
- Amphetamine (Dexedrine®)
- Amphetamine (Evekeo®)
- Droxidopa (Northera®)

Some children do not tolerate these drugs, but other medications boost blood pressure in the brain. They do not behaviorally overstimulate children because they do not penetrate the central nervous system. A limited course of midodrine (Proamantine®) is preferred in patients suffering from symptoms associated with low brain blood pressure.

Drugs that Only Boost Blood Pressure
- Midodrine (Proamantine®)
- Fludrocortisone (Florinef®)

Midodrine was approved in the U.S. for treating low blood pressure (orthostatic hypotension) resulting from autonomic dysfunction in adults in 1996. The drug stimulates sympathetic receptors in the body and boosts blood pressure in the brain.

Adult patients with low blood pressure with autonomic dysfunction often feel anxious, have difficulty focusing or concentrating, have increased hunger and thirst, and have trouble sitting very long. These symptoms are remarkably similar to children with autism and developmental disorders.

The use of midodrine in treating adults with these autonomic symptoms often greatly improves their symptoms without causing excessive mental stimulation or exacerbation of their anxiety.

Midodrine works equally well in children. Midodrine is typically dosed first thing in the AM after waking with another dose midway between waking and going to bed for the night. This second dose is often around 1-3 PM.

The medication works within 25-30 minutes of the first dose so that the positive effects can be immediately apparent. Because of the typical up-and-down variation in a child's behavior during the week, it might take a few days for the parents to appreciate its positive impact. Like all aspects of The Nemechek Protocol®, parental patience is critical.

Midodrine should be considered a bridging therapy. It is to be used for the limited time between needing to control the excessive behaviors better until the child recovers enough to control their blood pressure and emotions without substantial midodrine.

Midodrine also only works for about six hours. Hence, a parent must only stop the medication on any given day to observe the child's behavior without the medication the following day.

The dose and use of midodrine are tapered as the autonomic nervous system recovers. Before discovering how to get the autonomic nervous system to recover, using midodrine was common for adult patients with bothersome symptoms from low brain blood pressure. Midodrine is prescribed only for short periods because my patients often recover enough within a few months that midodrine is no longer necessary.

Fight or Flight Versus Childhood Road Rage

In addition to adequately regulating blood pressure, the ANS also influences how we handle the intensity of our emotional response to certain situations to keep us safe. The ANS constantly scans the environment for safety, danger, and life-threatening situations. This threat assessment and response system was coined "neuroception" by Dr. Stephen Porges and is a central tenet of his Polyvagal Theory.

When our ANS determines that our environment is safe, our defensive responses are suppressed, and we feel calm. When a threat or potential danger is perceived, the sympathetic branch of the ANS increases our sense of vigilance. It will trigger protective responses that make the individual more aggressive and willing to fight or flee from the perceived threat.

The threat assessment and response system operates below the radar of your awareness, but you can physically feel its presence. People often refer to this system when describing an inner voice or intuition about a situation that makes them fearful. Injuries to the ANS can cause the threat assessment and response system to work incorrectly.

If the brain cannot recover fully and cumulative brain injury occurs, consistent irregularities in a person's ability to correctly perceive what is threatening and what is not will result in the brain not knowing how to respond to situations appropriately.

The term "road rage' is often used when discussing the excessive reaction of automobile drivers in stressful traffic situations. Road rage occurs when the threat assessment and response system has been damaged from a brain injury and causes individuals to overreact to perceived threats.

When working correctly, the threat assessment and response system regulates a person's vigilance when driving. Whether driving on an isolated country road or a busy highway with highspeed traffic, the threat assessment and response system constantly monitors the potential danger of the present situation and forces the driver to apply the proper amount of vigilance to allow them to operate the automobile safely.

For example, on a country road, people may drive somewhat relaxedly because they travel at lower speeds with little traffic and often plenty of visibility because of the wide-open spaces. But when driving at higher speeds on a highway, there is more danger, and the driver's threat assessment and response system will increase their level of vigilance.

Being more careful on a busy highway may seem common sense, but the ANS's threat assessment and response system subconsciously produces much of the increased vigilance one experiences when driving.

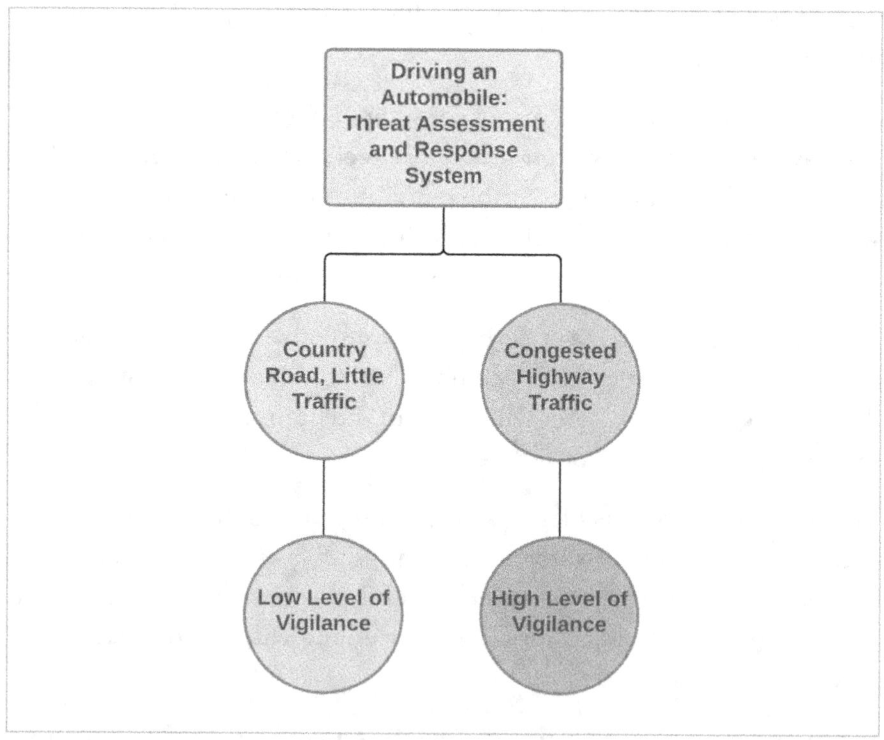

Threat Assessment and Response System of the ANS

A healthy ANS will not allow a person to drive casually or unsafely on a busy highway like a country road. Driving casually on a busy highway is too dangerous, and the ANS is designed to protect and keep them alive. The threat assessment and response system forces the driver to maintain focus and vigilance by scanning traffic, keeping within a reasonably safe speed, and maintaining control of the steering wheel.

Their vigilance increases as the intensity of the traffic increases. When somebody pulls in front of them in a potentially dangerous manner, their threat assessment and response system helps them react quickly to avoid a collision. Importantly, as the external threat increases, the level of vigilance and heightened reaction also increases in an appropriate and measured manner.

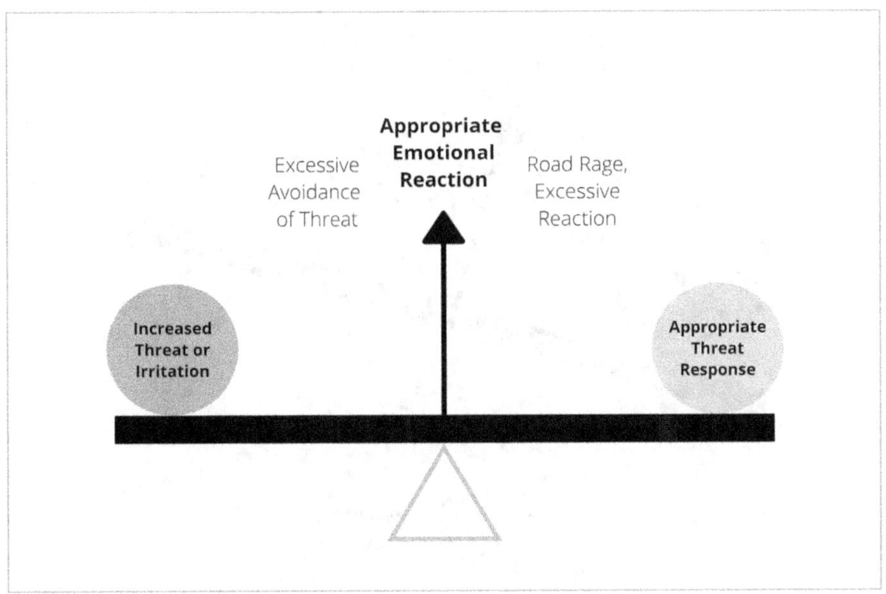

A Balanced Appropriate Emotional Reaction

Damage to the threat assessment and response system can prevent someone from being able to raise their vigilance enough such that they can no longer drive on the highway. Although they can handle the low-stress traffic of a country road or city street, their injury prevents them from increasing their vigilance enough to drive on the highway. I have seen this several times in adults who report that they inexplicably could not drive on the highway shortly after a traumatic event.

They feel that some inner force prevents them from doing so because their anxiety levels would rise to intolerable levels if they drove on the highway. They report that the damage they sustained from their brain injury has adversely affected their threat assessment and response system. Because of this injury, they are now incapable of increasing their threat management response to manage the potential threat of driving their automobile at higher speeds.

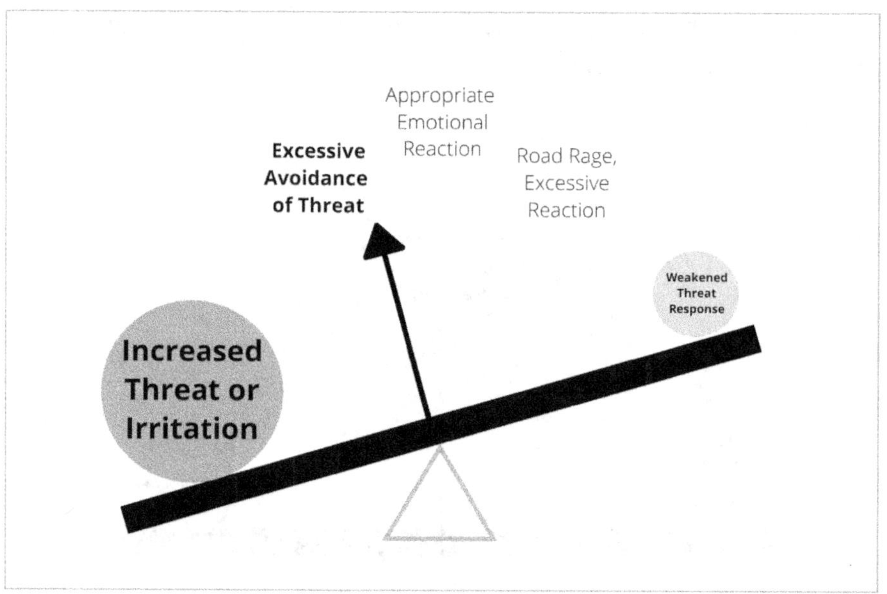

Excessive Avoidance of Threat

Sometimes, injuries can have the opposite effect. Instead of being unable to increase the level of vigilance to match the stressful event, the threat assessment and response system over-responds, and the driver demonstrates an excessively aggressive response commonly referred to as road rage.

Aggressive road rage behaviors occur when another driver's behavior strikes the individual with a damaged threat assessment and response system as irritating or even dangerous. Their response to the event is excessive. Instead of simply feeling annoyed or frightened and trying to lessen the danger of the moment, the driver with road rage will have an exaggerated response that might involve yelling, aggressive gesturing, and even chasing the other driver.

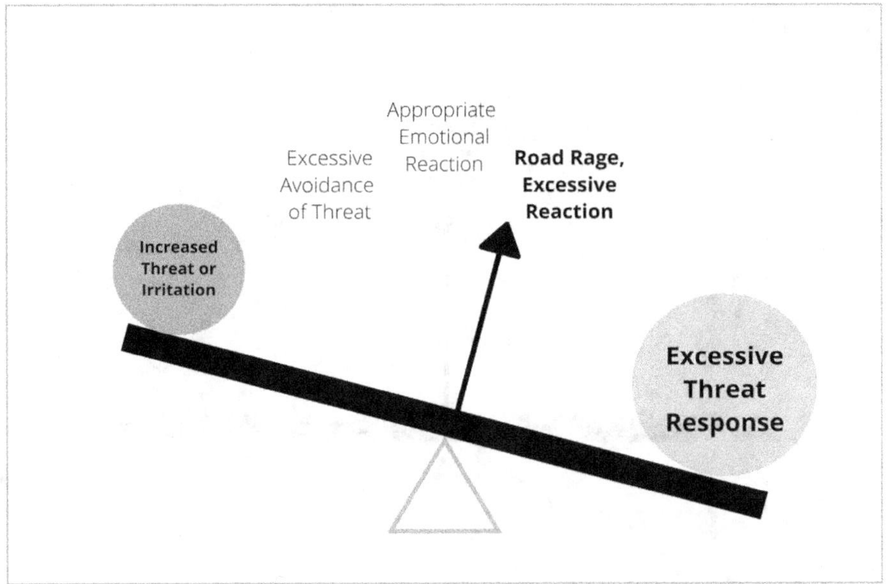

Excessive Against Threat

It often surprises people when I discuss road rage from an ANS damage perspective because it is not uncommon with my adult patients, and most recover nicely with The Nemechek Protocol®. As the chronic damage to their nervous system is repaired, their anxiety or aggression when driving on the highway often dissipates.

Road Rage for Children

From a child's perspective, a threatening situation can arise when another child attempts to take their toy (conflict management), when there is an unanticipated change in the schedule of events (transition issues), or when they are given a command to do something they do not want to do (time to put the iPad away).

If their autonomic threat assessment and response system works correctly, their reaction to these scenarios will be measured and appropriate. They follow the command but may pout or mildly show their displeasure but still follow through.

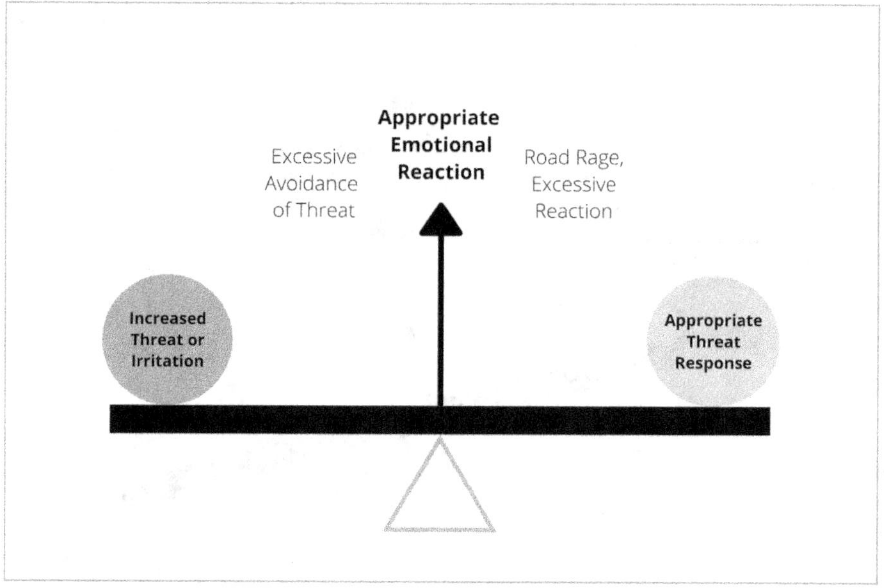

A Balanced Appropriate Emotional Reaction

However, when the ANS is not working correctly because of a brain injury, the response to these situations can result in either an excessive avoidance response or an excessively aggressive response of the threat assessment and response system.

In children, a weakened management response to the potential threats might cause the child to retreat to a different room when strangers or even their siblings enter the same room they presently occupy.

The child retreats to a different room because a prior injury to the threat assessment and response system cannot increase vigilance to manage the situation's complexity. This is a typical response in children with autism and developmental disorders.

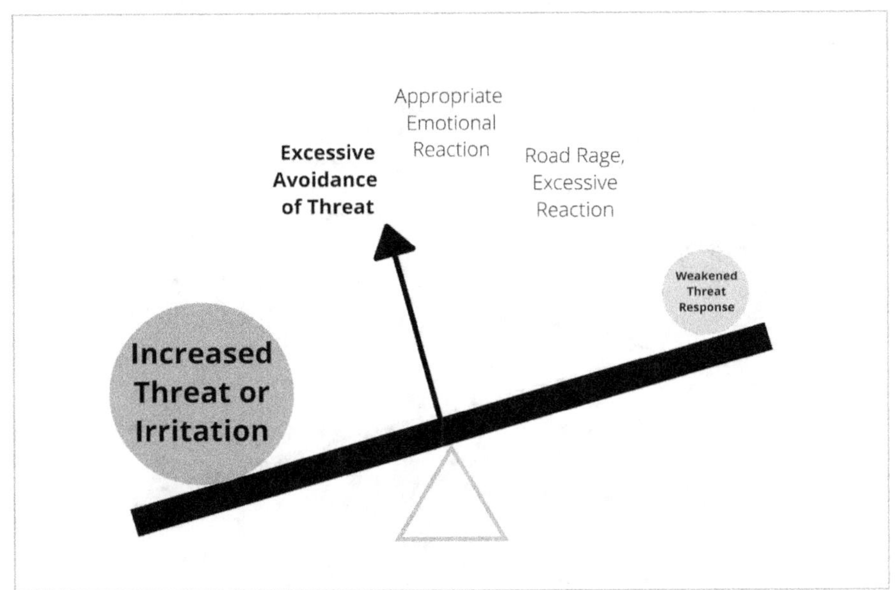

Excessive Avoidance of Threat

Occasionally, the child's damaged threat assessment and response system will trigger an excessive response similar to road rage. When another person tries to take away an item, the child is interested in at the moment (toy, iPad, etc.) or if there is a sudden change in the schedule, or there is any request by a parent, therapist, or teacher that the child does not welcome, the child reacts with excessive aggression similar to road rage. Hair pulling, biting, scratching, kicking, and punching result from an excessively primitive response by the threat assessment and response system.

This reaction is often referred to as a problem with transitioning. Road rage arises from an irritating situation because the aggression is not triggered if a child transitions to a favored activity, such as receiving ice crease or a cookie.

This is a common situation in some children with autism or developmental issues. Fortunately, the neurological damage leading to this response can be repaired with The Nemechek Protocol®, just like in adults.

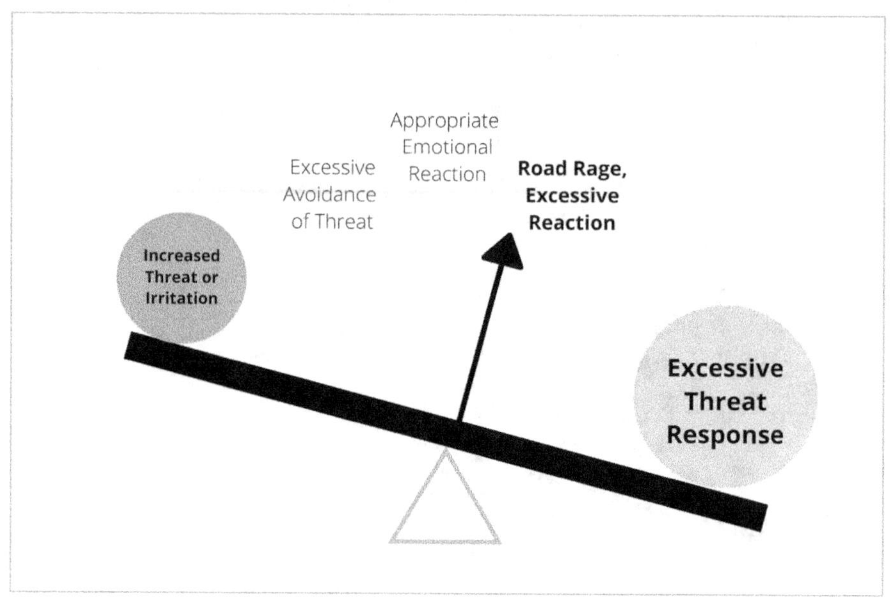

Excessive Against Threat

The aggressive behaviors may also be mislabeled as "defiance," as if the child has a willful, controllable role in the reaction. Children may be diagnosed as having oppositional defiance disorder or ODD. Behavior modification techniques are often unsuccessful in controlling these reactions because these events are not about the child's chosen desire to behave aggressively.

These negative reactions are an excessive, uncalibrated, aggressive biological response that is primitive and powerful and that most children cannot control. The child wants to please their parents or therapists and does not wish them harm. Like many parents whose child behaves in such a manner, the children almost universally show remorse for the harm they may have caused someone.

These aggressive moments of road rage are very primitive in design and are being triggered at a subconscious level. The child has limited control over them and often demonstrates remorse after their reaction harms another.

Identifying Road Rage from Low Blood Pressure Anxiety

To effectively manage the child's emotional ups and downs, it is necessary to differentiate between low blood pressure's fight or flight reaction and the aggressive responses of "road rage." Both involve a heightened emotional state with what can appear to be anxiety, aggression, or anger and can easily be confused with each other.

The protocol will help the autonomic nervous system recover both defects substantially. Until then, the difference in managing the events is quite different for the parent.

Low blood pressure can be avoided or managed with increased fluid or salt intake, moving the child into a horizontal position (lying on the couch or the floor to read or play), or using midodrine to boost blood pressure. If the anxious, aggressive event seems to be triggered without any irritant, this is likely a fight or flight reaction from excessively low brain blood pressure.

These events might occur if the child is sitting in a chair or the car too long, has a mild infection, becomes too hot, or has not had enough to eat or drink recently. Kids with poor blood pressure are often quite fidgety or hyperactive and seem frequently thirsty or hungry.

When an excessively aggressive response is triggered by phrases such as "time to put that away," "we can't (do what the child wants)," or "you are going to (the expected event)," this is likely a road rage response from a damaged threat assessment and response system. Road rage events might be managed with better transition planning or distraction from precipitating irritants. In more severe cases, behavior-modifying medications are required until the protocol allows enough recovery for the medications to be tapered.

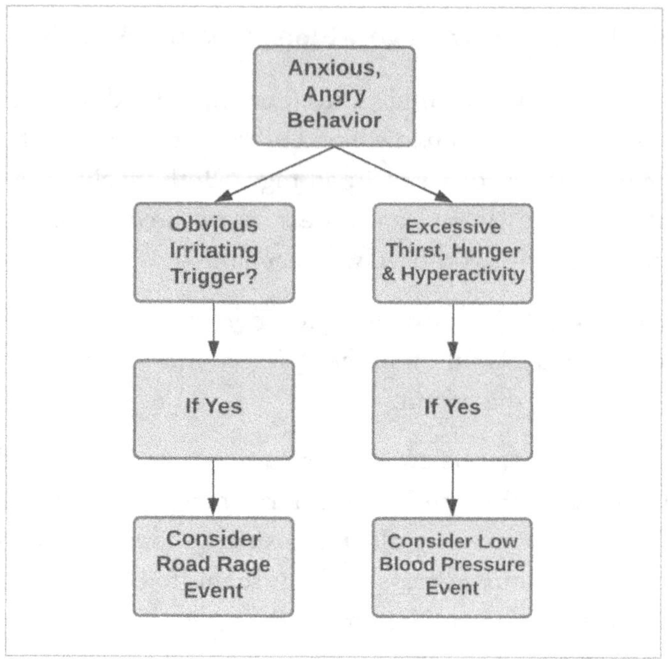

Low Blood Pressure vs. Road Rage

It's not unusual for kids to have some features of both forms of aggression, but the children with the most serious and even dangerous road rage events tend to do so in or approaching their teenage years.

The parents of a child with a history of being hyperactive and frequently hungry or thirsty have learned to manage the child's mode by keeping plenty of fluids or snacks handy. A slang term for this observation is "hangry," a combination of the words "hungry" and "angry." Then, as some children age, a different pattern of recognizable road rage aggression begins, often without any apparent cause to the parents.

The parents, therapists, and teachers often look for causes that would trigger excessive anger in a typically rational individual with a healthy, functioning threat assessment and response system. When they fail to find a reason, they often discuss defiance issues with labels such as Oppositional Defiance Disorder. They should instead be looking for a potentially traumatic event that damaged the autonomic threat assessment and response system.

<u>Potential Traumas Leading to Road Rage</u>

- **Physical Injury:** concussion or sub-concussive events

- **Inflammatory Injury:** surgery, vaccinations, fractures

- **Emotional Trauma:** moving to a new home, change in trusted therapist, bullying

When interviewing the parents about the time frame immediately before the onset of the road rage aggression, I can frequently identify potential emotional or physical traumas that could have further injured the autonomic nervous system.

More often than not, the unavoidable emotional trauma jumps out as the most likely cause. Some tantrums might be appropriate for the approximate maturity level of the child, but these tend to be self-limited, never aggressive, and have an obvious cause.

Regardless of the source of the trauma, The Nemechek Protocol® can help the child repair the damaged autonomic threat assessment and response system, and the events will decrease and often ultimately cease altogether.

Management of Road Rage in a Child

After determining that the patient has the road rage type of aggressive episodes, Dr. Nemechek has a treatment plan to help minimize the events and help them recover as soon as possible before they cause serious injury to themselves or another person.

The first step is to start the child with excessive aggression issues on The Nemechek Protocol®, including vagus nerve stimulation, because it increases the chances that the child will have the broadest improvement of these potentially dangerous outbursts. As the ANS recovers, the road rage aggression will lessen in intensity and frequency until the rage events ultimately stop.

The second step to avoiding or limiting the frequency of aggressive outbursts is to recognize that they do not come from willful, self-directed desires but from an involuntary impulse designed by evolution to help us survive.

The child's emotional responses are simply misfiring because of underlying autonomic damage. It is important to remember this is not from a lack of love or desire. They are often incapable of the impulse control required to suppress these behaviors.

Trying to reason with a child during an autonomic road rage event will often prove futile and frustrating for everyone. Suppose you have ever been in an automobile with someone exhibiting road rage. In that case, you understand that rationalizing with them rarely ever has any impact on their impulsive behavior at that moment.

What is needed is a consistent, predictable schedule of events that is flexible from a time perspective and recognition that the child needs to be in a positive mindset for any necessary changes to the schedule. In other words, minimize the irritating moments of conflict as much as possible. A parent may plan a schedule for the day for the child so they can comprehend it and post it somewhere that the child sees it.

If reading skills are lacking, consider using pictures or symbols to represent the activity instead of words and using pictures of school or meal-times (breakfast, lunch, and dinner) as reference points instead of time. While this isn't always practical, this example is just one strategy to manage the environment of the child until such time that the protocol can sufficiently repair the threat assessment and response system and the excessive road rage behaviors cease to occur.

Finally, if the aggressive episodes are dangerous to the child or those caring for them, prescription medications may be justified to control the dangerous behaviors. These medications should be prescribed under the guidance of a physician, preferably one who understands the brain's responses to inadequate oxygen delivery from autonomic dysfunction.

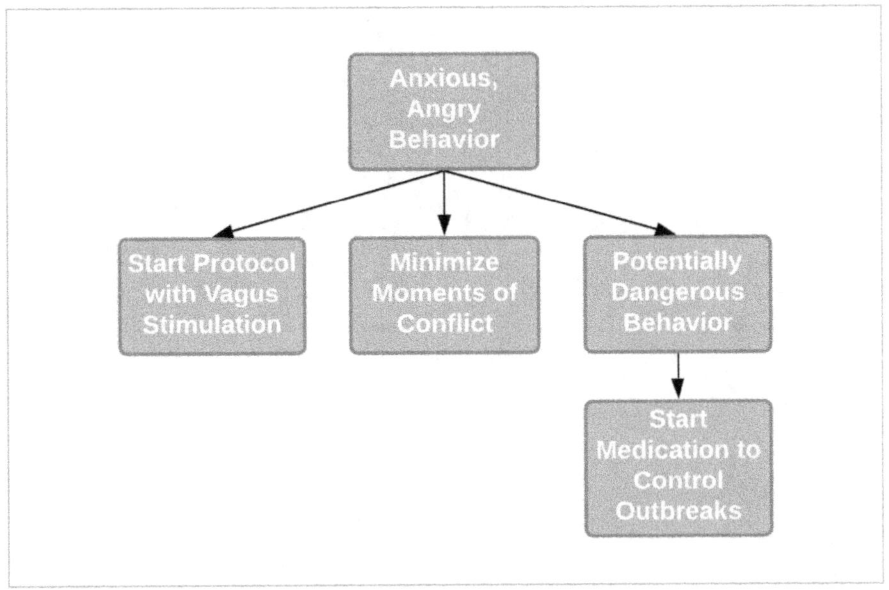

Managing Excessive Aggression

Many children initially prescribed one or two potent medications to control their aggressive behavior could, ultimately, be weaned off the medications without increasing aggressive behavior within six to twelve months of starting the protocol. Weaning of any of these medications should be done with the guidance of the prescribing physician.

These children and young adults will occasionally experience an increasing sense of self-awareness when the fight or flight and the road rage episodes from autonomic damage subside. Some have asked their parents, "What happened to me? How come I don't remember middle school?" Others will deny their prior behaviors occurred despite seeing video graphic evidence to the contrary.

Remember that the injured brain may not have been able to create memories from these past moments. This phenomenon is similar to what we witness in some recovering Alzheimer's patients who regain their sense of presence and self-awareness.

PART V

———

THE SCIENCE BEHIND THE NEMECHEK PROTOCOL®

15

PRIMED MICROGLIA: A RESIDUAL EFFECT OF SIBO

This chapter will explain in greater detail some key concepts. Hence, you understand how we got to this modern-day healthcare crisis and why the components of The Nemechek Protocol® are effective when used consistently together.

Normal Brain Development

The Nemechek Protocol® can help many childhood issues such as autism, developmental disorders, ADD/ADHD, POTS, PANS, PANDAS, and mood disorders because they all have a similar origin of chronic overgrowth of intestinal bacteria and omega-6:omega-3 imbalance that fuels inflammation.

Normal brain development requires a healthy environment for the brain to develop fully and quickly, and for a child to develop neurologically, they need to be able to prune neurons, repair brain injuries, and form neural networks.

As explained previously, a child is born with approximately one hundred billion neurons, and they must trim these to fifty billion neurons. The excess neurons provide developmental flexibility for the brain to acquire a new skill or ability. Most excess neurons are pruned away within the first five to six years of life. Failure to trim the neurons fast enough is a major cause of developmental issues.

If the failure to prune is mild and the neurons are not trimmed away fast enough, we often refer to this as developmental delay. If the neuronal trimming process has severely slowed or even stopped completely, the child may be classified as having developmental arrest.

A common cause of altered neuronal pruning is the impaired functioning of a specialized central nervous system white blood cell known as a microglia. Microglia are called the 'master gardener' because one of their primary roles is to tend to the neurons that branch throughout the brain like the branches of plants throughout a garden. Microglia grow to the neuron branches by either pruning them away like branches of a tree or by protecting and repairing them.

The initial distribution of neurons is somewhat random as the child's brain has to discover a connection between bodily movements and brain function. The developmental process involves forming the pathways that will allow your child to track your face with their eyes or roll over in their crib. These behaviors occur only when the child's brain finds the neurons that connect the thought (follow the mother's face) to the action (move my eyes and head). Microglia sense these neuronal pathways are critical and start nurturing and protecting them. If other neurons are not used meaningfully, they will eventually be eliminated as excess.

The process of pruning away the excessive neurons is necessary for the brain to survive. Neurons consume large amounts of energy. It is inefficient for the human body to spend energy on pathways that are not important for survival. At birth, the brain consumes nearly 85% of all oxygen and calories, but by the time a person reaches eighteen years of age, it has been "pruned down" to an organ that only consumes 20% of all oxygen and calories. Evolutionarily, this is a much more manageable percentage of energy consumption.

The neuronal pruning process continues throughout the child's life as they learn to crawl, stand upright, talk, walk, run, read, calculate, and mature into young adults. When children run, play, and mentally engage in challenging activities, the pruning process tries to refine the neurological pathways that support these activities. The microglia not only trim and maintain the normal sequence of maturation, but they also help repair the brain injuries that can occur from common physical (concussion and sub-concussive injuries), emotional (bullying, absence of a parent, intense fear, etc.), and inflammatory (surgery, fractures, vaccinations) traumas.

If the brain is correctly pruned and repaired, then collections of neurons will begin forming as the child learns new skills, social behaviors, and life skills. These collections of neurons are referred to as neural networks. The formation of neural networks occurs when one learns to play the piano (or any other complex skill, for that matter). Your understanding of music and the dexterity to play starts slowly, and one can only manage the simplest tune. This happens because a small grouping of neurons is connected in a neural network. The neural network will expand by "crowd-sourcing" more and more neurons as you learn to play more complex musical scores. The expanding number of neurons within the neural network allows someone to ultimately play a very complex musical score, such as Chopin on the piano.

Learning the social skills necessary to become a mature eighteen-year-old occurs similarly. Over time, children slowly learn to share, be patient, and follow social rules expected from the family and community. Just as the skills required to play Chopin require many years, developing neural networks for socialization will also require many years.

So collectively, children must be able to prune neurons, repair neurons, and build neural networks to normally develop neurologically and form the complex neural networks required to function in society. What is happening globally now is that bacterial overgrowth within the small intestine can fully disrupt the process of neurological maturation.

This is not a temporary problem. Microglia function can be permanently and adversely altered by five different events, leading to a form of microglia that no longer prunes nor repairs the neurons.

Bacterial overgrowth, also known as SIBO (small intestine bacterial overgrowth), and the excessive concentration of bacteria overwhelms the integrity of the small intestine. It leads to the leakage of lipopolysaccharide (LPS), a molecular component of a bacteria's outer shell, and is only found in bacteria that live in the colon. A scientific term for the LPS-releasing bacteria is "gram-negative rod bacteria."

A study on overweight and obese children found that over 70% had evidence of SIBO.

Bacterial Overgrowth Leads to Neurological Problems

Bacterial overgrowth is when the person's normal intestinal bacteria live in the wrong place. They are not foreign or "bad" bacteria; they are bacteria that should normally live within the colon but now are in the upper or small intestine. The species of bacteria normally living within the small intestine differ from those living normally within the large intestine (also known as the colon).

As explained briefly in Chapter 2, the two types of bacteria within the small and large intestines are so different from one another that it is easiest to think of one type as birds (the normal residents of the small intestine) and the other type as fish (the normal residents of the colon).

Maintaining the normal number of bacterial species within the upper and lower intestinal tract is possibly the most important factor in preventing bacterial overgrowth. The bacteria themselves are actively involved in maintaining their separation. Studies of patients with recurrent bacterial overgrowth with *Clostridium difficile* demonstrated that individuals with the lowest species counts are those most likely to have recurrent bacterial overgrowth. This is referred to as having low biodiversity of the intestinal microbiome.

Two other significant factors contributing to bacterial overgrowth include proper acidity of the small intestine and maintaining a normal level of forward intestinal propulsion or motility of the intestinal tract. Disruption of intestinal acidity with potent antacids and slowing of the forward propulsion that can occur after brain trauma, medications (anesthetics, pain medications), intestinal or abdominal surgery, or certain medical conditions (renal failure, scleroderma) are all well-documented triggers of intestinal bacterial overgrowth.

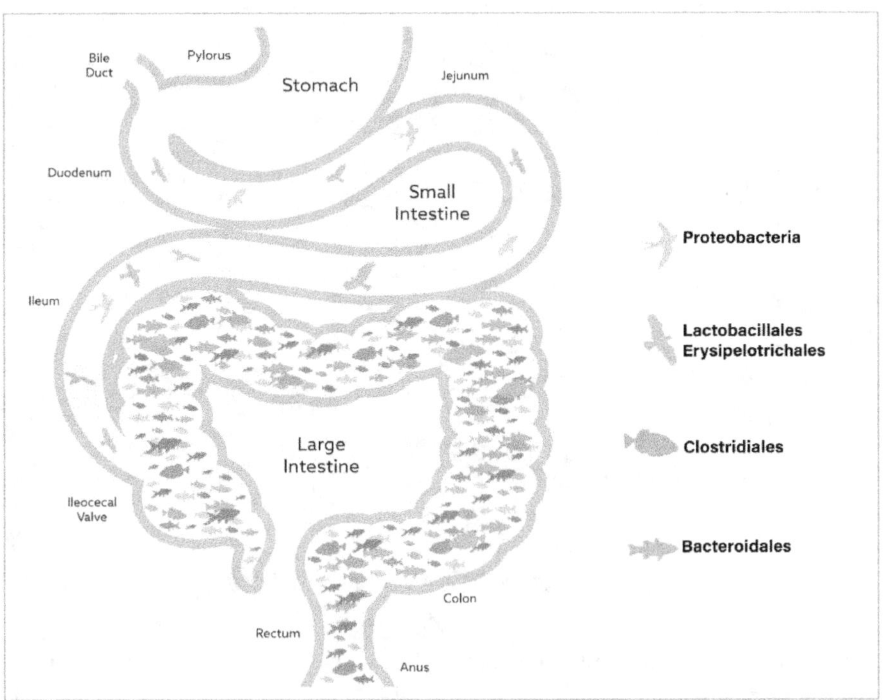

Normally Balanced intestinal Bacteria

There is an exceptionally large difference in the concentration of the number of bacteria living within the small intestine compared to the large intestine. For every individual "bird" bacterium in the upper small intestine, there are usually a hundred million "fish" bacteria living in the lowest portion of the colon, an enormous 1:100,000,000 difference in bacterial concentrations.

Bacterial intestinal overgrowth occurs when a single species of "fish" bacteria living in the large intestine migrates upstream into the small intestinal tract and replicates out of control among the "bird" bacteria. Just as everyone understands that fish should not live where birds live, large intestine bacteria should not be found in the small intestine where the "bird" bacteria live.

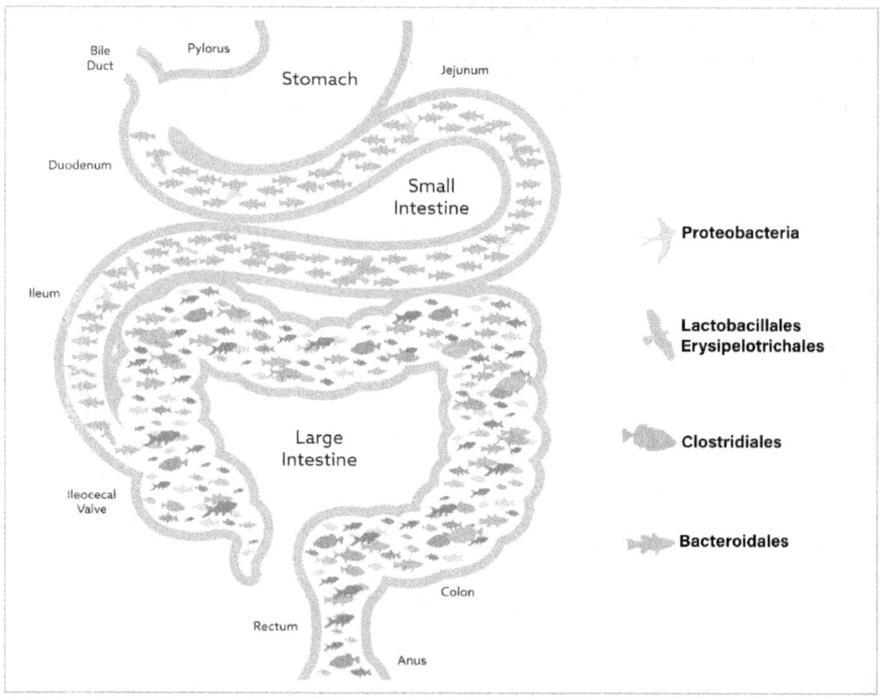

Bacterial Overgrowth of the Small Intestine (SIBO)

After the "fish" bacteria have migrated into the small intestine, there are not enough other bacteria to prevent them from growing out of control. Their overwhelming numbers overwhelm the design of the small intestine and allow the leakage of molecules into the surrounding tissue in a process known as bacterial translocation or "leaky gut." It is important to state that despite the common beliefs to the contrary, there is no scientific evidence that yeast, fungi, candida, or parasites cause a "leaky gut." The leakage of molecules from digested food and bacterial cell walls can trigger the release of a substantial amount of pro-inflammatory cytokines throughout the body. The stress from these pro-inflammatory cytokines alters the normal function of cells throughout the body.

Bacterial translocation may also trigger the abnormal release of various hormones, histamine, short-chain fatty acids, and potential toxins. They can also trigger abnormal reactions to common foods (tomatoes, bananas, milk, citrus, etc.), cause skin reactions (psoriasis, rosacea, eczema, hives, rashes), and send signals to the brain, potentially altering almost every aspect of brain, body, and cellular function.

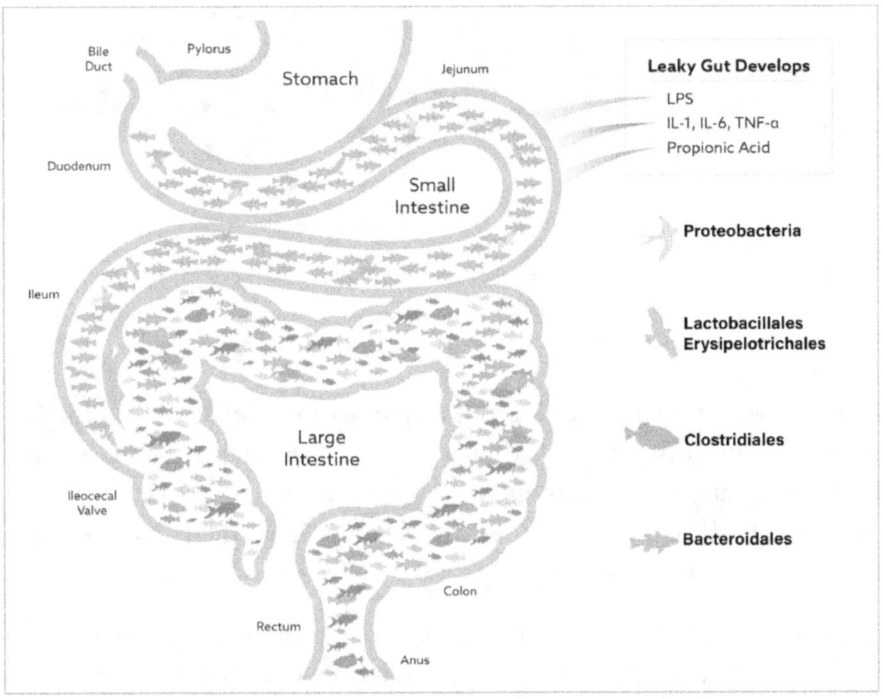

Bacterial Overgrowth Leads to Leaky Gut (Bacterial Translocation)

When bacterial translocation from overgrowth occurs, fragments of the bacteria cell membrane called lipopolysaccharide (LPS) leak into the bloodstream, causing an exceptionally large release of pro-inflammatory cytokines and can permanently alter the function of a particular white blood cell within the brain known as microglia.

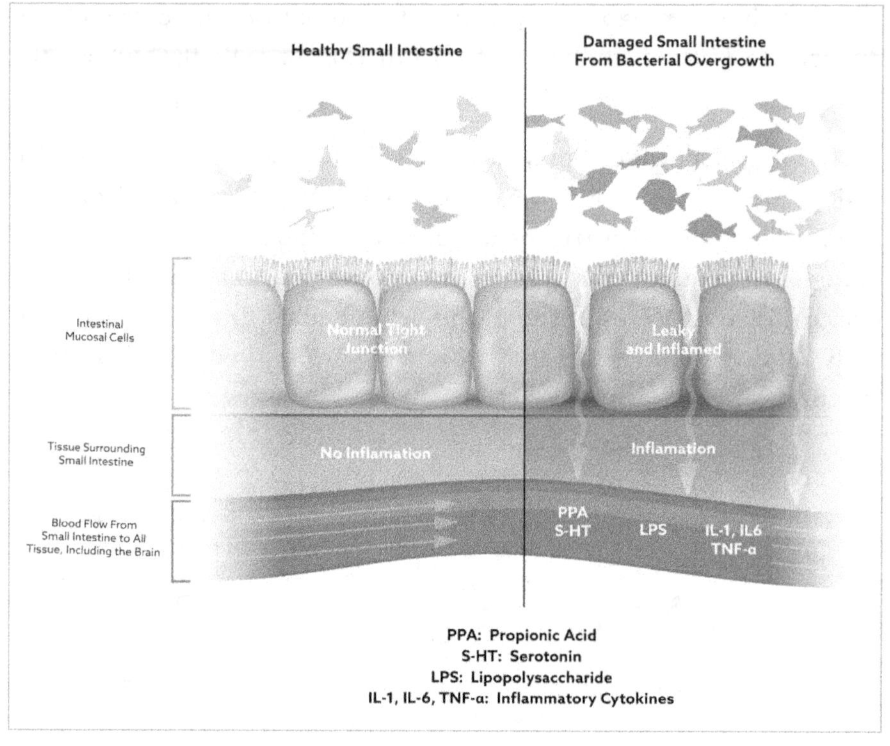

Inflammation from Leaky Gut

The altered microglia are called "primed M1-microglia," their function changes from a helpful cell that prunes healthy neurons and repairs damaged neurons into a permanently inflammatory cell that prevents normal childhood development and magnifies the damage from common brain traumas.

Suppose LPS priming and the release of pro-inflammatory cytokines occurs before the age of five or six. In that case, children will experience developmental problems (delay of milestones, sensory issues, motor delay, intellectual delay) and manifest problems associated with the poor repair of injuries (constipation, hyperactivity, poor focus, anxiety, and aggression).

If LPS priming and the release of pro-inflammatory cytokines occur after the age of 6 or so, the pruning of the brain will have been completed. Consequently, there will be no evidence of developmental problems. The brain will still have difficulty repairing injuries, and the children may experience attention issues (ADD), hyperactivity, anxiety, postural orthostatic tachycardia syndrome (POTS), recurrent headaches, lightheadedness, passing out (syncope), constipation, abdominal cramping, reflux (GERD), and even premenstrual syndrome (PMS).

Other less common factors capable of triggering the primed M1-microglia include a severe brain infection referred to as encephalitis (e.g., Ebola, Dengue), a high frequency of concussions (e.g., American football or hockey), excessive exposure and inhalation to 2.5-micron particulate matter ($PM_{2.5}$ diesel exhaust, tobacco smoke, burning wood, candles, cleaning products, air fresheners) and high levels of maternal inflammation during pregnancy of the child (i.e., the mother is hospitalized with septic shock).

Common childhood injuries such as insignificant falls and bumps to the head occur in all children as they crawl, walk, play, interact with siblings, and explore their environment. We have all had a similar experience of a crying child at the family reunion or the park because they hit their head while playing. This is a typical type of injury that children use to recover from naturally fully. Children would cry for a while, be comforted, calm down, and seem okay. We understand now that these simple head injuries likely cause minor brain damage that is fully repaired with healthy microglia.

Presently, the same minor injury is not fully repaired by the excessive pro-inflammatory cytokines and primed M1 microglia triggered by exposure to LPS released from bacterial overgrowth. Instead of recovering fully, the child is left with imperceptible residual damage that accumulates injury by injury over time in a process called cumulative brain injury.

One Hundred Years of Intestinal Bacterial Damage

In the womb, a child's intestinal tract contains little to no bacteria. It is only after birth that a child's intestinal tract becomes fully colonized by bacteria inhabiting the mother's intestinal tract. The two most important factors in the complete transmission of the mother's intestinal bacteria to her child are vaginal delivery and breastfeeding.

Studies suggest that humans have successfully passed the same blend of intestinal bacteria from mother to child for at least three million years. The only present-day individuals with relatively normal varieties of intestinal bacteria consist of a few very primitive tribes (Yanomami, Guahibo Amerindians, Malawians, and African hunter-gatherers), and the loss of intestinal bacteria is believed to have begun around the turn of the last century.

Since the turn of the last century, each sequential maternal generation has had their intestinal bacterial blend damaged uniquely, compounding the previously damaged bacteria blend they received from their mother at birth. By examining the bacteria contained within the intestinal tracts of the entombed royalty of Genoa, Italy, stool specimens from ancient tombs as well as 1,000-year-old frozen humans discovered in glaciers, scientists have determined that the human biome has had the same mixture of bacterial species until around 1900.

From this point forward, every maternal generation has potentially lost additional bacterial species due to pesticide exposure, antibiotics, and other chemicals. The damage to our intestinal microbiome has probably accelerated in the last 50 years as more potent antibiotics have been developed and commonly used for otherwise routine, minor infections.

Additionally, if a child is born by caesarian section (c-section) and is bottle-fed, the mother's microbiome will not be fully transferred to her infant child, and long-lasting differences between the child's and mother's intestinal bacteria can occur. If the mother's bacterial blend is already somewhat depleted before delivery, the child's bacterial blend may be weakened even further if born by cesarean section or if they are solely bottle-fed.

The bacterial issue is not just a mother-child issue. Both parents may contribute to the likelihood of bacterial overgrowth occurring and its potential impact on the child's health. Which bacteria may overgrow the small intestine, or what those bacteria might do once they overgrow, might be determined by genes the father and mother contributed. It is a complex combination of the mother's bacterial blend and genes from both parents, as well as a multitude of life events after birth (antibiotic exposure, probiotics, diet, environmental chemicals, injury, surgery, food preservatives, and other unknown factors) that may result in an unhealthy blend of intestinal bacteria and the development of bacterial overgrowth.

Presently, most individuals have less than expected numbers of intestinal bacterial species after being born compared to people over one hundred years ago. This is referred to as having decreased microbiome diversity. As the number of unique species decreases further and further with each maternal generation, the bacteria seem to have less capacity to maintain the usual separation of the different bacteria within the small and large intestines.

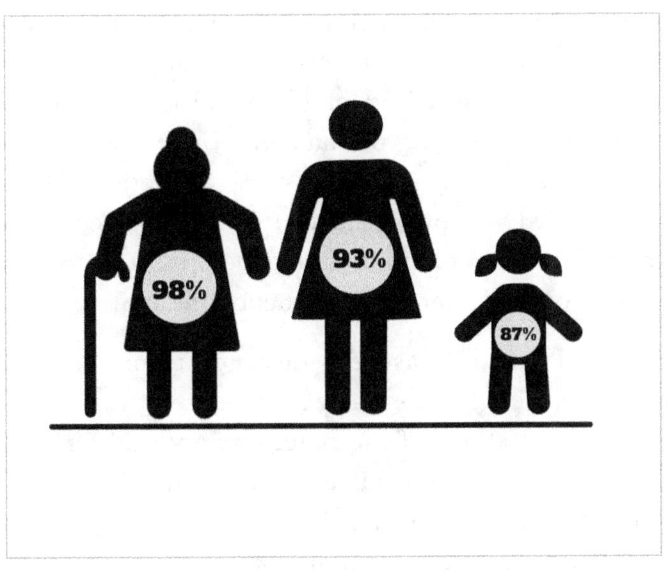

Decreasing Generational Microbiome Diversity

The decreased capacity to maintain the intestinal balance is compounded further when the function of the intestinal tract is further altered by brain trauma, intestinal infections, antibiotics, vaccines, antacids (proton pump inhibitors), probiotics, general anesthesia, abdominal surgery, and other medical procedures.

The collective effect of low biodiversity and these other factors increases the likelihood of children and adults developing small intestine bacterial overgrowth (SIBO). Once overgrowth occurs, the small intestine cannot withstand the stress of the increased bacterial load. Small molecules from bacterial cell walls and food particles can then leak into the surrounding tissue in a process referred to as bacterial translocation or "leaky gut." Bacterial translocation can trigger a surge of pro-inflammatory cytokines. Seventy percent of the immune system, including white blood cells and mast cells, is estimated to reside in the tissues immediately surrounding the small intestine, referred to as GALT (gastrointestinal-associated lymphoid tissue).

In addition, highly inflammatory molecules such as LPS may escape into the bloodstream, enter the central nervous system, and alter the normal function of microglia within the brain. As discussed earlier in this chapter, microglia are instrumental in pruning neurons in children and repairing the neurons in both children and adults. Once exposed to LPS, the microglia become permanently inflammatory, and their pruning and repairing of neurons stops altogether. However, the behavior of primed M1 microglia can be normalized with various experimental chemical compounds and devices. This change in the behavior of microglia is referred to as phenotypic shifting.

The Nemechek Protocol® has been designed to prevent primed M1-microglia from causing further damage. The use of vagus nerve stimulation, high concentrations of the omega-3 fatty acid DHA, and extra virgin olive oil have been shown in animal models to cause primed M1-microglia to shift their behavior into an anti-inflammatory, tissue-repairing M2-microglia. Not all children are destined to develop bacterial overgrowth even if they have low biodiversity of their intestinal bacteria. If bacterial overgrowth never occurs, their neurological development and recovery from brain traumas should continue normally.

Primed M1-Microglia Magnify Brain Injury

The unregulated and permanent inflammatory behavior of primed M1 microglia magnifies the degree of damage caused by common brain injuries. It prevents stem cells and other repair mechanisms (neurotrophins) from repairing the damage that would have fully recovered with normal functioning microglia.

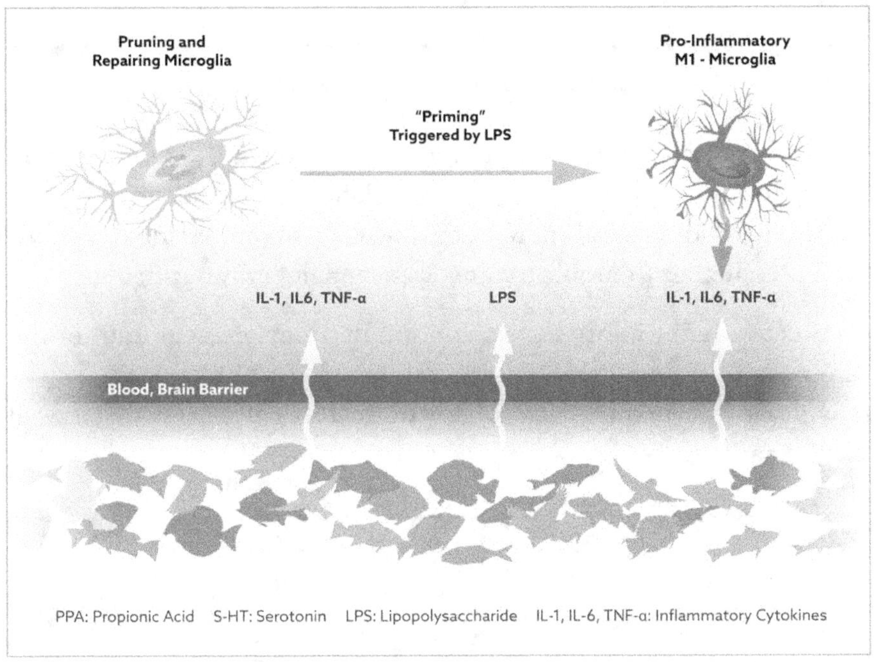

Triggering of Primed Microglia

The impairment of microglia may also be responsible for the abnormal white matter structure within the brain that seems to be associated with sensory perception disorders.

The magnified damage and incomplete recovery caused by primed M1 microglia are the hallmarks of a pathological process called cumulative brain injury or CBI.

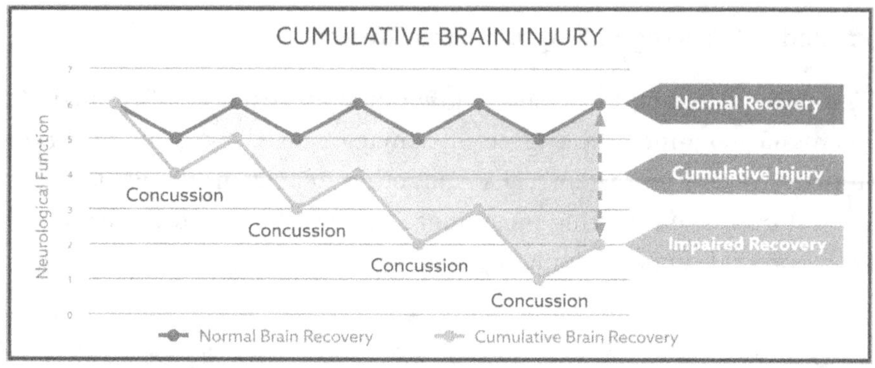

Cumulative Brain Injury from Physical Brain Trauma

Cumulative brain injury from primed M1 microglia is occurring in an epidemic fashion throughout the population. It is the predominant feature behind the well-publicized problem of professional football players contracting chronic traumatic encephalopathy (CTE).

Cumulative brain injury develops not only from physical injuries but can occur from emotional trauma and the release of high levels of pro-inflammatory cytokines from surgery or fractures of large bones, as well as vaccinations.

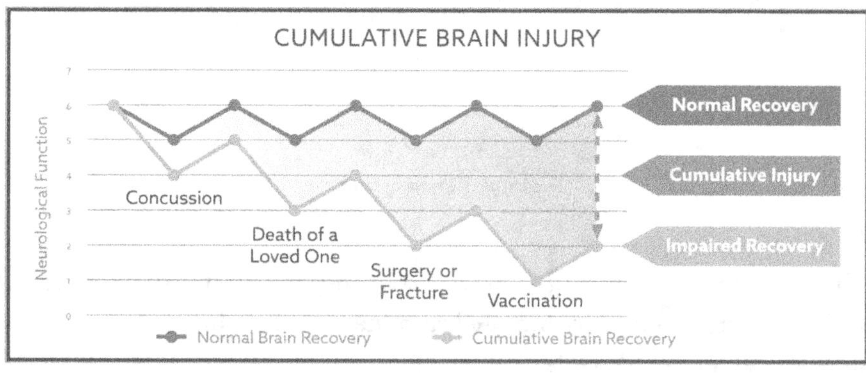

Cumulative Brain Injury from a Variety of Brain Traumas

In addition to primed M1 microglia not pruning neurons correctly and causing varying developmental delay, the cumulative brain injury effect from primed microglia also allows minor brain injuries to stack upon previously unresolved brain injuries.

Cumulative brain injury from primed MI-microglia is also a suspected factor in the development of attention-deficit/hyperactivity disorder (ADD/ADHD), POTS, PMS, most autonomic dysfunction, Alzheimer's dementia, Parkinson's disease, chronic depression, bipolar disorder, schizophrenia, and post-traumatic stress disorder.

When bacterial overgrowth occurs before the age of five, it will trigger developmental delays ranging from mild to severe. In addition to developmental delay, the child may accumulate damage via CBI to the autonomic nervous system.

A dysfunctional autonomic nervous system is responsible for many common childhood problems such as constipation, IBS, reflux, ADD, ADHD, POTS, fidgety movements, toe-walking, headaches, persistent hunger, and anxiety.

The increase of inflammation released from primed MI-microglia and the intestinal tract can lower the seizure threshold and increase both the likelihood and the frequency of epileptic seizures. This effect is often seen in children younger than one year of age as febrile seizures, its most benign form. A febrile seizure is a relatively harmless event in very young children that lasts less than a minute and occurs when the child is running a temperature.

This is an "out of the blue" event in an otherwise healthy child. In this situation, the child develops an inflammatory response and a fever after contracting a common viral infection. The inflammation then lowers the seizure threshold, causing the child to have a seizure. These seizures do not return unless the fever and inflammatory reaction occur again. Fortunately, children usually grow out of this pattern by their first birthday once their nervous system matures.

Once bacterial overgrowth occurs in the child, the cascade of LPS leakage, microglia priming, failure of neuronal pruning, and increased pro-inflammatory cytokine levels has now set the stage for developmental delay and cumulative brain injury, so now all it takes is one more pathological twist and autism occurs.

The feature differentiating a child with ADD, headaches, and anxiety from a child with PANS or PANDAS is the over-production of a short-chain fatty acid called propionic acid by colonic bacteria, which are now replicating out of control within the small intestine.

16

—————

THE HISTORY OF BALANCING THE INTESTINAL TRACT

Although bacterial overgrowth of the small intestine (SIBO) has garnered growing attention recently, intestinal bacterial overgrowth is a medical problem discovered approximately sixty years ago.

While The Nemechek Protocol® is a relatively new approach to reversing the toxic and inflammatory effects of bacterial overgrowth to treat children with a variety of neurological challenges, the techniques and medications described in this book were developed over many decades in treating adults with other forms of bacterial overgrowth.

This chapter aims to highlight the parallels between existing and widely accepted techniques for treating bacterial overgrowth and the use of rifaximin in The Nemechek Protocol® for the same purpose.

Bacterial Overgrowth has a Long History

Some of the first medical studies involved the treatment of bacterial overgrowth in patients with advanced cirrhosis of the liver (hepatic encephalopathy) in the 1960s and later with overgrowth of a particular bacterium, *Clostridium difficle* (*C. difficle* enterocolitis and pseudomembranous colitis) in the late 1970s.

Since untreated hepatic encephalopathy and *C. difficle* enterocolitis are potentially deadly, a great deal of medical research exists on managing bacterial overgrowth associated with these conditions medically.

The use of antibiotics (vancomycin and metronidazole) for the management of *C. difficle* enterocolitis will be discussed in parallel with the use of rifaximin to control overgrowth in children with autism, developmental delay and cumulative brain injury to show that the medical community has widely accepted this approach to bacterial overgrowth for years.

Clostridium difficle Enterocolitis

Clostridium difficle (C. difficle) is a bacteria that can be found living harmlessly within the lower portion of the intestinal tract (i.e., large intestine or colon) along with a thousand or so other bacterial species.

When restricted to the lower intestine, *C. difficle* is harmless because its growth is regulated by the counterbalancing effects of the other bacteria living within the colon.

When a bacterial overgrowth of the small intestine occurs, the overgrowth is generally from a single species of bacteria that usually lives within the colon but is now growing in much greater numbers within the small intestine.

Usually, the small intestine has very few bacteria within it, so it cannot restrict the growth of the intruding bacterium from the colon.

The intruding colonic bacterium will grow unregulated, increasing its concentration to 10,000-100,000 times the normal bacteria live within the small intestine. Excessive bacteria within the small intestine will damage tissue, leading to nutrient malabsorption and inflammation from bacterial translocation (i.e., leaky gut). Overgrowth can also disrupt the body's nervous, hormone, and immune systems.

These excessive bacteria have the potential to begin producing abnormal types or amounts of chemicals that are programmed into their genetic material. As the concentrations of these chemicals increase, they end up circulating in the bloodstream and produce adverse effects on the body. In the specific case of *C. difficle*, the chemicals produced from the overgrowth are called Toxin A and Toxin B.

When released, Toxin A and Toxin B trigger a severe inflammatory reaction that damages the small intestine and colon, resulting in fever, fatigue, abdominal pain, and severe diarrhea. If left untreated, it will eventually lead to shock and death.

Clostridium enterocolitis is bacterial overgrowth with one strain of deadly bacteria called *Clostridium difficle*.

Similarities Managing SIBO with The Nemechek Protocol® and Enterocolitis

The escalating frequency of rifaximin use I recommend with my protocol is similar to the escalating frequency of courses of antibiotics used in *C. difficle* enterocolitis.

In patients suffering from *C. difficle* enterocolitis, antibiotics help control *C. difficle*. The initial approach is to treat with a single ten-to-fourteen-day course of antibiotics.

Many patients' diarrhea, fever, and abdominal pain will resolve and never return. Similarly, an initial approach of The Nemechek Protocol® in adults is to use a single course of rifaximin.

In *C. difficle* enterocolitis, some patients quickly relapse after discontinuing the antibiotics. The relapses then require physicians to use repeated courses of antibiotics to control *C. difficle*. Eventually, the relapses of *C. difficle* overgrowth in most patients will cease after a few to several cycles of antibiotics.

Single Course of Antibiotic -> Several Cycles of Antibiotics

Adults with SIBO also experience relapses of bacterial overgrowth and may require repeated courses of rifaximin. I have my adult patients repeat their 10-day course of rifaximin whenever their symptoms return (heartburn, diarrhea, joint or abdominal pain, etc.) for more than 10-14 days. Similar to *C. difficle* enterocolitis, patients with

SIBO will eventually stop relapsing after a few to several cycles of rifaximin.

My approach to treating children with relapsing bacterial overgrowth is similar but different in one respect. Children are often unable to readily communicate the internal symptoms that improve with a course of rifaximin and, likewise, cannot communicate when the symptoms have returned.

Unfortunately, they may relapse before their parents can observe any outward improvements. Therefore, the determination of when to repeat rifaximin as determined by the parents proved ineffective.

Since the inflammatory stress of intestinal bacterial overgrowth prevents any further neurological recovery, I concluded that the children who did not show increased recovery after a single course of rifaximin were relapsing very quickly. I devised a system of monthly cycles of rifaximin to maintain the balance of bacteria within their intestinal tract.

But even cycles of antibiotics might not be enough to eventually stop the relapses common with *C. difficle* enterocolitis or bacterial overgrowth in children and adults.

In the case of rapidly recurring enterocolitis, infectious disease specialists might prescribe continuous antibiotics for one to several months. The Nemechek Protocol® takes the same approach with children.

Cycles of Antibiotics -> Continuous Course of Antibiotics

If a child is not demonstrating substantial neurological recovery with *monthly* cycles of rifaximin, they are experiencing a relapse of bacterial overgrowth often within a week after completing the rifaximin.

This was first observed with some highly aggressive autistic patients. Within a few days of starting rifaximin, the violent tendencies in some of these patients significantly diminished. Still, the aggression would return within a week after finishing the 10-day course of rifaximin.

The return of aggression after every cycle of rifaximin was consistent round after round. Once continuous rifaximin was begun, the aggression was consistently improved. Significant signs of neurological recovery began within two to three months, indicating that bacterial overgrowth was finally suppressed.

After twelve months of rifaximin therapy, most patients could be tapered back from monthly cycles to intermittent rifaximin or from continuous to monthly cycles of rifaximin and then eventually to intermittent rifaximin.

Tapering Can Begin after 12 Months
Continuous Rifaximin -> Monthly Rifaximin -> Intermittent Rifaximin

In conjunction with the other aspects of The Nemechek Protocol®, a child's recovery with more aggressive use of rifaximin has been exceptionally positive. Many parents are opting to maintain some controlling rifaximin regimen (monthly or continuous) to avoid relapses and continue the exciting recovery path their child is experiencing.

FMT and C. Difficle Enterocolitis

There are patients with *C. difficle* enterocolitis who do not even respond to continuous antibiotics and will eventually deteriorate and die of septic shock. For decades, treatment-resistant enterocolitis killed thousands of patients in the U.S. annually.

Within the last several years, a treatment referred to as fecal microbiota transplant (FMT) has been discovered to control treatment-resistant enterocolitis. FMT entails increasing the diversity of bacteria within the patient's intestinal tract with a specimen of fecal stool from a healthy donor.

Antibiotic-Resistant Entercolitis -> Fecal Microbiota Transplant

By recolonizing the bacteria in this manner, patients near death from treatment-resistant *C. difficle* miraculously recover within a few days. It was discovered that the patients who eventually require FMT often have very low levels of bacterial biodiversity within their intestinal tract.

The effectiveness of FMT in this scenario underscores the importance of how the other intestinal bacteria are a critical component in the re-establishment of bacterial balance within the intestinal tract.

Rifaximin and other antibiotics do not force bacterial intestinal balance to occur; they shift the balance of bacteria back in the right direction so the remaining bacteria can regulate the balance themselves.

Aside from a dramatic improvement in patients with treatment-resistant *C. difficle* enterocolitis, FMT has had relatively limited success in treating patients with inflammatory bowel disease, obesity, or diabetes.

In my experience, rarely, a child does not respond to either inulin or rifaximin (cycling or continuous). Therefore, I am uncertain if FMT has any significant utility in children.

In support of my skepticism, intestinal bacterial studies of children with autism do not detect low levels of biodiversity as found in adults with recurrent *C. difficle* enterocolitis. Furthermore, I have many children under my care who have been treated with FMT by other physicians with little to no significant success.

Applying Old Science to a New Scenario

As we have reviewed, how The Nemechek Protocol® recommends either a single course, monthly cycles, or a continuous course of rifaximin to control disabling bacterial overgrowth in children parallels what has been done for decades in adults.

The focus of The Nemechek Protocol® is to safely induce neurological recovery in children by controlling inflammation and bacterial overgrowth with techniques developed over decades for adults.

17

PANS, PANDAS AND PROPIONIC ACID

DIFFERENT FACES OF THE SAME DISORDER

The last few decades have seen an alarming increase in acquired neurological disorders among children. Children increasingly develop conditions such as autism, developmental delay, sensory problems, emotional disorders, attention disorders (ADD/ADHD), post-concussion syndrome, tics, Tourette's syndrome, PANS, and PANDAS. Acquired neurological conditions develop after birth and are viewed differently from congenital disorders that may have a genetic component or have occurred before birth.

Consequently, researchers are grappling to understand each of these conditions, but unfortunately, they often focus on individual disorders and not the bigger picture. There is little to no research on understanding why such a large variety of neurological conditions increasingly affect children over the same time frame.

Commonly Acquired Neurological Conditions

Tics
Autism
PANS/PANDAS
Attention Disorders
Emotional Disorders
Tourette's Syndrome
Developmental Disorders
Post-Concussion Syndrome

When assessing an individual who develops a variety of symptoms within a relatively narrow timeframe, a physician is trained not to view each problem or symptom separately but to look for a single cause that might be responsible for all their symptoms. Applying the same logic to children's increased acquired neurological issues, small intestine bacterial overgrowth (SIBO) could be the single common factor contributing to these conditions.

SIBO is a condition in which bacteria that typically live within the colon are found in high concentrations within the small intestine. The small intestine typically has relatively few bacteria, but SIBO results in bacterial counts ranging from 1,000 – 100,000 times the amount normally found. Besides contributing to some digestive issues such as diarrhea, reflux, and food intolerance, SIBO results in the leakage of molecules of nutrients and bacteria into tissue layers surrounding the small intestine.

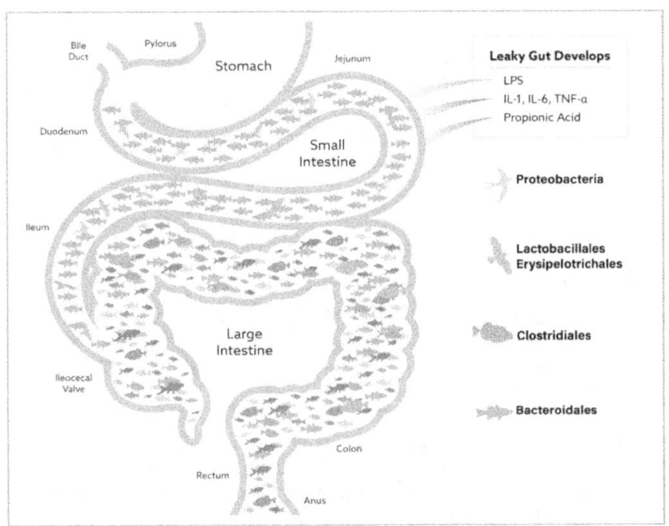

The small intestine wall disruption is called bacterial translocation (i.e., leaky gut) since only bacteria cause this. Yeast (i.e., fungi, Candida), viruses, and protozoa (i.e., parasites) may grow in excess within the small intestine, but there is no evidence they contribute to the leaky gut problem.

I can explain SIBO's ability to trigger various neurological disorders in children through two factors: when bacterial overgrowth first occurs and whether or not the overgrowing bacteria can produce a behavior-altering substance such as propionic acid.

For normal neurological development in a child to occur, the brain's neuron mass is pruned from approximately 100 billion neurons down to 50 billion by the time the child is five years old. Inflammation from SIBO can prevent the pruning from occurring correctly. If SIBO occurs before five years of age, the child will have some developmental or sensory issues. If it occurs after five years of age, no developmental problems arise because the pruning is already complete.

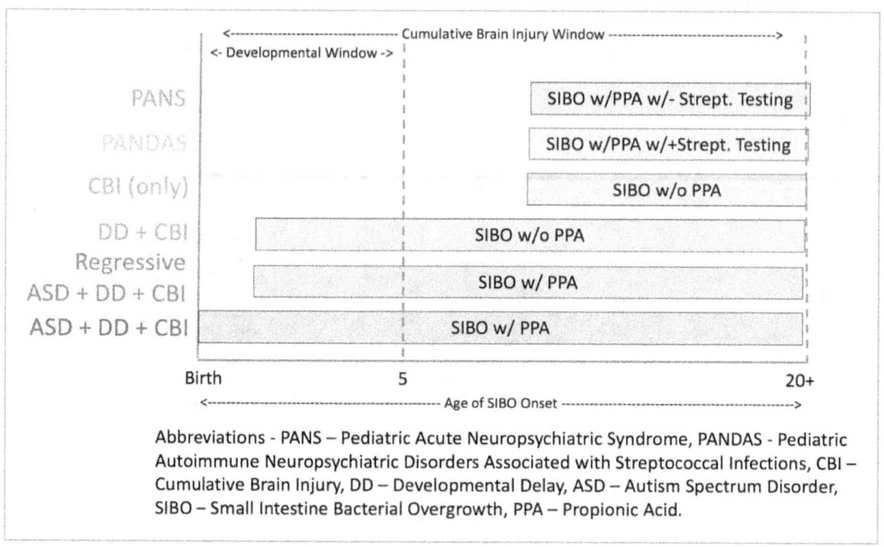

Abbreviations - PANS – Pediatric Acute Neuropsychiatric Syndrome, PANDAS - Pediatric Autoimmune Neuropsychiatric Disorders Associated with Streptococcal Infections, CBI – Cumulative Brain Injury, DD – Developmental Delay, ASD – Autism Spectrum Disorder, SIBO – Small Intestine Bacterial Overgrowth, PPA – Propionic Acid.

The inflammation from SIBO also impairs the nervous system's ability to fully repair itself after injuries resulting from physical, inflammatory, emotional, and chemical (propionic acid) insults. After an injury, a portion of the damage is repaired, but some residual neurological damage remains after each injury. Over time, the residual damage from repeated traumas will build on top of each other, resulting in a phenomenon referred to as cumulative brain injury (CBI) or minor repetitive traumatic brain injury.

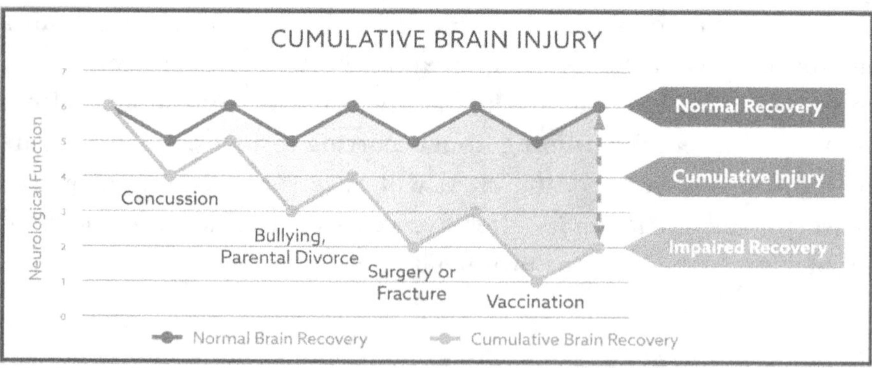

As the damage from CBI accumulates, symptoms begin to appear, with some of the most common being hyperactivity, anxiety, chronic depression, excessive aggression, poor focus, heartburn, reflux, and constipation.

<u>**Symptoms of Cumulative Brain Injury in Children**</u>
Bloating
Insomnia
Anxiety/OCD
Constipation
Hyperactivity
Heartburn/Reflux
Chronic Depression
Focus/Attention Disorders
Aggression/Temper Tantrums
Increased Levels of Thirst or Hunger

Unlike the pruning process, cumulative brain injuries can occur throughout life. Therefore, whether or not the inflammation from SIBO occurs before or after age five, CBI increases with each additional injury.

SIBO Before 5 Years of Age

If SIBO occurs after age 5-6, a child can only develop cumulative brain injury. If SIBO happens before age 5, the child will experience CBI and developmental delay. Depending on the intensity of the inflammatory strain caused by SIBO, the developmental issue can be mild or severe.

Propionic acid is found in high concentration in the tissues of children with advanced autism and has a sedating and, at times, almost hallucinatory effect on the children. Propionic acid production depends on the specific colonic bacteria that is overgrown within the small intestine. Since not all colonic bacteria produce propionic acid, the excess production of propionic acid depends on whether or not the overgrowing species is capable of excreting it. If the overgrowing bacteria produce propionic acid, the child will have a decreased level of awareness, poor eye contact, and may engage in strange behaviors such as staring transfixed at spinning objects.

A child younger than five years old with SIBO with a propionic acid-producing species of bacteria will have developmental issues, cumulative brain injury symptoms, and behaviors uniquely associated with autism. If younger than five, when SIBO occurs with a bacteria that does not produce propionic acid, the child will not have these unique autistic behaviors and will only be diagnosed with developmental delay and cumulative brain injury.

SIBO After 5 Years of Age

After age five, SIBO without propionic acid production will result in cumulative brain injury symptoms and no developmental issues. In the event the child is older than five years old, SIBO occurs with PPA-producing bacteria, they will manifest in conditions commonly referred to as PANS (pediatric acute-onset neuropsychiatric syndrome) or PANDAS (pediatric autoimmune neuropsychiatric disorder associated with streptococcal infections).

The symptoms commonly associated with PANS and PANDAS consist of high anxiety levels, often resulting in obsessive-compulsive behaviors (i.e., OCD) and other neurological and psychiatric symptoms. The main difference is that PANS has a rapid onset, often within 24-48 hours. In contrast, PANDAS is thought not to develop rapidly and is associated with colonizing streptococcal bacteria in the pharynx (i.e., a positive strep throat swab). PANS and PANDAS can mysteriously disappear as quickly as they appear and reappear months or years later.

I believe both PANS and PANDAS are simply the occurrence of SIBO with propionic acid-producing bacteria and are not separate medical conditions. In animal studies, SIBO increases anxiety-like behavior, and I have witnessed this same effect in my private practice. A subset of my adult patients will also experience high anxiety levels after SIBO develops. The anxiety can rapidly resolve after treatment of SIBO with rifaximin (Xifaxan®). Many of these adults had their anxiety initially escalate very rapidly after an infection, a course of antibiotics, surgery, or a brain injury, all of which are well-known triggers of SIBO.

The general state of subtle to profound confusion associated with PANS and PANDAS is most likely due to the release of propionic acid in a fashion similar to very young children diagnosed with autism.

The confusion with PANS and PANDAS is that the spontaneous resolution of these conditions after a course of antibiotics lies in commonly used antibiotics, such as amoxicillin or trimethoprim/sulfamethoxazole, which have a 20-30% chance of reversing SIBO. Thus, their use can sometimes lead to rapid improvement of SIBO-derived symptoms and even complete remission.

Suppose a physician managing a child with PANS or PANDAS is not tracking every single course of antibiotics that any other physicians might have prescribed the same patient for a routine middle ear or dental infection. Or the physician prescribed one of these antibiotics to "clear the strep" from the pharynx. The common antibiotics used in these instances can reverse SIBO, halt the release of propionic acid into the bloodstream, and trigger an improvement in the patient's PANS or PANDA symptoms. Physicians commonly miss the underlying reason for the child's improving symptoms and consider their progress as "spontaneous" or a consequence of some other treatment (vitamins, homeopathy, anti-yeast therapy, anti-mold therapy, heavy metal therapy, etc.).

I have witnessed many children under my care quickly improve from PANS or PANDAS by simply rebalancing the intestinal bacteria with either inulin or rifaximin.

Positive Strep Tests Don't Always Mean What You Think

Also, the diagnosis of PANDAS requires the presence of a positive strep-tococcal throat test or culture in children. Approximately 10-14% of all children within the U.S. are carriers of harmless strains of streptococcus. They will test positive with rapid strep tests or throat cultures but do not have any throat symptoms. Infectious disease specialists advise against treating these children with antibiotics because they often cannot clear the streptococcus, and treatment does not benefit their health.

Because of the high carrier rate, 10-14% of children with any diagnosis or common symptoms will test positive for strep because they are carriers. Because of this, streptococcus can mistakenly be linked to almost any disease process by finding streptococcus growing in the back of their throat (pharynx). What further leads physicians down this path of mistaken therapy is that prolonged courses of antibiotics they treat children with can partially suppress SIBO and reduce propionic acid production, resulting in some improvement in the child's symptoms.

The faulty logic of "giving antibiotics for streptococcus bacteria leads to improvement; therefore, the problem must be caused by streptococcus" is understandable but incorrect. They are treating the same child with rifaximin results in a better and longer-lasting positive response. And since rifaximin is only active within the small intestine and does not enter the bloodstream, the positive impact from rifaximin cannot be because it cleared the throat's streptococcus infection.

Autoimmune Versus Autoinflammatory

While I agree that children diagnosed with PANS or PANDAS have excess inflammation within their brains, I disagree that this is an autoimmune process; the children suffer from an autoinflammatory process. Inflammation from an autoimmune process targets specific types of tissue in the body. For example, rheumatoid arthritis is an autoimmune disorder in which inflammation is primarily targeted at a few particular joints of the hands. Think of autoimmunity as a sharpshooter who can hit the center of a bullseye when shooting a bullet without damaging other bodily systems.

Autoinflammation releases inflammatory chemicals into the bloodstream, which have wide-ranging adverse effects on the body's tissue. In the case of the hands, almost all the joints of the hand would hurt, not just a specific few joints, as seen in rheumatoid arthritis. Instead of a sharpshooter, think of autoinflammation as a shotgun that cannot just hit the target's center but scatter its effect across a much larger area.

When SIBO is present, the leakage through the small intestine walls can activate up to 70% of all white blood cells. These cells, in turn, release inflammatory chemicals called cytokines into the bloodstream and potentially harm any cell from head to toe.

The reversal of SIBO with rifaximin causes a rapid reduction in a high level of autoinflammation and a reduction in circulating propionic acid levels and results in the sudden improvement of my patients diagnosed as being affected with PANS and PANDAS. Historically, treating most autoimmune disorders results in a slow, not rapid, reversal of a patient's symptoms.

The Effectiveness of the Nemechek Protocol®

I have assisted in caring for over 1,000 children with autism, developmental delay, sensory issues, and cumulative brain injury, many of which had been previously diagnosed and treated for PANS or PANDAS. The Nemechek Protocol® is solely focused on reducing inflammation, most notably through the reversal of SIBO using either the prebiotic fiber inulin or the non-absorbable antibiotic rifaximin.

My protocol allows more than 80% of the children under my care to maintain a rate of neurological recovery that parents, teachers, and therapists find unequaled. My protocol's true power and success lie within the human body's natural ability to neurologically recover if the body is maintained in a healthy, non-inflammatory state.

18

ADD, ADHD AND POTS

s discussed in the preceding chapter, the overgrowth of bacteria within the small intestine (SIBO) results in the release of inflammatory cytokines into the bloodstream. If these cytokines penetrate the central nervous system, they will impair the brain's ability to recover from physical, inflammatory, emotional, and chemical injuries. As a result, injuries are only partially repaired, with the residual damage building with each new injury in a process called cumulative brain injury.

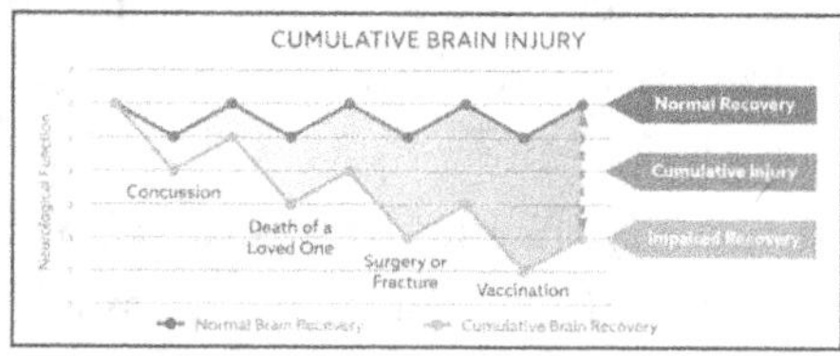

After concussions, the symptoms people often complain of are the result of damage to the autonomic nervous system and are the result of two basic mechanical processes in the body: slowing of the intestinal tract and decreased blood pressure in the brain. Slowing of the intestinal tract will result in food sticking in the esophagus, poor emptying of stomach acid leading to nausea, heartburn and reflux,

176

cramping of the small intestine (i.e., irritable bowel syndrome), and commonly, constipation.

The second mechanical effect of an injury is a decreased ability of the brain to maintain proper blood pressure within the central nervous system. Maintaining normal blood flow to the brain depends on the patient having normal blood volume (no anemia, dehydration, or kidney problems) and functioning neurological reflexes that help maintain blood pressure.

Through a complex interaction of signals between the brain, pressure sensors in the carotid artery and aorta, nerve impulses, and networks of arteries and veins, the body can maintain near-perfect blood flow to the brain and scalp muscles despite sometimes widely fluctuating blood pressures experienced by the rest of the body.

When functioning normally, blood flow in the brain is nearly unchanged when someone goes from the lying to standing position, even though gravity causes approximately 1/3 of the body's entire blood volume to move from the upper portion of the body to the lower portion. But when the segment of the autonomic nervous that regulates blood pressure is injured and not working well, the body cannot keep proper blood flow and oxygen levels to the brain.

ADD and ADHD

If an injury results in low brain blood pressure (scientifically referred to as cerebral hypoperfusion), the oxygen carried in red blood cells cannot fully transfuse into neurons within the brain. The inadequate release of oxygen results in our neurons not functioning correctly, leading to symptoms of poor focus, brain fog, and, more formally, the diagnosis of either attention deficit disorder (ADD) or attention deficit hyperactivity disorder. Low brain blood pressure is also a common source of fatigue, abnormal balance, poor vision, chest tightness, abdominal pain, headaches, and neck tightness, referred to as coathanger pain.

When the autonomic nervous system cannot correctly push blood upwards against the force of gravity, the blood tends to pool in the skeletal muscles of the legs. Through Pavlovian conditioning, the brain learns that if it (the brain) can get the subject (the child) to move or constrict their muscles, pressure improves, and oxygen delivery to the brain is improved. This conditioned internal drive is very powerful. It results in children becoming fidgety, toe walking, drawing their legs up to their chests when sitting, or becoming so fidgety they are diagnosed now with ADHD instead of ADD. Children often seek out a horizontal position when sitting on the sofa or are constantly slouched sideways when seated in a chair.

It is worth noting that the primary action of medications used to treat ADD or ADHD (methylphenidate or amphetamine/dextroamphetamine) is to *boost blood pressure in the brain.* They are considered stimulants, which is correct; they stimulate the nervous system to increase brain blood pressure, thereby increasing brain oxygen delivery.

POTS

Postural orthostatic tachycardia syndrome (POTS) is another diagnosis given to children and adults with damage to their autonomic nervous system. POTS also occurs from cumulative brain injury, as does ADD and ADHD, with one major exception: instead of the single overriding problem of low brain blood pressure in ADD and ADHD, POTS has two problems. Low brain blood pressure combined with damage to how the autonomic nervous system has the heart compensates for the low brain blood pressure.

Think of the heart as a hydraulic pump whose purpose is to pump blood through the body and, most importantly, maintain proper blood pressure within the brain. In subjects with ADD or ADHD, the low brain blood pressure elicits a normal, compensatory increase in the heart rate, increasing to 80-100 beats per minute (normal ranges from 60-70 BPM). Individuals with POTS will have an exaggerated increase in heart rate to 130-150 beats per minute when experiencing low brain blood pressure.

POTS often have similar focus and attention issues as those diagnosed with ADD or ADHD. It's just that the diagnosing physicians frequently do not see the similarities and will not give both diagnoses. Most patients with poor brain blood pressure will have multiple issues from the cumulative brain injury. For example, many will also have problems with constipation, bloating, or reflux problems due to other forms of autonomic nervous system damage.

Diagnosing Low Brain Blood Pressure

When taken at the arm, patients with low brain blood pressure occasionally exhibit a low reading. Unfortunately, the same individual may also have a normal blood pressure midday and a high blood pressure reading within the same day.

This is because the autonomic nervous system often increases blood pressure in the large arteries within the upper arm to drive more blood pressure upwards into the brain. This is referred to as the vagal reflex and commonly results in transient increases in blood pressure readings in the arm to help improve blood pressure readings in the brain.

Our understanding of suboptimal brain blood pressure and perfusion pressure in individuals with ADD, ADHD, or POTS comes from scientific studies using specialized MRI scanning techniques or ultrasound devices that can measure blood pressure through the bone of the skull.

The essential diagnostic elements for autonomic dysfunction are the presence of ADD, ADHD, or POTS without any significant laboratory abnormalities (severe anemia), cardiac problems (congestive heart failure or abnormal heart rhythms), dehydration (hyperglycemia, excessive vomiting or diarrhea), or medications known to lower blood pressure.

19

DEPRESSION, ANXIETY, OCD AND ODD

As the prevalence of autism, ADD, or ADHD has grown in children, so too have other mental health disorders. Children are more frequently experiencing chronic depression, obsessive-compulsive disorder (OCD), generalized anxiety, bipolar disorder, or oppositional defiance disorder (ODD).

While I respect the academic attention being focused on these problems, they are all considered separate problems, each with a unique underlying cause. However, after working with many children carrying these diagnoses, I have observed that the vast majority also are dealing with symptoms of autonomic dysfunction, as I've discussed in prior chapters.

Most of these children also have a co-diagnosis of ADD or ADHD, are fidgety, excessively fatigued, and have constipation or heartburn due to autonomic dysfunction. When discussing the child's medical history with their parents in detail, many of these individual medical problems correlate with a past brain injury. It often didn't occur to the parent or their pediatrician that their child was experiencing brain injury other than concussions that were the cause or aggravating factor of worsening emotional problems.

Physical Brain Injuries Can Alter Emotions and Behavior

As discussed in earlier chapters, brain injuries that can alter nervous system function are not restricted to concussions. A concussion is an injury that damages neurons, causing symptoms that persist for more than 24 hours but do not cause bleeding in the brain; therefore, the MRI or CT scan of the brain will appear normal. However, some physical injuries will damage neurons but do not lead to symptoms lasting more than 24 hours. An example is when a child heads a soccer ball in a match, neurons will be damaged without lingering symptoms.

Called subconcussive brain injuries, these events are very common in childhood and aren't recorded in our memory as something significant we should report to the pediatrician. Our parents and grandparents taught us that children with concussions and subconcussive injuries during their lifespan, high levels of inflammation from SIBO, and other causes were nearly non-existent, and all children would recover without any residual damage or symptoms.

The injuries will be repaired fully if the brain is healthy and without excessive inflammation. But suppose the brain has elevated levels of inflammatory cytokines from bacterial overgrowth (SIBO) or a high dietary intake of inflammatory omega-6-rich oil. In that case, the injuries are only partially repaired, and residual symptoms may remain in a process called cumulative brain injury. These injuries can occur anywhere within the brain. If they occur in the region of the brain responsible for regulating emotions (i.e., the hippocampus), the child may begin experiencing depression, anxiety, or OCD. In athletics, the development of depression, anxiety, or OCD after a sports-related concussion is a common occurrence.

Non-Physical Brain Injuries Can Also Alter Emotions and Behavior

Physical injuries are the only jury that can damage the brain and trigger chronic emotional and behavioral problems. Injuries can arise from surges in inflammatory cytokines released by white blood cells and the emotional stress from experiencing emotionally traumatic or threatening events.

White blood cells will release chemicals referred to as inflammatory cytokines in response to a wide variety of events, such as a fracture of a large bone (femur, humerus, pelvis), the stress of a surgical incision (abdominal or chest surgery), an abnormally strong reaction to vaccinations and from certain illnesses such as COVID or sepsis. The surge in inflammatory cytokines from any of these events will cause cellular damage within the brain.

But by far, the most common brain injury children and adults experience is from emotionally traumatic events in life. These events can be significant, such as the death of a loved one, sexual assault, a near-death experience, bullying, a toxic workplace, and abandonment. These and other minor emotional events will also contribute to the cumulative brain injury and lead to chronic emotional or behavioral dysregulation.

Emotional or psychological trauma has been demonstrated in animals to cause cellular damage, causing hippocampus neurons to malfunction. This damage is visible in a microscope from an emotional or psychological stressor; it is cellular in origin, not simply behavioral.

Common Depressive Episodes Are Injuries That Are Repaired

What I have outlined above should be placed in the context of a routine episode of depression that an individual recovers from and that we all are familiar with. For example, in an individual whose spouse dies unexpectedly, the surviving spouse often will experience symptoms of depression and anxiety.

We now understand the intense emotional grief and sorrow experienced by the surviving spouse will damage neurons within the hippocampus, leading to symptoms recognized as depression and anxiety. Suppose the surviving spouse is generally healthy and has no excessive inflammatory cytokines within this region of the brain. In that case, the natural repair and rejuvenation mechanisms within the hippocampus will repair the cellular damage from the emotional trauma within a few weeks to a few months.

The symptoms of depression are often physical and will persist until the damage is fully repaired. After a few months, the surviving spouse may function normally from a physical standpoint, but if they reflect on the passing of their spouse, they may become very emotional. This intermittent emotional distress when reflecting on memories is from grief and is not felt to be due to cellular damage.

If someone experiences the death of their spouse or some other emotional trauma but cannot recover from the chronic effects of depression, they more than likely are experiencing chronic inflammation within the hippocampus. Most modern antidepressants are understood to alter hormone levels such as serotonin and lower inflammation within the hippocampus, allowing this region of the brain to recover and the symptoms to improve. The Nemechek Protocol also lowers inflammation, allowing the hippocampus to recover and the symptoms of depression and anxiety to resolve.

The Nemechek Protocol holds the same potential of allowing children to recover from various emotional and behavioral problems. It carries far less risk than a child being placed on chronic psychiatric medications.

My

20

UNDERSTANDING HOW THE PROTOCOL WORKS IN 3 STEPS

Step One: Rebalancing the Intestinal Tract

The excessive production of inflammatory cytokines fuels cumulative brain injury and is the core pathophysiological factor of many childhood neurological conditions. Therefore, establishing control over inflammation resulting from bacterial overgrowth is the most critical step of The Nemechek Protocol.

Some children and adults with intestinal bacterial overgrowth will show signs or symptoms of the overgrowth, but many will not. Common symptoms of bacterial overgrowth include reflux or heartburn, specific food intolerance (tomatoes, spices, citrus, coffee, chocolate, etc.), watery or urgent stool, anxiety, or eczema.

It is not unusual for a child or an adult with bacterial overgrowth to not have any particular intestinal symptoms. Approximately 20-30 % of adults with intestinal bacterial overgrowth have no obvious intestinal symptoms. Although there may be no noticeable intestinal symptoms, bacterial overgrowth can prevent brain injury repair through elevated brain inflammation and abnormal microglia function. Because of these reasons, all children with chronic neurological issues deserve treatment to address small intestine bacterial overgrowth.

Preferred Method to Balance Intestinal Bacteria in Younger Children:

Inulin Prebiotic Fiber Supplementation
1/8 -1/2 teaspoon of inulin powder, once per day

Inulin is an over-the-counter (OTC) prebiotic fiber that comes from a variety of natural plant sources. Inulin derived from agave, chicory root, and Jerusalem artichoke are all acceptable forms of inulin. Inulin prebiotic powder is inexpensive and is sold by a variety of manufacturers.

Use inulin to balance intestine bacteria if the child is under eight. If the child is between eight and fourteen, begin with either inulin or rifaximin. Some children may fluctuate in behavior or intestinal function for a week or two after starting the inulin fiber.

Beyond the dose of 1/2 teaspoon a day, it is rare to see any added improvement in symptoms, and the higher dose can potentially increase hyperactivity, hunger, thirst, anxiety, or aggression. It may cause discomfort from excessive gas, cramping, or bloating.

Inulin powder is odorless and has a slightly sweet taste. Inulin powder may be taken with or without food and mixed with hot or cold liquids or solids. Inulin is the only prebiotic fiber that I use with my patients.

Over the years, different prebiotic fibers have been tested, but none reduced bacterial overgrowth enough to allow brain recovery in children.

Inulin increases the acidity of the small intestine, which results in suppressed growth of the colonic bacteria within the small intestine. When the growth of the colonic bacteria is suppressed, propionic acid production is dramatically reduced.

Prebiotic fibers are very different from probiotic bacteria. Inulin is *not* a probiotic and should *not* be used with a probiotic. One should immediately stop using all probiotics before starting The Nemechek Protocol®.

In an earlier chapter, it was explained how the bacteria in the small intestine are so different from the bacteria living down in the colon that you could think of one type of them as birds (small intestine bacteria) and the other as fish (colon bacteria).

Using the birds and fish illustration of SIBO, inulin fiber is best thought of as food for the healthy "bird" bacterial within the small intestine: inulin feeds the birds (the beneficial bacteria that should be there). Still, it does not feed the fish (the invading bacteria). Inulin gummies because it seems some children seem to react negatively to dyes or other ingredients in a gummy.

After starting the child on daily inulin, fish, and olive oil, parents often ask how they will know whether this is the right amount for their young child. The first treatment goal is to determine if the inulin effectively reverses bacterial overgrowth or if rifaximin is necessary.

Determining if Inulin is Effective

If the reversal of bacterial overgrowth with inulin leads to a decline in propionic acid, it will result in what is referred to as the awakening, especially in younger patients. The awakening occurs within the first 1-2 weeks and is manifested by the children showing more eye contact, alertness, and engagement.

Once the awakening occurs, the dose of inulin is adequate because the sudden improvement in the child's behavior is evidence that the bacteria have been suppressed. No further increases in inulin dosage are necessary if the awakening occurs.

Suppose the dosage of inulin is increased very slowly or the children are older. In that case, their awakening behaviors change so slowly that they are not noticed despite suppressing propionic acid.

Improvements in neurological development will begin to occur at an increased pace over the following three to six months. If there is no significant improvement after three to six months, the inulin is ineffective, and the child will need to be treated with rifaximin.

Pointers and FAQ's:

What type of inulin do I prefer? I prefer pure inulin powder for children (inulin is not very effective at controlling bacterial overgrowth in older teens and adults). When buying powdered inulin, I recommend buying Nemechek Blue Organic Inulin (NemechekProtocol.com) or Inulin from NOW Foods. Many other brands are less effective than Nemechek Blue or NOW Foods. A list of Nemechek-approved brands is listed in the appendix.

How fast of a pace might recovery occur?

Some studies indicate that developmental delay recovers at about a rate of two to three months for every calendar month that brain inflammation is lowered. Some children may recover this fast, while other children take considerably longer. No matter the child's age, the most essential factor to consider is whether the protocol has increased the rate of improvement compared to the pace of any gains before the protocol.

How long must my patients stay on inulin and the rest of The Nemechek Protocol®? Brain recovery is a long-term process, and each aspect of the protocol (intestinal balance, olive oil, and fish oil) has different timelines. Since we still do not understand how to completely prevent bacterial overgrowth from occurring, there will be an ongoing need to maintain the intestinal balance and reverse overgrowth should it occur.

The deficiency of omega-3 fatty acids and excess omega-6 fatty acids within the food supply make the regular supplementation with omega-3 fatty acids from fish oil (at present) and olive oil a long-term health requirement.

Do intestinal symptoms change after starting inulin?

Sometimes, a patient's constipation or bloating worsens after starting inulin. Constipation, heartburn, and bloating are signs of their underlying autonomic dysfunction and not a direct consequence of inulin. These only seem to "worsen" because inulin stops the watery or frequent stools associated with bacterial overgrowth, making underlying constipation or bloating more apparent.

Constipation and bloating will eventually resolve as The Nemechek Protocol® continues to improve autonomic function. If the child is uncomfortable or experiencing pain from constipation, the use of a non-fiber, non-digestive enzyme supplement such as magnesium (milk of magnesia) or MiraLAX® is recommended.

Suppose the child is not having daily bowel movements but is comfortable and without pain. In that case, using these products only as needed is recommended, not to create a bowel movement daily.

What if the inulin worsens stimming?

If there seems to be excessive stimming after starting the inulin, it is recommended to decrease the inulin dose by 1/8 of a tsp per day and see if things improve. It can sometimes take a week or two before the dosage reduction results in improved behaviors.

What if the child is having painful cramping or mucous in stool?

If the child is experiencing cramping or mucous in stool, stop using probiotics, digestive enzymes, or supplements. If these additional supplements are not being used, consider stopping the inulin for a week and restarting it at a lower dose. If the symptoms still do not stop, have the child's pediatrician evaluate the child.

What if the child cannot tolerate inulin?

If a child cannot tolerate inulin, consider using a course of the prescription rifaximin to balance the intestinal tract.

What about other products for bacterial overgrowth?

Please do not use any other fibers, probiotics, vitamins, minerals, herbs, or enzymes for bacterial overgrowth for my patients. It is also not necessary to use supplements to reverse leaky gut as it will spontaneously repair itself within a few weeks of starting inulin (or treating with rifaximin)

Is testing for bacterial overgrowth, propionic acid, or types of bacteria in stools useful?

No. Although intriguing, medical science is nowhere close to understanding how to do these tests accurately, nor do we understand the results in such a way that we could use the results to improve the treatment response in the child.

Warning:

Do not take probiotics during or after the use of inulin. The reason is that once the gut bacteria is rebalanced and the birds and the fish have shifted back to their respective environments, it is important to avoid introducing foreign bacteria (like lizards) for the birds to deal with. There is growing evidence that the indiscriminate application of probiotics may worsen the overall blend of intestinal bacteria.

Preferred Method to Balance Gut Bacteria in Older Children and Adults:

Non-Absorbable Antibiotic
Rifaximin 550 mg twice daily for 10 days.

As children age, inulin is less and less effective at controlling the balance of intestinal bacteria. By twenty, inulin is rarely effective enough to assist in brain recovery.

If the child is between eight and fourteen, you can start with inulin or rifaximin. Still, if the child is fifteen or older, consider starting with rifaximin because of the low likelihood that inulin will be effective.

As children age, the inulin becomes less and less effective at controlling bacterial overgrowth. This may be due to the natural maturation of the intestinal bacteria as children mature into adulthood. We are not just trying to suppress "gut bacteria" as a singular entity. We must suppress and balance over a thousand species within the large intestine, all with unique characteristics.

The species of bacteria that tend to overgrow in the small intestine of a younger child (let us call them species A) may be more sensitive to the prebiotic effects of inulin. As a result, inulin is more effective in younger children.

As the child's intestinal bacteria naturally mature with age, species less sensitive to the effects of inulin (let's call these species B) might be more likely to cause overgrowth and make inulin seem to lose its effectiveness in balancing the intestinal bacteria.

Suppose inulin fiber loses effectiveness over time, or the side effects (hyperactivity, anxiety, aggression) are intolerable. In that case, it is recommended to use rifaximin (brand name of Xifaxan® in the U.S.) 550 mg two times daily for ten days every month or twice daily to reduce the excessive colonic bacteria from the small intestine in my patients.

Rifaximin will remove the presence of any colonic bacteria (species A and species B) that have overgrown within the small intestine yet do not harm the remaining colonic bacteria. This prescription drug must be prescribed and supervised by a physician. This pharmaceutical treatment may need to be repeated periodically as bacterial overgrowth relapses can occur frequently.

Principles of Recovery

It is essential to understand that treatment with inulin or rifaximin alone will not repair a child's brain injury, will not control the primed M1 microglia, and recovery will be limited. Aside from contributing an unhealthy amount of inflammatory stress within the brain, bacterial overgrowth also triggers the formation of primed M1 microglia that inhibit neuronal pruning, migration, and repair.

Supplementation with fish and olive oil and vagus nerve stimulation (VNS) may all be required to regulate inflammation and overcome the negative effects of the primed M1 microglia.

It is also important to mention that FMT (fecal microbiota therapy) has no direct effect on bacterial overgrowth of the small intestine or the primed M1 microglia. As such, FMT will predictably have minimal effect on restoring neuronal pruning, neuronal migration, and cellular repair. FMT is not recommended for pediatric patients.

The key pathophysiological features of autism involve both brain inflammation and intestinal overgrowth, and consistent effort is required to control both over the long term. The power of the protocol is in its collective impact on reducing inflammation within the brain.

Other than increasing the fish and olive oil doses as the child ages, altering or reducing the doses of individual components of the protocol often leads to confusion and may even reduce the protocol's effectiveness if mistakes are made.

Assessing Effectiveness

After completing the 10-day course of rifaximin and starting the fish and olive oil, parents will ask how they determine whether the doses are correct for their child. There are two things to look for when assessing the effectiveness of treatment.

First, reversing bacterial overgrowth with one course (10 days) of rifaximin will lead to a drop in propionic acid and often the awakening period. This is a period where the child becomes more aware and has more eye contact, alertness, and engagement but may have more stimming or insomnia.

As stated before, the older the child, the less likely the parent will notice an awakening. This might be because the bacteria responsible for overgrowth in older children tend not to produce excessive propionic acid, or the species overgrowing the small intestine is not producing any propionic acid.

Secondly, if the intestinal bacteria blend has been rebalanced and the proper amounts of fish oil and olive oil are given, there should be a noticeable increase in the rate of neurological development within the next few months.

If there is no significant improvement after 2-3 months, assume the intestinal bacteria are rapidly relapsing, and more frequent dosing of rifaximin is needed.

Monitoring

Bacterial overgrowth of the small intestine is only sometimes detectable with a quantitative bacterial culture or PCR analysis of fluid aspiration from the small intestine or by the abnormal metabolism of sugars with a hydrogen and/or methane breath test. Treatment with rifaximin often results in the reversal of the findings on these tests.

From a practical standpoint, these tests are not helpful, and I do not recommend using them. Quantitative culture and PCR analysis require a complicated endoscopy procedure each time a sample might be needed. The breath test has so many variables affecting its accuracy that the results are often more of a source of confusion than helpful.

Instead of these tests, keep detailed notes about the clinical improvements of intestinal, psychiatric, musculoskeletal, and neurological improvements your child experienced within the first month after treatment with inulin or rifaximin. This collective set of symptoms is referred to as the SIBO fingerprint.

Use this list of symptom improvements to check for bacterial overgrowth relapses because a relapse will often result in the return of many of the same symptoms that were resolved initially on inulin or rifaximin.

Unfortunately, many children often cannot communicate enough to help us decode what they may be experiencing. It is too often difficult for the parents to gauge any immediate changes by observation, and the SIBO fingerprint approach becomes less useful.

Because of this challenge, parents must use deductive reasoning to help decide if the intestine's bacteria have been successfully balanced. If inulin or rifaximin have been successful, noticeable developmental gains will become apparent within four to eight weeks.

Suppose this does not occur, especially by the third month. In that case, it can reasonably concluded that the inulin is ineffective or the child's bacterial overgrowth has rapidly relapsed after finishing the rifaximin.

. . .

Pointers and FAQ's:

Follow-up use of inulin after rifaximin is sometimes used if intestinal symptoms such as diarrhea, post-meal stool urgency, or food intolerance are still present. If inulin does not make any significant difference in these situations, discontinue using it.

> *Rifaximin is a prescription medication that a physician should only administer and supervise.*

Never add probiotics to your child's treatment program after rebalancing intestinal overgrowth with rifaximin. Adding probiotics can easily make things worse for the patient, even if the probiotic seemed to help before using rifaximin. At times, adding foreign strains of bacteria (probiotics) may increase the child's level of inflammation, intestinal distress, depression, and other psychological symptoms.

Except when using inulin for continued diarrhea, etc., the ongoing use of prebiotic fibers such as inulin, probiotics, or digestive enzymes after taking rifaximin is generally discouraged because they may cause a worsening of symptoms after intestinal bacterial re-balancing is achieved.

Step Two: Reduction of Brain Inflammation

In the earlier chapter, we discussed how cytokines from bacterial translocation are reduced by rebalancing intestinal bacteria in Step 1 with inulin or rifaximin. This section will review the components involved in further reducing inflammation with The Nemechek Protocol®.

In addition to the release of pro-inflammatory cytokines from bacterial overgrowth, four unique sources of inflammation need to be addressed.

Lowering Four Additional Sources of Inflammation

- Shift M1-Microglia towards the Anti-Inflammatory M2-Microglia Phenotype

- Balance Omega-6 and Omega-3 Fatty Acids
- Reduction of Dietary Linoleic, Arachidonic, and Palmitic Acids
- Improving Vagus Nerve Function

Shifting M1-Microglia to the Anti-Inflammatory M2-Phenotype

Increasing the intake of omega-3 fatty acids is a critical step and must be performed to shift inflammatory primed M1-microglia to the anti-inflammatory M2-microglial phenotype.

The M1 to M2 shift maximizes the brain's natural ability to restore proper neurological development by re-initiating synaptic pruning, neuronal migration, and neuronal repair, ensuring maximum recovery.

The human body requires a blend of omega-3 fatty acids, the core nutrients that earlier generations obtained in everyday foods but are now commonly lacking in the modern food supply.

There are three types of omega-3, and each has distinct functions: DHA, EPA, and ALA. DHA is docosahexaenoic acid, EPA is eicosapentaenoic acid, and ALA is alpha-linolenic acid.

All three types of omega-3 are essential, but for this part of The Nemechek Protocol®, we focus on the DHA component, particularly its ability to aid in repairing brain damage from inflammation and injury. DHA is the only omega-3 fatty acid that substantially penetrates the brain and is found in variable amounts in fish oil.

Patients must supplement with DHA to shift their primed M1-microglia cells back into the M2-microglia type, which allows proper brain development and recovery from cumulative brain injury. There are no substitutes for DHA omega-3 fatty acid supplementation.

The amounts of daily DHA that I use with my patients may be taken all at once, or they may be taken in divided doses throughout the day. They can also be taken with or without food. Although important in its own right, the specific amount of accompanying EPA paired with the DHA component in fish oil is less critical. This might be because EPA does not readily penetrate the central nervous system.

Nemechek Silver high-concentration DHA fish oil capsules or liquids available from NemechekProtocol.com are the recommended fish oil. Fish oils from NOW® Foods or Nordic Naturals®. are also acceptable—these brands I preferentially use to help my patients recover from various neurological impairments and injuries.

I recommend against using the new high DHA concentration formulations that contain little to no EPA. Although little EPA enters the central nervous system, its presence in the fish oil blend is essential for the proper function of cells outside the central nervous system.

Balancing Omega-3 and Omega-6 Fatty Acids

This chart contains the dosage of Nordic Naturals Ultimate Omega fish oil, which I commonly recommend for my patients based on age.

Age and Daily Omega-3 (EPA+DHA) Dosage:

0-6 Months Old: 150 mg (EPA+DHA) daily*
7-12 Months Old: 300-450 mg (EPA+DHA) daily*
1-5 Years Old: 450-600 mg (EPA+DHA) daily*
5-7 Years Old: 600-1,000 mg (EPA+DHA) daily*
8-10 Years Old: 1,000-1,500 mg (EPA+DHA) daily*
11-14 Years Old: 1,500-2,000 mg (EPA+DHA) daily*
15-18 Years Old: 2,000-3,500 mg (EPA+DHA) daily*

Older than 18 years of age – Supplementation MUST contain a least 3,000 mg of the DHA fraction.*

---

*The mg. shown represents the total of the EPA + DHA omega-3 fatty acid content in fish oil. This number is not the total mg. from everything else in the fish oil itself. It is necessary to look at the back label to calculate the total EPA plus DHA amounts in any product, this is usually lower than the total omega-3 which is advertised or listed on the product.

Alternatively, teens and adults who can swallow fish oil capsules can use high-concentration DHA capsules found at NemechekProtocol.com.

Pointers:

Does fish oil cause intestinal distress?

Sometimes, patients may experience loose stools that can occur when first starting their fish oil. This is often due to their intestinal tract being irritated from bacterial overgrowth or being unable to absorb the sudden increase of oil being ingested.

If loose stools occur, I will have my patients stop their fish oil for two to three weeks until rebalancing their intestinal bacteria with inulin or rifaximin gives their intestinal tract a chance to repair itself. Then, after a few weeks, my patients can restart their fish oil at 1/4 of the full dose.

They may slowly increase the dosage by adding another ¼ dose every week until they reach the full dose. This is because by slowly increasing the amount of fish oil, we essentially train the intestinal tract to improve its ability to absorb the fatty acid molecules in the oil.

Do I ever add vitamins or other products besides fish oil?

No. Adding supplements such as glutamine, digestive enzymes, biofilm agents, or anti-fungal medications is unnecessary for intestinal bacteria recovery from bacterial overgrowth or the absorption of fish oil.

An exception to this rule is a medical physician's supplementation of iron or a particular vitamin in response to documented low levels.

Do I ever use fermented fish oil with my patients?

No. I do not recommend fermented fish oil.

Do I ever use krill oil with my patients?

No. Krill oil is a different molecule than fish oil molecule. Our ancestors evolved on the shorter molecule found in fish oil, not the longer molecule found in krill oil. I use the same molecules and core nutrients that kept our ancestor's brains strong and resilient. These are much less expensive in the doses we require than commonly available from krill oil.

Is there a vegetarian option if your patients are allergic to fish or do not want to ingest a fish byproduct?

Maybe. Algae-derived DHA might be beneficial, but I have never seen a patient on algae-derived DHA significantly improve.

Autonomic improvement and recovery were believed to be medically impossible until I developed The Nemechek Protocol® and have only been realized with marine-based DHA. The lack of EPA in algae-derived DHA might be a reason for it not seeming to work.

Can another form of omega-3 (EPA or ALA) substitute for the DHA from fish?

No. Other forms of non-marine omega-3 fatty acids, such as flax oil (ALA), do not readily penetrate the central nervous system and do not have the same impact on inflammation or microglia function as DHA.

The Additional of Alpha-Linoleic Acid (ALA)

The third component of omega-3 is ALA (alpha-linolenic acid), which is plant-based omega-3. Some research suggests ALA may help DHA penetrate the brain.

If my patients choose to consume nuts as part of The Nemechek Protocol®, I instruct them to eat a minimum of ¼ cup of nuts per day. All tree nuts have adequate ALA supplies, including almonds, pecans, pistachios, cashews, and walnuts. Dry or roasted peanuts (which are legumes and not tree nuts) are also an acceptable ALA source.

If my patient decides to consume ALA by ground flaxseed or chia seeds, they will supplement with 1/2 to 1 tablespoon per day. If they consume flax oil in liquid or soft gel form, the recommended amount is between 500 to 1,000 mg once daily.

Reducing the Dietary Intake of Omega-6 Fatty Acids

Reducing pro-inflammatory cytokines with The Nemechek Protocol® also requires decreasing the patient's dietary intake of high-concentration omega-6 fatty acid cooking oils.

This is done by no longer cooking with them (vegetable oils, margarine, shortening) and eliminating foods that contain high linoleic acid oils as primary ingredients.

I instruct my patients to avoid or limit the consumption of food products whenever possible that contain omega-6 fatty acids. These oils **should be limited or avoided:**

- Soy (Soybean) Oil
- Sunflower Oil
- Corn Oil
- Safflower Oil
- Cottonseed Oil
- Grapeseed Oil
- Peanut Oil
- Margarine
- Shortening

Foods containing soy milk, soy protein, or lecithin are allowed if they do not list any prohibited oils on the label. In these first stages of The Nemechek Protocol®, reducing omega-6 oils from foods is often the most demanding thing for my patients.

If the food product contains any prohibited oils listed above, I recommend reducing their intake as much as is practical or replacing them with a different brand with an acceptable oil. There are a few oils that have a healthier balance of omega-6 to omega-3 fatty acid ratio and are **acceptable:**

- Canola Oil
- Coconut Oil
- Avocado Oil

- Palm Kernel Oil

Once my patients start reading labels for omega-6 oils, it becomes clear to them the extent to which these oils now appear in foods they eat daily, such as salad dressings and bread. Omega-6 oils can be found in foods that we may otherwise consider clean, organic, and healthy. They even appear as ingredients in pet foods.

Pointer:

Memorizing the acceptable oils is more straightforward than learning the longer list of prohibited oils. Canola is increasingly being used in store-bought foods because of its healthier profile. One of my mottos is, "My patients *can* have *can*ola oil."

Some products will say they contain either a prohibited or an acceptable oil (e.g., "may contain soybean oil or canola oil"). The consumer is left to wonder which oil is used in the product. Err on the side of caution and try to avoid products whose ingredients are uncertain.

Prevention of Brain and Systemic Inflammation from Dietary Linoleic, Arachidonic and Palmitic Acids

While on The Nemechek Protocol®, I recommend patients try to avoid omega-6 fatty acids in cooking oils and foods but also to protect themselves from omega-6 that they cannot control.

Three specific omega-6 fatty acids are common within the food supply and should be avoided if possible because excessive intake can contribute to inflammation.

- Linoleic acid is commonly found in the unnatural vegetable oils added to the foods we purchase in the market.
- Arachidonic acid is found in elevated concentrations in dietary meats fed grains such as soybeans or corn.
- Palmitic acid - found in high quantities in processed and grain-fed foods.

Patients find these hard to control because they may be unable to see them on an ingredient label. They may not know what was fed to the meat or fish they eat, or they do not know what type of cooking oils are being used by a restaurant.

Fortunately, the omega-9 fatty acid oleic acid can block the inflammatory toxicity of these omega-6 fatty acids, and high quantities of oleic acid are present in authentic extra virgin olive oil.

Daily consumption of omega-9-rich olive oil is essential in protecting the body from excessive omega-6 fatty acid toxicity.

Daily Supplementation with Olive Oil

In addition to decreasing the consumption of high-concentration omega-6 fatty acid cooking oils and foods, I ask my patients to increase their daily consumption of extra virgin olive oil (EVOO). EVOO contains approximately 70% oleic acid, and oleic acid can reduce the underlying inflammation resulting from excessive dietary intakes of linoleic, arachidonic, and palmitic acid.

Several studies show that adults benefit from the daily consumption of two or more tablespoons (30 ml or more) of extra virgin olive oil daily. Increasing your intake of EVOO can be done by topping foods with olive oil in the traditional manner or by simply drinking it straight as if it were a medicine.

Heating olive oil while cooking does not damage the oleic acid molecule nor lower the amount contained within the oil.

For children younger than three, using EVOO when cooking foods should be adequate. Starting at age three, I recommend supplementing the diet by adding EVOO to food or directly consuming it. These are the following guidelines:

- If under 2 years of age, cooking food daily in EVOO should be adequate.
- If between 2 to 4 years old, give ¼-½ of a teaspoon (1.25-2.5 ml) of EVOO daily

- If between 4 to 8 years old, give 1 teaspoon (5 ml) of EVOO daily
- If between 9 to 12 years old, give 2 teaspoons (10 ml) of EVOO daily
- If between 13 to 17 years old, give 1 tablespoon (15 ml) of EVOO daily
- If 18 years or older, give 2 tablespoons (30 ml) of EVOO daily.

Pointer:

EVOO may be mixed into a variety of liquids or taken by spoon. Some of my older patients cut the taste with balsamic or lemon juice.

EVOO is not well regulated in the U.S., and the risk of buying oils that are not extra virgin or are tainted with other oils is a significant concern for my patients. Some olive oils may be diluted with a high percentage of soy or other vegetable oils, which we are trying to avoid.

Because of the considerable risk of buying fraudulent imported olive oils, patients on The Nemechek Protocol® are recommended to use extra virgin olive oils certified by the California Olive Oil Council (COOC; www.cooc.com for more information).

COOC certification is the only certification process in the U.S. that requires laboratory testing of olive oil to prove the purity and quality of the oil. You can find approved COOC-certified producers and their certification of EVOO off the COOC.com website and have the products shipped to your home.

Improving Vagus Nerve Function

The vagus nerve is the tenth cranial nerve and carries information from the parasympathetic branch of the autonomic nervous system. Neurological signals on the vagus nerve travel upwards into the brain and downwards to all the organs in the body. Signals traveling upwards can induce neuroplasticity, while signals traveling downward improve organ function and help suppress abnormal levels of inflammation.

Transcutaneous auricular vagus nerve stimulation (taVNS) is a treatment that involves extremely low electrical impulses to the vagus nerve. Vagus nerve stimulators have been implanted in patients in the U.S. since the late 1990s, but it is also possible to stimulate the nerve externally.

I use a portable vagus nerve stimulator as part of The Nemechek Protocol® that many autistic and non-autistic patients use at home.

VNS results in the suppression of inflammation as well as increased neuroplasticity, especially when paired with a cognitive (speech, reading, mathematics training), sensory (integration therapy), or motor (physical therapy or gait training) activity.

The use of taVNS for 5 minutes per day is a potent and effective tool for the suppression of inflammation as well as for the induction of neuroplasticity. Suppressing inflammation within the brain improves microglia's brain repair and neuronal pruning abilities.

I may add taVNS to a child's treatment later in The Nemechek Protocol® if their recovery is incomplete or unusually slow. Once recovery has begun, tVNS treatment may help expand the breadth of a child's recovery.

While all children are treated with identical stimulation parameters, my adult patients use taVNS with various settings based on several factors that I take under consideration as their doctor.

Transcutaneous auricular VNS can cause harm if the stimulation settings are incorrect. I am a leading expert in the clinical application of taVNS, and many of my patients travel to my office in Arizona to be prescribed a portable transcutaneous vagus nerve stimulator they can use at home.

I do not prescribe or perform any other non-electrical methods of vagus stimulation because other methods are less effective at keeping the healthy shift in microglia function.

Pointer:

The need for taVNS increases with the severity of developmental impairment as well as the age of the patient. By the early teen years, it seems most children with autism or developmental disorders may require taVNS to obtain a complete, broad level of neurological recovery.

Warning:

I also strongly recommend against any taVNS do-it-yourself approach using other devices such as TENS units because of the potential harm that may occur if not set or used correctly. The vagus nerve may be permanently damaged if stimulation is done incorrectly.

PART VI

THINKING ABOUT THE FUTURE

21

POTENTIAL OPPORTUNITIES FOR PREVENTION

Now that I have discovered a process that can reverse or improve key features in many other childhood neurological disorders, I naturally consider whether this process may be used in a potentially preventive manner. If I can make a change in the children of today, what about making a change in the children of tomorrow?

The prevention of inflammation and bacterial overgrowth are key targets in preventing many childhood developmental disorders. In the case of autism, the first challenge is whether we can prevent the excessive production of propionic acid from bacterial overgrowth, as it is the unique pathological feature that delineates autism from most other disorders.

If we can keep a child's intestinal bacteria balanced without overgrowth in the small intestine and excessive propionic acid production, autism, developmental delay, and cumulative brain injury in most children would likely not occur. I believe the same holds for conditions that occur after a child has met all their developmental milestones (ADD, ADHD, PANS, PANDAS, Depression, Anxiety, OCD, POTS, ODD).

In this chapter, I have included the recommendations I discuss with my patients that address potential methods to limit or reduce the risk of a child from developing clinically harmful overgrowth of intestinal bacteria.

None of my prevention suggestions in this chapter are "proven" because human clinical trials have been performed. My theories come from my experiences and observations after treating adults of all ages, children with autism and developmental disorders, and women before and after pregnancy with The Nemechek Protocol®.

I have been able to reverse or significantly improve bacterial overgrowth in child-bearing-age women and children of all ages. There is reasonable potential that the same methods that prevent bacterial overgrowth might also prevent or limit the occurrence of autism, developmental delay, and cumulative brain injury since they are commonly the consequence of bacterial overgrowth.

Any readers of this book who are learning about the treatment modalities and suggestions that I give to my patients must thoroughly discuss any of these potential treatment modalities and suggestions with their healthcare providers before initiating them at any time before conceiving, during pregnancy, or after delivery.

Considerations Before Pregnancy

Women considering pregnancy need to be aware that pro-inflammatory cytokines (IL-1, IL-6, TNF-alpha) that are produced within their body can cross the placenta and cause potential harm to their unborn child.

Pro-inflammatory cytokines can disrupt normal brain development and activate genes in their child while still in the womb and after birth. After birth, they may even be capable of causing new mutations within the child's DNA. These cytokines are also associated with increased pregnancy complications such as miscarriage and eclampsia.

I recommend my female patients who are considering becoming pregnant work towards normalizing their body's inflammatory status many months before planning to conceive. The Nemechek Protocol® for Autonomic Recovery (for adults) is designed to specifically reduce a person's excessive levels of pro-inflammatory cytokines to improve or restore autonomic nervous system dysfunction.

Waiting until a woman becomes pregnant before starting the process of general inflammation reduction is not a good strategy because it may take three or more months to achieve a lower or normal state of inflammatory cytokines, and both rifaximin and vagus nerve stimulation are prohibited from use during pregnancy and inulin supplementation is less effective in adults.

The higher dietary consumption of olive oil and fish as part of the Mediterranean diet is associated with favorable neurobehavioral outcomes in early childhood. There is no reason to believe the olive oil and fish oil recommended with The Nemechek Protocol® would not offer the same benefits.

The rifaximin medication I prescribe to my adult patients to reverse intestinal bacterial overgrowth is not a treatment option during pregnancy as it is not approved for use during pregnancy or breastfeeding.

The reduction of overall inflammation before pregnancy may improve fertility rates and limit complications such as pre-eclampsia and miscarriage during pregnancy. Supplementing with fish and olive oil can also increase the mother's neurological resilience against the intense physical and psychological stressors accompanying delivery.

Ensuring a woman does not have significant bacterial overgrowth and supplementing their diet with the correct balance of omega-3 and omega-6 fatty acids via The Nemechek Protocol® will go a long way towards maximizing their chances for a healthy and uncomplicated pregnancy.

Considerations During Pregnancy

Inflammation can affect the child's neurological development prior to birth while they are still developing within the womb. Excessive exposure of the fetus to elevated levels of pro-inflammatory cytokines is an important contributing factor that might also determine the presence or level of severity of autism or other developmental disorders at the time of birth.

Sources of pro-inflammatory cytokine exposure during pregnancy may include intestinal bacterial imbalance of the mother, inadequate omega-3 and excessive omega-6 fatty acid dietary intake, exposure to tobacco smoke, urban air pollution, periodontal disease, as well as excessive dietary AGEs (advanced glycation end-products) intake.

After birth, excessive pro-inflammatory cytokines can disrupt a child's normal neuronal development and inhibit the brain from repairing commonplace injuries that occur from physical, emotional, chemical, and inflammatory trauma.

Improving Omega-3 Fatty Acid Transfer in the Third Trimester

During pregnancy, the mother will transfer half of her omega-3 fatty acid stores to her child during the third trimester. This transfer gives the child enough omega-3 fatty acids for normal neurological development during their first year. This also signals how important the supply of omega-3 fatty acids is to healthy development.

The importance of omega-3 fatty acids is so significant that the child of a mother supplementing with high doses of omega-3 fatty acids from fish oil will give birth to a child with an I.Q. that is almost 10 points higher than they would have had if the mother did not supplement.

If the mother's diet is low in omega-3 fatty acids and high in inflammation-causing omega-6 fatty acids, the child may experience a similar imbalance of omega fatty acids during the third-trimester transfer. The omega fatty acid imbalance will further increase the inflammatory cytokine level within the mother and child and may additionally impair normal brain development in the child.

Supplementation with extra virgin olive oil is critical to reduce the inflammatory state of the mother even further during pregnancy. Extra virgin olive oil contains high amounts of omega-9 fatty acid called oleic acid that helps block and reverse the inflammatory damage caused by excessive dietary omega-6 fatty acid intake and saturated fatty acids such as palmitic acid.

I typically recommend that the expectant mothers under my care supplement with 2,000-3,000 mg of fish oil daily and consume 2 tablespoons of COOC-certified extra virgin olive oil. High intakes of fish and olive oil are routine in many regions of the Mediterranean and, as a natural consequence, are known to be safe during pregnancy.

Pregnant women should not take a high-concentration DHA fish oil (DHA mg. are greater than EPA mg.). The predominant intake of omega-3 fatty acids during evolution from fish had much more EPA than DHA. Although uncertain if biologically important, a relatively higher EPA concentration of fish oil should be consumed during pregnancy (EPA mg. are greater than DHA mg.) to help mimic our evolutionary exposure.

Improving Intestinal Bacterial Balance During Pregnancy

To improve intestinal balance during pregnancy, I recommend my patients supplement, if needed, with the over-the-counter prebiotic plant fiber inulin. Although not as effective as rifaximin, inulin may improve the intestinal symptoms of bacterial overgrowth, such as diarrhea, heartburn, nausea, and cramping.

Intestinal balance treatment options during pregnancy are limited to just the inulin fiber. The use of the non-absorbable antibiotic rifaximin to rebalance the intestinal bacteria has not been adequately studied during pregnancy and is never to be recommended for use during pregnancy.

Considerations After Delivery

As long as the infant child can maintain the proper balance of intestinal bacteria, they predictably will not develop inflammation nor excessive propionic acid production that occurs only from bacterial overgrowth of the small intestine.

Bacterial overgrowth in a newborn infant could potentially occur if their intestinal bacteria are disrupted by spending time in the NICU or by receiving antibiotics before discharge.

Since reversing intestinal bacterial imbalance and restoring the omega-3 to omega-6 fatty acid balance reverses many of the key features in autism, managing these issues upfront may theoretically help prevent regressive autism from occurring in some children.

If there is any suspicion of bacterial overgrowth in the mother or older siblings (since they would also be colonized with the mother's bacterial blend of my patient, the younger sibling), I generally recommend supplementing the newborn infant with 1/32 to 1/16 tsp of powdered inulin fiber daily.

Fish oil and olive oil are not required since the additional omega fatty acids needed from each will be provided through the mother's breast milk as long as she takes each.

When the child is old enough to eat regular food, I recommend they be supplemented in addition with fish oil and that their food be cooked in COOC-certified extra virgin olive oil to protect them from toxic omega-6 fatty acids that will inevitably seep into their diet.

22

HOPE IS ON THE HORIZON

The human brain has an enormous capacity for repair and rejuvenation. The microglia within the brain are proving to be capable of restarting their task of synaptic-neuronal pruning even after many years of being in a state of inflammatory paralysis.

The substantial reduction of pro-inflammatory cytokines within the brain is all that is necessary for the normal process of maturation and brain repair to begin anew.

We are also beginning to understand that once human genes are turned on by inflammation, they can ultimately be shut off again once the inflammatory environment within the body is significantly reduced.

My advice is the same for all my patients and their parents. Do your best to be patient, give The Nemechek Protocol® and my overall approach to lower inflammation a chance, and adopt a marathon mindset because brain recovery takes time and effort.

Because the path to recovery for many medical conditions is often five steps forward, and then often one or two steps backward, it is best to compare today's behavior in your child, to their behavior one to two months ago, not yesterday. Comparing today to yesterday will only serve to put you on an emotional roller coaster, and it could possibly lead you to make some incorrect decisions for your child.

The only thing required for continuous recovery is the consistent application of an inflammation-suppressing regimen and patience. Remember, the neurons within the human brain, like your hair, grow slowly and therefore your child's improvement will occur slowly but steadily.

23

INDEX

APPENDIX

NEMECHEK PROTOCOL-APPROVED BRANDS

DOSING REFERENCE GUIDE

Dosing Information for Children:

I recommend starting all the ingredients at the same time or as soon as they become available. A modification approach is to start the children on just the fish and olive oils for the first 4 weeks and then start the inulin or rifaximin. The delay will allow the oils to fully saturate the brain and be ready to assist in the recovery once the intestine overgrowth is reversed with either inulin or rifaximin.

Ingredient #1 – Daily Extra Virgin Olive Oil Dosage

Use only COOC-certified and give raw uncooked olive oil daily, either straight like medicine or mixed in food or drink. The minimal amount of olive oil is listed below.

- If under 4 years of age, give ¼-½ of a teaspoon (1.25-2.5 ml) of EVOO daily

- If 4 to 8 years old, give 1 teaspoon (5 ml) of EVOO daily
- If 9 to 12 years old, give 2 teaspoons (10 ml) of EVOO daily
- If 13 to 17 years old, give 1 tablespoon (15 ml) of EVOO daily
- If 18 years or older, give 2 tablespoons (30 ml) of EVOO daily

Ingredient #2 – Liquid Fish Oil Dosage

- Use the liquid form of fish oil produced by Nordic Natural called Ultimate Omega (NNUO)
- If under 4 years of age, give a 1/8 teaspoon (0.6 ml) of fish oil daily
- If 3 to 5 years old, give a 1/4 teaspoon (1.25 ml) of fish oil daily
- If 6 to 10 years old, give a 1/2 teaspoon (2.5 ml) of fish oil daily
- If 11 to 14 years old, give 1 teaspoon (5 ml) of fish oil daily or 2-3 DHA-500 tablets (NOW Foods)
- If 15 to 17 years old, give 2 teaspoons (10 ml) of fish oil daily or 4-5 DHA-500 tablets (NOW Foods)
- If 18 years or older, give 1 tablespoon (15 ml) of fish oil daily or 6 DHA-500 tablets (NOW Foods)

Ingredient #3 – Balance Intestinal Bacteria

Inulin and the prescription medication rifaximin (Xifaxan®) are two options to balance the intestinal bacteria. Starting with inulin is preferred in younger children while starting with rifaximin is recommended in older children because inulin is less effective in older children.

Choosing Between Inulin versus Rifaximin

- If under 8 years of age, use inulin to balance intestine bacteria
- If 8-14 years old, you can start with either inulin or rifaximin
- If 15 years of age or older, I recommend starting with rifaximin

Inulin Dosage

- Give a 1/8 teaspoon of powdered inulin (NOW Foods, Inc) once daily
- Can be mixed in food or drink
- Dosage does not change with age

Rifaximin (Xifaxan®) Dosage

- 550 mg twice daily for 10 days for ages five years and older
- Since the medication is not absorbed into the bloodstream, the dosage does not need to be adjusted for children 5-years-old and older.
- Medication can be crushed and mixed with food or drink if necessary
- This is a prescription medication and must be obtained through your physician

Notes on Adjusting the Inulin Dosage

As inulin reverses the bacterial overgrowth, the amount of propionic acid declines. Declining propionic acid levels leads to the awakening in which the child is more alert and cognizant of their surroundings.

If the initial dose of inulin does not trigger an "awakening" (more engaged, better eye contact, more aware of the world around them) then you may need to increase inulin slowly but do not exceed the ½ tsp dose. In my practice, I have not found that if a dose beyond ½ tsp produces meaningful results and I simply move on to Rifaximin.

Autistic children older than 10 and children who are not on the spectrum may not experience the "awakening". This does not mean that the protocol is not working.

Beyond just suppressing the production of propionic acid, the only true way to determine if the inulin is controlling the inflammatory stress produced by bacterial overgrowth is by observing improvements in the child's behavior and developmental issues over the ensuing 3 months.

If behaviors and neurological functions begin to improve, stay on this dose of inulin. If there is little to no improvement, the inulin is ineffective, and I recommend switching to monthly cycles of rifaximin.

Dosing Information for Adults (with and without Autism):

Ingredient #1 – Daily Extra Virgin Olive Oil (EVOO) Dosage

- Consume 30 ml (2 tablespoons) or more of EVOO per day
- Use only COOC-certified (California Olive Oil Certified) EVOO
- Olive oil should be raw and uncooked
- Can be mixed with food or drink

Ingredient #2 – Omega-3 Fatty Acids (EPA and DHA) from Fish Oil

- Adult patients require 3,000 mg of DHA daily. Although important, relatively little EPA penetrates the central nervous system and dosing is based upon the DHA fraction within the fish oil
- **Option 1** – Take 6 DHA-500 fish oil capsules (NOW Foods, Inc) per day
- **Option 2** – Take 15 ml (1 tablespoon) of Nordic Naturals Ultimate Omega liquid fish oil per day
- Either choice of fish oil may be taken with or without food, as a single dose or split into 2 doses

Ingredient #3 - Omega-3 Fatty Acids (ALA) from Nuts, Flax, or Chia

- **Option 1** – Consume a ¼ cup of nuts per day (almonds, pecans, pistachios, cashews, and walnuts)

- **Option 2** - Consume flax or chia seeds: 1/2 to 1 tablespoon per day.
- **Option 3** - Consume liquid flax oil: 500 to 1,000 mg once daily.

Ingredient #4 – Balance Intestinal Bacteria with Rifaximin

- Take 550 mg of rifaximin twice daily (in AM and PM) for 10 days
- Medication can be crushed and mixed with food or drink if necessary
- This is a prescription medication and must be obtained through your physician
- Repeated cycles of rifaximin may be required whenever the associated-intestinal symptoms return.

Ingredient # 5 – Vagal Nerve Stimulation

The purpose of vagus nerve stimulation in The Nemechek Protocol® is to suppress systemic and central nervous system inflammation. Lowering inflammation allows the nervous system to recover.

- Children and adults less than thirty years of age require only five minutes of continuous transcutaneous vagus nerve stimulation tVNS) per day
- At the proper settings, five minutes of tVNS is enough to significantly reduce inflammation throughout the body for at least 24 hours
- Between the ages of thirty and forty, five minutes of daily tVNS may not be enough and stimulation time may need to increase to one to two hours per day
- Patients over forty years of age almost universally need two hours of cycling tVNS

GLOSSARY

A Short Glossary of Scientific Terms

- **ALA, Alpha-Linolenic Acid** - An omega-3 fatty acid commonly supplemented in the form of nuts, flax, or chia.

- **Arachidonic Acid** - An omega-6 fatty acid that is part of the inflammation-producing process.

- **Autonomic Nervous System** - A large portion of the nervous system that regulates blood pressure, coordinates all organs (heart, intestines, bladder, etc.), controls inflammation, and regulates hormone production.

- **Bacterial Overgrowth** - Often used to refer to excessive bacterial growth within a segment of the intestinal tract. Less specific than the term SIBO which also implies a positive methane or hydrogen breath test or an abnormal quantification study from the small intestinal aspirate.

- **CBI** - Cumulative Brain Injury. The cumulative damage that results from the residual defects remaining after improperly repaired physical, inflammatory, or metabolic damage.

•**Concussion** - A physical injury to the brain that results in persistent symptoms for several days. Also referred to as a minor traumatic brain injury or mTBI.

•**Cumulative Brain Injury** - The cumulative damage that results from the residual defects remaining after improperly repaired physical, inflammatory, or metabolic damage.

•**Cytokines, Anti-Inflammatory** - Chemicals released from white blood cells that decrease the inflammatory response.

•**Cytokines, Pro-Inflammatory** - Chemicals released from white blood cells that increase the inflammatory response.

•**Developmental Delay** - The slowing of the normal rate of neurological and emotional maturation of a child. Often the result of excessive inflammation, nutritional deficiencies, and improper neuronal pruning.

•**Developmental Arrest** - The complete stoppage of the neurological and emotional maturation of a child. Often the result of excessive inflammation, nutritional deficiencies, and improper neuronal pruning.

•**DHA** - Docosahexaenoic acid (DHA) is an omega-3 fatty acid that is a primary structural component of the human brain, cerebral cortex, skin, and retina. Dietary sources include wild fish, fish oil, and meat from animals that feed on their natural food (e.g., grass-fed beef).

•**Digestive Enzymes** - Supplements often provided to improve digestion and intestinal symptoms.

•**Dysbiosis** - Refers to a general disruption of normal microbial balance within the intestinal tract. Dysbiosis can refer to any segment of the intestinal tract (mouth, small intestine, or colon), and although usually implies bacteria, may also be used in regard to protozoan, fungi, or archaebacteria.

•**EPA** - Eicosapentaenoic acid (EPA) is an omega-3 fatty acid. Dietary sources include wild fish, fish oil, and meat from animals that feed on their natural food (e.g., grass-fed beef).

•**EVOO** - Extra Virgin Olive Oil. EVOO is the highest quality of olive oil and is considered to have favorable flavor characteristics. It contains oleic acid which is an omega-9 fatty acid.

•**Inflammation** - A normal response by the immune system to fight infection or repair damaged tissues. Excessive inflammation can lead to damaging effects on the body.

•**Intestinal Bacterial Overgrowth** - Often used when referring to the excessive presence of bacteria within the small intestine. These bacteria often originate in the colon (lower or large intestine) and abnormally migrate up to the small intestine.

•**Inulin** - A prebiotic plant fiber derived from agave, onions, garlic, chicory is preferentially digested by the types of bacteria that normally inhabit the small intestine.

•**Linolenic Acid** - An omega-6 fatty acid that is part of the inflammation-producing process. Commonly found in plants and in high concentrations within a wide variety of cooking oils.

•**Microglia, M0** - These are a specialized form of white blood cells that live in the brain. They are often referred to as surveillance or pruning microglia.

•**Microglia, M1** - These are a specialized form of white blood cells that live in the brain. They promote inflammation and are part of the healthy repair process but can cause damage if they become primed.

•**Microglia, M2** - These are a specialized form of white blood cells that live in the brain. They shut off inflammation and are part of the healthy repair process.

•**Microglia, Primed** - These are microglia that permanently morph into M1-microglia and prevent the brain from fully repairing brain trauma. They also are a major source of inflammatory cytokines within the brain.

•**mTBI** - Minor (lower case letter M) traumatic brain injury. A brain injury that is relatively mild and is commonly referred to as a concussion.

•**MTBI** - Major (upper case letter M) traumatic brain injury. A brain injury that is cause significant cellular damage and is often associated with intracranial bleeding.

•**Neuron** - A cell within the brain that carries or stores neurological information.

•**Neuroplasticity** - The process through which the brain develops new neuronal pathways to perform certain tasks.

•**Oleic Acid** - An omega-9 fatty acid that is very plentiful in olive oil. Oleic acid blocks the brain damage that can result from excessive omega-6 fatty acids and palmitic acid.

•**Omega-3 Fatty Acid** - These nutrients are unsaturated fatty acids and are important for normal metabolism. They are classified as an essential nutrient because humans are unable to synthesize omega-3 fatty acids and require them in their diet in order to remain healthy.

•**Omega-6 Fatty Acid** - These nutrients are a family of pro-inflammatory and anti-inflammatory polyunsaturated fatty acids. They are commonly found in plants and are classified as essential nutrients.

•**Omega-9 Fatty Acid** - These are unsaturated fatty acids and are not essential nutrients. Oleic acid found within olive oil is one example of an omega-9 fatty acid.

•**Palmitic Acid** - This nutrient is the most common saturated fatty acid found in animals, plants, and microorganisms. Excessive amounts in the diets of humans results in increase inflammation within the brain.

•**Phenotype** - The phenotype is the visible characteristic of how an animal, cell, or plant looks or behaves. (Genotype is the potential characteristic coded in the organism's DNA).

•**Prebiotic** - A form of fiber that induces the growth or activity of beneficial microorganisms (e.g., bacteria and fungi). The most common example is in the gastrointestinal tract where the digestion of prebiotic fibers can alter the composition of organisms in the gut microbiome.

•**Probiotic** - Bacterial organisms that are ingested or added to foods and are potentially beneficial to health.

•**Propionic Acid** = A small chain fatty acid produced by bacteria within the intestinal tract.

•**RifaGut**™ - Another market brand name for rifaximin.

•**Rifaximin** - The generic term for the non-absorbable antibiotic sold under the brand name Xifaxan™, Rifagut™, Rifaximina™, and SIBOFix™.

•**SIBO** = Small Intestine Bacterial Overgrowth. A specific form of bacterial overgrowth that is designated by a positive methane or hydrogen breath test or an abnormal quantification study from a small intestinal aspirate.

•**SIBOFix**™ - Another market brand name for rifaximin.

•**Synapse** - A portion of a neuron (or nerve cell) that permits the neuron to pass an electrical or chemical signal to another neuron.

•**The Nemechek Protocol**® - a medical treatment program invented by Dr. Patrick M. Nemechek, D.O. relating to methods for preventing, reducing, or reversing acute and/or chronic autonomic damage by the suppression of pro-inflammatory cytokines which is useful in treating a variety of diseases or conditions (U.S. Patent No. 10,335,356).

•**Toxic Encephalopathy** - The medical state of a child whose brain has essentially been drugged with excessive propionic acid.

•**Traumatic Brain Injury, TBI** - The focal term for a physical injury to the head and results in symptoms lasting more than 24 hours. See mTBI and MTBI.

•**Vagus Nerve** - The 10th cranial nerve of the human body that carries the signals in the parasympathetic branch of the autonomic nervous system.

•**Vagus Nerve Stimulation, VNS** - This is a medical treatment that involves delivering electrical impulses to the vagus nerve in the autonomic nervous system. Therapeutically VNS reduces inflammation throughout the brain and body and is capable of inducing neuro-plasticity.

•**White Blood Cells (WBC)** - Cells of the immune system are often referred to as white blood cells or WBCs.

•**Xifaxan**^{TM} - This is the brand name of a time-released formulation of rifaximin sold within the United States.

SCIENTIFIC REFERENCES

We have provided a sampling of the many research articles that have helped shape the development of The Nemechek Protocol®.

Autonomic Dysfunction:

Taylor EC, Livingston LA, Callan MJ, Ashwin C, Shah P. Autonomic dysfunction in autism: The roles of anxiety, depression, and stress. Autism. 2021 Jan 24:1362361320985658. doi: 10.1177/1362361320985658. Epub ahead of print. PMID: 33491461.

Thapa R, Pokorski I, Ambarchi Z, Thomas E, Demayo M, Boulton K, Matthews S, Patel S, Sedeli I, Hickie IB, Guastella AJ. Heart Rate Variability in Children With Autism Spectrum Disorder and Associations With Medication and Symptom Severity. Autism Res. 2021 Jan;14(1):75-85. doi: 10.1002/aur.2437. Epub 2020 Nov 22. PMID: 33225622.

Baumann C, Rakowski U, Buchhorn R. Omega-3 Fatty Acid Supplementation Improves Heart Rate Variability in Obese Children. Int J Pediatr. 2018 Feb 26;2018:8789604. doi: 10.1155/2018/8789604. PMID: 29681953; PMCID: PMC5846363.

Hiura M, Nariai T, Sakata M, Muta A, Ishibashi K, Wagatsuma K, Tago T, Toyohara J, Ishii K, Maehara T. Response of Cerebral Blood Flow and

Blood Pressure to Dynamic Exercise: A Study Using PET. Int J Sports Med. 2018 Feb;39(3):181-188. doi: 10.1055/s-0043-123647. Epub 2018 Jan 22. PMID: 29359277.

Bjørklund G. Cerebral hypoperfusion in autism spectrum disorder. Acta Neurobiol Expo (Wars). 2018;78(1):21-29. https://www.ncbi.nlm.nih.gov/pubmed/29694338

Goodman B. Autonomic Dysfunction in Autism Spectrum Disorders (ASD). *Neurology* April 5, 2016 vol. 86 no. 16 Supplement P5.117. http://www.neurology.org/content/86/16_Supplement/P5.117

Anderson CJ et al. Pupil and Salivary Indicators of Autonomic Dysfunction in Autism Spectrum Disorder. *Developmental psychobiology.* 2013;55(5):10.1002/dev.21051. https://www.ncbi.nlm.nih.gov/pmc/articles/PMC3832142/

Goodman B et al. Autonomic Nervous System Dysfunction in Concussion. *Neurology* February 12, 2013 vol. 80 no. 7 Supplement P01.265. http://www.neurology.org/content/80/7_Supplement/P01.265

La Fountaine MF. et al. Autonomic Nervous System Responses to Concussion: Arterial Pulse Contour Analysis. *Frontiers in Neurology* 7 (2016): 13. https://www.ncbi.nlm.nih.gov/pmc/articles/PMC4756114/

Amhed K. Assessment of Autonomic Function in Children with Autism and Normal Children Using Spectral Analysis and Posture Entrainment: A Pilot Study. *J of Neurology and Neuroscience.* 2015. Vol. 6 No. 3:37. http://www.jneuro.com/neurology-neuroscience/assessment-of-autonomic-function-in-children-with-autism-and-normal-children-using-spectral-analysis-and-posture-entrainment-a-pilot-study.pdf

Bacterial Overgrowth:

Santos ANDR, Soares ACF, Oliveira RP, Morais MB. THE IMPACT OF SMALL INTESTINAL BACTERIAL OVERGROWTH ON THE GROWTH OF CHILDREN AND ADOLESCENTS. Rev Paul Pediatr. 2020 Jan 13;38:e2018164. doi: 10.1590/1984-0462/2020/38/2018164. PMID: 31939507; PMCID: PMC6958541.

Hoog CM, Lindberg G, Sjoqvist U. Findings in patients with chronic intestinal dysmotility investigated by capsule endoscopy. BMC Gastroenterol. 2007 Jul 18;7:29. doi: 10.1186/1471-230X-7-29. PMID: 17640373; PMCID: PMC1940016.

Wang L, Yu YM, Zhang YQ, Zhang J, Lu N, Liu N. Hydrogen breath test to detect small intestinal bacterial overgrowth: a prevalence case-control study in autism. Eur Child Adolesc Psychiatry. 2018 Feb;27(2):233-240. doi: 10.1007/s00787-017-1039-2. Epub 2017 Aug 10. PMID: 28799094.

Liu Z, Mao X, Dan Z, Pei Y, Xu R, Guo M, Liu K, Zhang F, Chen J, Su C, Zhuang Y, Tang J, Xia Y, Qin L, Hu Z, Liu X. Gene variations in autism spectrum disorder are associated with alteration of gut microbiota, metabolites and cytokines. Gut Microbes. 2021 Jan-Dec;13(1):1-16. doi: 10.1080/19490976.2020.1854967. PMID: 33412999; PMCID: PMC7808426.

Roussin L, Prince N, Perez-Pardo P, Kraneveld AD, Rabot S, Naudon L. Role of the Gut Microbiota in the Pathophysiology of Autism Spectrum Disorder: Clinical and Preclinical Evidence. Microorganisms. 2020 Sep 7;8(9):1369. doi: 10.3390/microorganisms8091369. PMID: 32906656; PMCID: PMC7563175.

Martín-Masot R, Molina Arias M, Diaz Martin JJ, Cilleruelo Pascual ML, Gutierrez Junquera C, Donat E, Román Riechmann E, Navas-López VM. Management of small intestinal bacterial overgrowth by paediatric gastroenterologists in Spain. Rev Esp Enferm Dig. 2020 Dec 29. doi: 10.17235/reed.2020.7582/2020. Epub ahead of print. PMID: 33371710.

Avelar Rodriguez D, Ryan PM, Toro Monjaraz EM, Ramirez Mayans JA, Quigley EM. Small Intestinal Bacterial Overgrowth in Children: A State-Of-The-Art Review. Front Pediatr. 2019 Sep 4;7:363. doi: 10.3389/fped.2019.00363. PMID: 31552207; PMCID: PMC6737284.

Adams JB et al. Gastrointestinal flora and gastrointestinal status in children with autism -- comparisons to typical children and correlation with autism severity. *BMC Gastroenterology*. 2011. https://www.ncbi.nlm.nih.gov/pubmed/21410934

Wang L. Hydrogen breath test to detect small intestinal bacterial overgrowth: a prevalence case control study in autism. *Eur Child Adolesc Psychiatry.* 2017 Aug 10. https://www.ncbi.nlm.nih.gov/pubmed/28799094

Hsiao EY et al. The microbiota modulates gut physiology and behavioral abnormalities associated with autism. *Cell.* 2013;155(7):1451-1463. https://www.ncbi.nlm.nih.gov/pmc/articles/PMC3897394/

Cryan JF et al. Mind-altering microorganisms: the impact of the gut microbiota on brain and behaviour. *Nat Rev Neurosci.* 2012 Oct;13(10):701-12. https://www.ncbi.nlm.nih.gov/pubmed/22968153

Cao X, Liu K, Liu J, Liu YW, Xu L, Wang H, Zhu Y, Wang P, Li Z, Wen J, Shen C, Li M, Nie Z, Kong XJ. Dysbiotic Gut Microbiota and Dysregulation of Cytokine Profile in Children and Teens With Autism Spectrum Disorder. Front Neurosci. 2021 Feb 10;15:635925. doi: 10.3389/fnins.2021.635925. PMID: 33642989; PMCID: PMC7902875.

Cumulative Brain Injury:

Chang HK, Hsu JW, Wu JC, Huang KL, Chang HC, Bai YM, Chen TJ, Chen MH. Traumatic Brain Injury in Early Childhood and Risk of Attention-Deficit/Hyperactivity Disorder and Autism Spectrum Disorder: A Nationwide Longitudinal Study. J Clin Psychiatry. 2018 Oct 16;79(6):17m11857. doi: 10.4088/JCP.17m11857. PMID: 30403445.

Bjørklund G, Kern JK, Urbina MA, Saad K, El-Houfey AA, Geier DA, Chirumbolo S, Geier MR, Mehta JA, Aaseth J. Cerebral hypoperfusion in autism spectrum disorder. Acta Neurobiol Exp (Wars). 2018;78(1):21-29. PMID: 29694338.

Cunningham C. Microglia and neurodegeneration: the role of systemic inflammation. *J Neurosci.* 2013 Mar 6;33(10):4216-33. https://www.ncbi.nlm.nih.gov/pubmed/22674585

Bilbo S, Stevens B. Microglia: The Brain's First Responders. Cerebrum. 2017 Nov 1;2017:cer-14-17. PMID: 30210663; PMCID: PMC6132046.

Olsen AB, Hetz RA, Xue H, Aroom KR, Bhattarai D, Johnson E, Bedi S, Cox CS Jr, Uray K. Effects of traumatic brain injury on intestinal contractility. Neurogastroenterol Motil. 2013 Jul;25(7):593-e463. doi: 10.1111/nmo.12121. Epub 2013 Apr 2. PMID: 23551971; PMCID: PMC3982791.

Wager-Smith, Karen, and Athina Markou. Depression: A Repair Response to Stress-Induced Neuronal Microdamage That Can Grade into a Chronic Neuroinflammatory Condition?*Neuroscience and biobehavioral reviews* 35.3 (2011): 742–764. https://www.ncbi.nlm.nih.gov/pubmed/208837188

Histamine:

Collins S, Reid G. Distant Site Effects of Ingested Prebiotics. *Nutrients.* 2016;8(9):523. https://www.ncbi.nlm.nih.gov/pmc/articles/PMC5037510/

Visciano P et al. Biogenic Amines in Raw and Processed Seafood. *Frontiers in Microbiology.* 2012;3:188. https://www.ncbi.nlm.nih.gov/pmc/articles/PMC3366335/

Feng c et al. Histamine (Scombroid) Fish Poisoning: a Comprehensive Review. *Clin Rev Allergy Immunol.* 2016 Feb;50(1):64-9. https://www.ncbi.nlm.nih.gov/pubmed/25876709

Jin X et al. Increased intestinal permeability in pathogenesis and progress of nonalcoholic steatohepatitis in rats. *World Journal of Gastroenterology: WJG.* 2007;13(11):1732-1736. https://www.ncbi.nlm.nih.gov/pubmed/17461479

Guo Y et al. Functional changes of intestinal mucosal barrier in surgically critical patients. *World Journal of Emergency Medicine.* 2010;1(3):205-208. https://www.ncbi.nlm.nih.gov/pmc/articles/PMC4129678/

Inflammation:

Zengeler KE, Lukens JR. Innate immunity at the crossroads of healthy brain maturation and neurodevelopmental disorders. Nat Rev Immunol. 2021 Jan 21. doi: 10.1038/s41577-020-00487-7. Epub ahead of print. PMID: 33479477.

Li YJ, Zhang X, Li YM. Antineuroinflammatory therapy: potential treatment for autism spectrum disorder by inhibiting glial activation and restoring synaptic function. CNS Spectr. 2020 Aug;25(4):493-501. doi: 10.1017/S1092852919001603. Epub 2019 Oct 29. PMID: 31659946.

Coomey R, Stowell R, Majewska A, Tropea D. The Role of Microglia in Neurodevelopmental Disorders and their Therapeutics. Curr Top Med Chem. 2020;20(4):272-276. doi: 10.2174/1568026620666200221172619. PMID: 32091337; PMCID: PMC7323119.

Mottahedin A, Ardalan M, Chumak T, Riebe I, Ek J, Mallard C. Effect of Neuroinflammation on Synaptic Organization and Function in the Developing Brain: Implications for Neurodevelopmental and Neurodegenerative Disorders. Front Cell Neurosci. 2017 Jul 11;11:190. doi: 10.3389/fncel.2017.00190. PMID: 28744200; PMCID: PMC5504097.

Madore C, Leyrolle Q, Lacabanne C, Benmamar-Badel A, Joffre C, Nadjar A, Layé S. Neuroinflammation in Autism: Plausible Role of Maternal Inflammation, Dietary Omega 3, and Microbiota. Neural Plast. 2016;2016:3597209. doi: 10.1155/2016/3597209. Epub 2016 Oct 20. PMID: 27840741; PMCID: PMC5093279.

Cao X, Liu K, Liu J, Liu YW, Xu L, Wang H, Zhu Y, Wang P, Li Z, Wen J, Shen C, Li M, Nie Z, Kong XJ. Dysbiotic Gut Microbiota and Dysregulation of Cytokine Profile in Children and Teens With Autism Spectrum Disorder. Front Neurosci. 2021 Feb 10;15:635925. doi: 10.3389/fnins.2021.635925. PMID: 33642989; PMCID: PMC7902875.

Inulin:

Kellow NJ et al. Effect of dietary prebiotic supplementation on advanced glycation, insulin resistance and inflammatory biomarkers in adults with pre-diabetes: a study protocol for a double-blind placebo-controlled randomized crossover clinical trial. *BMC Endocrine Disorders*. 2014;14:55. https://www.ncbi.nlm.nih.gov/pubmed/25011647

Hopkins MJ, Macfarlane GT. Nondigestible Oligosaccharides Enhance Bacterial Colonization Resistance against *Clostridium difficile* In

Vitro. *Applied and Environmental Microbiology*. 2003;69(4):1920-1927. https://www.ncbi.nlm.nih.gov/pmc/articles/PMC154806/

Collins S, Reid G. Distant Site Effects of Ingested Prebiotics. *Nutrients*. 2016;8(9):523. https://www.ncbi.nlm.nih.gov/pmc/articles/PMC5037510/

Slavin J. Significance of Inulin Fructans in the Human Diet. *Compre Rev in Food Science and Food Safety*. 2015 14;1: 37–47. http://onlinelibrary.wiley.com/doi/10.1111/1541-4337.12119/abstract

Microglia and Neuroinflammation:

Coomey R, Stowell R, Majewska A, Tropea D. The Role of Microglia in Neurodevelopmental Disorders and their Therapeutics. Curr Top Med Chem. 2020;20(4):272-276. doi: 10.2174/1568026620666200221172619. PMID: 32091337; PMCID: PMC7323119.

Petrelli F, Pucci L, Bezzi P. Astrocytes and Microglia and Their Potential Link with Autism Spectrum Disorders. *Frontiers in Cellular Neuroscience*. 2016;10:21. https://www.ncbi.nlm.nih.gov/pmc/articles/PMC4751265/

Norden, DM et al. Microglial Priming and Enhanced Reactivity to Secondary Insult in Aging, and Traumatic CNS Injury, and Neurodegenerative Disease. *Neuropharmacology* 96.0 0 (2015): 29–41. https://www.ncbi.nlm.nih.gov/pmc/articles/PMC4430467/

Calabrese, F et al. Brain-Derived Neurotrophic Factor: A Bridge between Inflammation and Neuroplasticity. *Frontiers in Cellular Neuroscience* 8 (2014): 430. https://www.ncbi.nlm.nih.gov/pmc/articles/PMC4273623/

Cunningham, Colm. Systemic Inflammation and Delirium – Important Co-Factors in the Progression of Dementia. *Biochemical Society Transactions* 39.4 (2011): 945–953. https://www.ncbi.nlm.nih.gov/pubmed/21787328

Paolicelli RC et al. Synaptic pruning by microglia is necessary for normal brain development. *Science* 2011 Sep 9;333(6048):1456-8. https://www.ncbi.nlm.nih.gov/pubmed/21778362

Omega Fatty Acids:

Simopoulos AP. The importance of the omega-6/omega-3 fatty acid ratio in cardiovascular disease and other chronic diseases. Exp Biol Med (Maywood). 2008 Jun;233(6):674-88. doi: 10.3181/0711-MR-311. Epub 2008 Apr 11. PMID: 18408140.

Madsen L, Kristiansen K. Of mice and men: Factors abrogating the anti-obesity effect of omega-3 fatty acids. *Adipocyte*. 2012;1(3):173-176. https://www.ncbi.nlm.nih.gov/pmc/articles/PMC3609096/

El-Ansary AK et al. On the protective effect of omega-3 against propionic acid-induced neurotoxicity in rat pups. *Lipids in Health and Disease*. 2011;10:142. https://www.ncbi.nlm.nih.gov/pmc/articles/PMC3170231/

Chang, P et al. Docosahexaenoic Acid (DHA): A Modulator of Microglia Activity and Dendritic Spine Morphology. *Journal of Neuroinflammation* 12 (2015): 34. https://www.ncbi.nlm.nih.gov/pmc/articles/PMC4344754/

Patterson E et al. Health Implications of High Dietary Omega-6 Polyunsaturated Fatty Acids. *Journal of Nutrition and Metabolism*. 2012;2012:539426. https://www.ncbi.nlm.nih.gov/pubmed/22570770

Harvey, LD. et al. Administration of DHA Reduces Endoplasmic Reticulum Stress-Associated Inflammation and Alters Microglial or Macrophage Activation in Traumatic Brain Injury. *ASN Neuro* 7.6 (2015): 1759091415618969. https://www.ncbi.nlm.nih.gov/pmc/articles/PMC4710127/

Liu, JJ. et al. Pathways of Polyunsaturated Fatty Acid Utilization: Implications for Brain Function in Neuropsychiatric Health and Disease. *Brain research* 0 (2015): 220–246. https://www.ncbi.nlm.nih.gov/pmc/articles/PMC4339314/

Titos E et al. Resolvin D1 and its precursor docosahexaenoic acid promote resolution of adipose tissue inflammation by eliciting macrophage polarization toward an M2-like phenotype. *J Immun.* 2011 Nov 15;187(10):5408-18. https://www.ncbi.nlm.nih.gov/pubmed/22013115

Chen S et al. n-3 PUFA supplementation benefits microglial responses to myelin pathology. *Scientific Reports.* 2014;4:7458. https://www.ncbi.nlm. nih.gov/pubmed/25500548

Minkyung K et al. Impact of 8-week linoleic acid intake in soy oil on Lp-PLA2 activity in healthy adults. *Nutr & Metab.* 2017. 14:32. https://www. ncbi.nlm.nih.gov/pmc/articles/PMC5422895/

Christian LM et al. Body weight affects ω-3 polyunsaturated fatty acid (PUFA) accumulation in youth following supplementation in post-hoc analyses of a randomized controlled trial. *PLoS ONE.* 2017;12(4):e0173087. https://www.ncbi.nlm.nih.gov/pmc/articles/PMC5381773/

Igarashi M et al. Dietary N-6 Polyunsaturated Fatty Acid Deprivations Increases Docosahexaenoic Acid (DHA) in Rat Brain. *Journal of Neurochemistry.* 2012;120(6):985-997. https://www.ncbi.nlm.nih.gov/pmc/arti cles/PMC3296886/

Grundy T et al. Long-term omega-3 supplementation modulates behavior, hippocampal fatty acid concentration, neuronal progenitor proliferation and central TNF-α expression in 7 month old unchallenged mice. *Frontiers in Cellular Neuroscience.* 2014;8:399. https://www.ncbi.nlm. nih.gov/pmc/articles/PMC4240169/

Mazahery H, Stonehouse W, Delshad M, Kruger MC, Conlon CA, Beck KL, von Hurst PR. Relationship between Long Chain n-3 Polyunsaturated Fatty Acids and Autism Spectrum Disorder: Systematic Review and Meta-Analysis of Case-Control and Randomised Controlled Trials. Nutrients. 2017 Feb 19;9(2):155. doi: 10.3390/nu9020155. PMID: 28218722; PMCID: PMC5331586.

Prevention:

Chu DM et al. Maturation of the Infant Microbiome Community Structure and Function Across Multiple Body Sites and in Relation to Mode of Delivery. *Nature medicine.* 2017;23(3):314-326. https://www.ncbi.nlm. nih.gov/pubmed/28112736

Arslanoglu S et al. Early supplementation of prebiotic oligosaccharides protects formula-fed infants against infections during the first 6 months of life. *J Nutr.* 2007 Nov;137(11):2420-4. https://www.ncbi.nlm.nih.gov/pubmed/17951479

Helland IB et al. Maternal supplementation with very-long-chain n-3 fatty acids during pregnancy and lactation augments children's IQ at 4 years of age. *Pediatrics.* 2003 Jan;111(1):e39-44. https://www.ncbi.nlm.nih.gov/pubmed/12509593

Desai et al. Depletion of Brain Docosahexaenoic Acid Impairs Recovery from Traumatic Brain Injury. Annunziato L, ed. *PLoS ONE.* 2014;9(1):e86472. https://www.ncbi.nlm.nih.gov/pubmed/24475126

Carlson SE et al. DHA supplementation and pregnancy outcomes. *The American Journal of Clinical Nutrition.* 2013;97(4):808-815. https://www.ncbi.nlm.nih.gov/pubmed/23426033

Carvajal JA. Docosahexaenoic Acid Supplementation Early in Pregnancy May Prevent Deep Placentation Disorders. *BioMed Research International.* 2014;2014:526895. https://www.ncbi.nlm.nih.gov/pubmed/25019084

Fukuda H et al. Inhibition of sympathetic pathways restores postoperative ileus in the upper and lower gastrointestinal tract. *J Gastroenterol Hepatol.* 2007 Aug;22(8):12939. https://www.ncbi.nlm.nih.gov/pubmed/17688668

Perring S et al. Assessment of changes in cardiac autonomic tone resulting from inflammatory response to the influenza vaccination. *Clin Physiol Funct Imaging.* 2012 Nov;32(6):437-44. https://www.ncbi.nlm.nih.gov/pubmed/23031064

Jae SY et al. Does an acute inflammatory response temporarily attenuate parasympathetic reactivation? *Clin Auton Res.* 2010 Aug;20(4):229-33. https://www.ncbi.nlm.nih.gov/pubmed/20437076

De Wildt DJ et al. Impaired autonomic responsiveness of the cardiovascular system of the rat induced by a heat-labile component of Bordetella pertussis vaccine. *Infection and Immunity.* 1983;41(2):476-481. https://www.ncbi.nlm.nih.gov/pmc/articles/PMC264665/

Kashiwagi Y et al. Production of inflammatory cytokines in response to diphtheria-pertussis-tetanus (DPT), *haemophilus influenzae* type b (Hib), and 7-valent pneumococcal (PCV7) vaccines. *Human Vaccines & Immunotherapeutics.* 2014;10(3):677-685. https://www.ncbi.nlm.nih.gov/pmc/articles/PMC4130255/

Akiho H et al. Cytokine-induced alterations of gastrointestinal motility in gastrointestinal disorders. *World Journal of Gastrointestinal Pathophysiology.* 2011;2(5):72-81. https://www.ncbi.nlm.nih.gov/pmc/articles/PMC3196622/

Vantrappen G et al. The Interdigestive Motor Complex of Normal Subjects and Patients with Bacterial Overgrowth of the Small Intestine. *Journal of Clinical Investigation.* 1977;59(6):1158-1166. https://www.ncbi.nlm.nih.gov/pmc/articles/PMC372329/

Jacobs C et al. Dysmotility and PPI use are independent risk factors for small intestinal bacterial and/or fungal overgrowth. *Alimentary pharmacology & therapeutics.* 2013;37(11):1103-1111. https://www.ncbi.nlm.nih.gov/pmc/articles/PMC3764612/

Miyano Y et al. The Role of the Vagus Nerve in the Migrating Motor Complex and Ghrelin- and Motilin-Induced Gastric Contraction in Suncus. Covasa M, ed. *PLoS ONE.* 2013;8(5):e64777. https://www.ncbi.nlm.nih.gov/pmc/articles/PMC3665597/

Propionic Acid and Autism:

Choi J, Lee S, Won J, Jin Y, Hong Y, Hur TY, Kim JH, Lee SR, Hong Y. Pathophysiological and neurobehavioral characteristics of a propionic acid-mediated autism-like rat model. PLoS One. 2018 Feb 15;13(2):e0192925. doi: 10.1371/journal.pone.0192925. PMID: 29447237; PMCID: PMC5814017.

El-Ansary AK et al. Etiology of autistic features: the persisting neurotoxic effects of propionic acid. *Journal of Neuroinflammation.* 2012;9:74. https://www.ncbi.nlm.nih.gov/pubmed/22531301

McFabe DF et al. Neurobiological effects of intraventricular propionic acid in rats possible role of short chain fatty acids on the pathogenesis and characteristics of autism spectrum disorders. *Behav Brain Res.* 2007. Jan 10:176(1);149-69. https://www.ncbi.nlm.nih.gov/pubmed/16950524

Xiong X, Liu D, Wang Y, Zeng T, Peng Y. Urinary 3-(3-Hydroxyphenyl)-3-hydroxypropionic Acid, 3-Hydroxyphenylacetic Acid, and 3-Hydroxyhippuric Acid Are Elevated in Children with Autism Spectrum Disorders. *BioMed Research International.* 2016. https://www.ncbi.nlm.nih.gov/pmc/articles/PMC4829699/

MacFabe DF. Short-chain fatty acid fermentation products of the gut microbiome: implications in autism spectrum disorders. *Microbial Ecology in Health and Disease.* 2012;23:10. https://www.ncbi.nlm.nih.gov/pubmed/23990817

Rifaximin:

Ponziani FR et al. Eubiotic properties of rifaximin: Disruption of the traditional concepts in gut microbiota modulation. *World Journal of Gastroenterology.* 2017;23(25):4491-4499. https://www.ncbi.nlm.nih.gov/pmc/articles/PMC3747729/

Gao, J et al. Rifaximin, gut microbes and mucosal inflammation: unraveling a complex relationship. Gut Microbes. 2014 Jul 1;5(4):571-5. https://www.ncbi.nlm.nih.gov/pubmed/25244596

Yao CK. The clinical value of breath hydrogen testing. *J Gastroenterologists Hepatol.* 2017 Mar;32 Suppl 1:20-22. https://www.ncbi.nlm.nih.gov/pubmed/28244675

Muniyappa P, Gulati R, Mohr F, Hupertz V. Use and safety of rifaximin in children with inflammatory bowel disease. J Pediatr Gastroenterol Nutr. 2009 Oct;49(4):400-4. doi: 10.1097/MPG.0b013e3181a0d269. PMID: 19668011.

Ghoshal UC et al. Utility of hydrogen breath tests in diagnosis of small intestinal bacterial overgrowth in malabsorption syndrome and its relationship with orocecal transit time. *Indian J Gastroenterol.* 2006 Jan-Feb;25(1):6-10. https://www.ncbi.nlm.nih.gov/pmc/articles/PMC4175689/

Muniyappa P et al. Use and safety of rifaximin in children with inflammatory bowel disease. *J Pediatricians Gastroenterol Nutr.* 2009 Oct;49(4):400-4. https://www.ncbi.nlm.nih.gov/pubmed/19668011

Pimentel M, Cash BD, Lembo A, Wolf RA, Israel RJ, Schoenfeld P. Repeat Rifaximin for Irritable Bowel Syndrome: No Clinically Significant Changes in Stool Microbial Antibiotic Sensitivity. *Digestive Diseases and Sciences.* 2017;62(9):2455-2463. https://www.ncbi.nlm.nih.gov/pmc/articles/PMC5561162/

Guslandi M. Rifaximin in the treatment of inflammatory bowel disease. World J Gastroenterol. 2011 Nov 14;17(42):4643-6. doi: 10.3748/wjg.v17.i42.4643. PMID: 22180705; PMCID: PMC3237300.

Vagus Nerve Stimulation:

van Hoorn A, Carpenter T, Oak K, Laugharne R, Ring H, Shankar R. Neuromodulation of autism spectrum disorders using vagal nerve stimulation. J Clin Neurosci. 2019 May;63:8-12. doi: 10.1016/j.jocn.2019.01.042. Epub 2019 Feb 4. PMID: 30732986.

Levy ML, Levy KM, Hoff D, Amar AP, Park MS, Conklin JM, Baird L, Apuzzo ML. Vagus nerve stimulation therapy in patients with autism spectrum disorder and intractable epilepsy: results from the vagus nerve stimulation therapy patient outcome registry. J Neurosurg Pediatr. 2010 Jun;5(6):595-602. doi: 10.3171/2010.3.PEDS09153. PMID: 20515333.

Yap JYY, Keatch C, Lambert E, Woods W, Stoddart PR, Kameneva T. Critical Review of Transcutaneous Vagus Nerve Stimulation: Challenges for Translation to Clinical Practice. Front Neurosci. 2020 Apr 28;14:284. doi: 10.3389/fnins.2020.00284. PMID: 32410932; PMCID: PMC7199464.

Badran BW, Jenkins DD, Cook D, Thompson S, Dancy M, DeVries WH, Mappin G, Summers P, Bikson M, George MS. Transcutaneous Auricular Vagus Nerve Stimulation-Paired Rehabilitation for Oromotor Feeding Problems in Newborns: An Open-Label Pilot Study. Front Hum Neurosci. 2020 Mar 18;14:77. doi: 10.3389/fnhum.2020.00077. PMID: 32256328; PMCID: PMC7093597.

Manning KE, Beresford-Webb JA, Aman LCS, Ring HA, Watson PC, Porges SW, Oliver C, Jennings SR, Holland AJ. Transcutaneous vagus nerve stimulation (t-VNS): A novel effective treatment for temper outbursts in adults with Prader-Willi Syndrome indicated by results from a non-blind study. PLoS One. 2019 Dec 3;14(12):e0223750. doi: 10.1371/journal.pone.0223750. PMID: 31794560; PMCID: PMC6890246.

Komegae EN, Farmer DGS, Brooks VL, McKinley MJ, McAllen RM, Martelli D. Vagal afferent activation suppresses systemic inflammation via the splanchnic anti-inflammatory pathway. Brain Behav Immun. 2018 Oct;73:441-449. doi: 10.1016/j.bbi.2018.06.005. Epub 2018 Jun 5. PMID: 29883598; PMCID: PMC6319822.

Koopman FA, Chavan SS, Miljko S, Grazio S, Sokolovic S, Schuurman PR, Mehta AD, Levine YA, Faltys M, Zitnik R, Tracey KJ, Tak PP. Vagus nerve stimulation inhibits cytokine production and attenuates disease severity in rheumatoid arthritis. Proc Natl Acad Sci U S A. 2016 Jul 19;113(29):8284-9. doi: 10.1073/pnas.1605635113. Epub 2016 Jul 5. PMID: 27382171; PMCID: PMC4961187.

Marshall R, Taylor I, Lahr C, Abell TL, Espinoza I, Gupta NK, Gomez CR. Bioelectrical Stimulation for the Reduction of Inflammation in Inflammatory Bowel Disease. Clin Med Insights Gastroenterol. 2015 Dec 6;8:55-9. doi: 10.4137/CGast.S31779. PMID: 26692766; PMCID: PMC4671545.

Huston JM, Gallowitsch-Puerta M, Ochani M, Ochani K, Yuan R, Rosas-Ballina M, Ashok M, Goldstein RS, Chavan S, Pavlov VA, Metz CN, Yang H, Czura CJ, Wang H, Tracey KJ. Transcutaneous vagus nerve stimulation reduces serum high mobility group box 1 levels and improves survival in murine sepsis. Crit Care Med. 2007 Dec;35(12):2762-8. doi: 10.1097/01.CCM.0000288102.15975.BA. PMID: 17901837.

Zhang Q, Lu Y, Bian H, Guo L, Zhu H. Activation of the $\alpha7$ nicotinic receptor promotes lipopolysaccharide-induced conversion of M1 microglia to M2. Am J Transl Res. 2017 Mar 15;9(3):971-985. PMID: 28386326; PMCID: PMC5375991.

NOTES

ABOUT THE AUTHORS

Dr. Patrick M. Nemechek, D.O. was born in Tucson, Arizona. He graduated with a B.S. in Microbiology from San Diego State University (1982) and obtained his Doctorate in Osteopathic Medicine from the University of Health Sciences, Kansas City, Missouri (1987).

Dr. Nemechek completed his training in internal medicine at UCLA School of Medicine (1990) where he had the distinguished honor of being named Chief Resident and later Clinical Instructor for the Department of Medicine at UCLA.

Dr. Nemechek's mentor at UCLA was Albert Einstein's nephew who encouraged him to go into the particularly complex field of HIV Medicine, which was the medical mystery of that time, where Dr. Nemechek would have the challenging freedom to save people's lives.

While at UCLA, Dr. Nemechek was recognized with the Robert S. Mosser Award for Excellence in Internal Medicine for his outstanding academic performance and instrumental role in starting UCLA's first HIV clinic at Kern Medical Center, Bakersfield, California.

In 1994, Dr. Nemechek moved to Kansas City, Missouri where he opened an HIV treatment and research facility named Nemechek Health Renewal.

It was at this point that Dr. Nemechek started work in earnest as a classically trained internal medicine "scientist-physician", entering the field of HIV when there was no diagnostic test, no treatment, and no answers.

Those early decades transformed Dr. Nemechek into an innovator who followed the latest research, looked at problems on a cellular and metabolic level, and became one of the first doctors develop treatment for wasting syndrome as well as other HIV-related complex problems.

Dr. Nemechek's innovative approach to the complexities of HIV disease garnered him honors such as being chosen as a "Site of Clinical Excellence" by Bristol Myers Squibb Company & KPMG Peat Marwick, being named one of the top HIV physicians in the U.S. by POZ magazine and receiving several nominations for the Small Business of the Year Award by the Greater Kansas City Chamber of Commerce.

During his 20 years in the Midwest, Dr. Nemechek authored, co-authored or co-collaborated on 72 scientific abstracts and publications, participated in 41 different clinical studies, and in 1999 became a founding investigator for the HIV Research Network, a consortium of 18 different universities and HIV treatment facilities funded by the U.S. Department of Health and Human Services.

He has served on numerous editorial, professional, and advisory boards as well as founding two non-profit HIV health advocacy organizations, the Bakersfield Aids Foundation and Fight Back KC.

By 2004, many of Dr. Nemechek's HIV patients were stable and leading normal lives but strangely they were starting to die of sudden cardiac events due to Cardiac Autonomic Neuropathy (CAN).

Dr. Nemechek set out to learn more about the lethal phenomena and in 2006 purchased new technology called spectral analysis that allowed him to tune into the communication signal between the heart and the brain, quantifying the balance and tone of the two branches of the autonomic nervous system.

Dr. Nemechek received additional training in autonomic testing and analysis at the Universidade De Lisboa, in Lisbon, Portugal, one of the top autonomic research facilities in the world.

Dr. Nemechek has now performed and analyzed thousands of autonomic patterns of damage. The more Dr. Nemechek learned about the field of Autonomic Medicine, the more he realized that it is the failure of the brain that sets into motion the failure of the body.

With his extensive research experience and expertise in metabolism, immunology, and the autonomic nervous system, Dr. Nemechek returned to his home state of Arizona in 2010 with his wife Jean and opened Nemechek Consultative Medicine, an Internal Medicine and Autonomic Medicine practice.

[Image: Jean Book Photo 2018 (1).jpg]

Jean Nemechek is uniquely qualified to run the business and co-author with Dr. Nemechek as she graduated with a B.A. in Communications and a B.S. in Journalism from the University of Kansas (1988, 1989) and a Juris Doctorate from Washburn School of Law (1993).

After relocating back home to Arizona, Dr. Nemechek was once again treating children and adults of all ages for routine matters. He was shocked at how incredibly sick the general population had become in just a few decades. The disease continuum had moved up about 40 years it seemed, and diseases that had once struck only the elderly were routinely occurring in middle age or early adulthood.

Dr. Nemechek could recall when he was a medical student and his instructor called him into an exam room to see a person in their 50's who had diabetes. It was unheard of in those days to have someone "so young" with type II diabetes. Tragically, that disease is now quite commonplace in middle age as we have become collectively sick and old at an accelerated pace.

Dr. Nemechek realized that many of his routine patients were suffering from the early stages of disease and autonomic dysfunction (heartburn, headaches, fatigue), small intestine bacterial overgrowths – SIBO (intestinal distress, food intolerances), and their children were increasingly experiencing the symptoms arising from autonomic dysfunction and SIBO (anxiety, ADD, autism, and digestive and intestinal issues).

That is when Dr. Nemechek began, once again, to make history. He knew he had to change the practice of modern medicine back to the goals of healing the patient and reversing disease. Dr. Nemechek began to approach his regular patients with same the investigative research angle that he once did with HIV, he pushed beyond the disease labels to understand and resolve the underlying problem.

Dr. Nemechek started using all available scientific and medical tools to induce the nervous system and organs to repair themselves by normalizing inflammation control mechanisms, inducing natural stem cell production, and reactivating innate restorative mechanisms.

Starting in 2010, Dr. Nemechek embarked on an extraordinary path that involved altering and improving intestinal bacteria and reducing pro-inflammatory cytokines within the central nervous system and witnessed an unprecedented recovery in all five stages of autonomic dysfunction without long term medication. This is unheard of in our time.

As the years passed, Dr. Nemechek also began working with various current and former professional athletes whose brain symptoms resolved (Autonomic Advantage™ Brain Injury Recovery Program), and he began incorporating bioelectric medicine, specifically electromodulation of the vagus nerve, with his patients.

Dr. Nemechek found the key to treatment and reversal of many of the common diseases affecting people today is reversing dysfunction of the autonomic nervous system in combination with the renewal of stem cell production and neurogenesis through the reduction of metabolic inflammation.

Because of his efforts and career experiences, Dr. Nemechek invented an effective program to prevent, reduce, or reverse autonomic nervous system damage through a combination of natural neurochemical supplements, short term prescription medications, dietary restrictions, and neuromodulation of the Vagus nerve.

Dr. Nemechek's treatment approach is extremely effective in the recovery of autonomic function from a variety of neuroinflammatory conditions including traumatic brain injury, concussion, chronic traumatic encephalopathy (CTE), post-concussion syndrome (PCS), Alzheimer's disease, Parkinson's disease, essential tremor, post-traumatic stress disorder (PTSD), chronic depression, treatment-resistant epilepsy, autism, developmental delay, Asperger's syndrome, and sensory and motor disorders.

In 2016, Dr. Nemechek filed a patent application to protect his groundbreaking formula that is now known as "The Nemechek Protocol®" or The Nemechek Protocol for Autonomic Recovery (Patent No. 10,335,356).

In response to his unique expertise in clinical autonomics and the development of The Nemechek Protocol® for Autonomic Recovery, the practice was renamed (dba) Nemechek Autonomic Medicine in 2017.

This book explains the main tools used by Dr. Nemechek in his work with autistic and developmental delay patients in his medical practice using certain parts of The Nemechek Protocol®. His approach with these patients is now also commonly referred to as "The Nemechek Protocol for Autism", and it has spread throughout the world.